Settlers, Servants & Slaves

Aboriginal and European Children in
Nineteenth-century Western Australia

PENELOPE HETHERINGTON

University of Western Australia Press

First published in 2002 by
University of Western Australia Press
Crawley, Western Australia 6009
www.uwapress.uwa.edu.au

Publication of this book was supported by funding assistance from the
Western Australian History Foundation.

National Library of Australia
Cataloguing-in-Publication entry:

Hetherington, Penelope.
    Settlers, servants and slaves: Aboriginal and European children
    in nineteenth-century Western Australia.

    Bibliography.
    Includes index.
    ISBN 1 876268 73 5.

    1. Aborigines, Australian—Children—Employment—Western
    Australia. 2. Child labor—Western Australia. 3. Aborigines,
    Australian—Western Australia—Treatment. I. Title.

331.34699915

Cover photographs: Group of Aboriginal children in the goldfields,
1890s, courtesy Battye Library, 5990P; the Storey children, courtesy
Fremantle City Library Local History Section, print no. 3654.

Produced by Benchmark Publications, Melbourne
Consultant editor Amanda Curtin, Curtin Communications, Perth
Series design by Robyn Mundy Design, Perth
Cover design by Ron Hampton, Pages in Action, Melbourne
Typeset in 9½pt Garamond Light by Lasertype, Perth
Printed by Brown Prior Anderson, Melbourne

Penelope Hetherington has published widely on the history of women and children of Western Australia, as well as on African history. Before her retirement in 1993, she was a Senior Lecturer in History at The University of Western Australia, where she taught African history and historiography. She now concentrates on research and writing.

CONTENTS

TABLES

CONVERSIONS

References to weights and measures are given in the way in which they were expressed at the time, in imperial units. Conversions to the metric system are as follows:

1 acre	0.405 hectare
1 square mile	2.59 square kilometres
1 foot	30.5 centimetres
1 mile	1.61 kilometres
1 pound	454 grams
1 ton	1.02 tonnes

Currency

Australian currency changed from pounds, shillings and pence to dollars and cents in 1966. Because of variations in currency values over time, actual conversions are difficult. At the time of the currency changeover, the following conversions applied:

1 penny (1d)	1 cent
1 shilling (1s)	10 cents
1 pound (£1)	2 dollars

I wish to thank the Western Australian History Foundation for a grant of $4,000 towards the cost of the publication of this book.

INTRODUCTION

Understanding childhood
in nineteenth-century Western Australia

THIS book belongs with an expanding literature about colonizing settler societies in various parts of the world. There are some histories of children in Australian colonial societies, most of them focusing entirely on the children of the immigrant communities.[1] This volume, however, seeks to link the very different experiences of European and Aboriginal children in nineteenth-century Western Australia. Many children from both descent groups, as well as children of mixed descent, were used as unpaid labour by the settler colonists. In the North West, the work of Aborigines of all ages—sometimes in family groups in the pastoral industry, sometimes as forced labour in the pearling industry—laid the foundation for the wealth and power of a small elite of immigrant families. The male authority figures in this nineteenth-century capitalist society erected a complex legal web that allowed them to control and exploit the majority of the population, both immigrant and Aboriginal.

The question of what is meant by 'childhood' has to be examined historically.[2] Throughout the nineteenth century, English laws concerning questions of marriage and property enshrined the idea that the full duties and privileges of adult life belonged to the period after 21 years of age, and all persons below that age were, in legal jargon, referred to as 'infants'. As late as 1949, the standard reference on English law stated that 'infants are persons under the age of twenty one years, and such persons have always been protected by law and have only a limited legal responsibility'.[3] Persons under the age of 21 years were protected in certain circumstances in contract law and in the law concerning civil wrongs, and 21 was the age for the making of legal wills and for representing oneself in court. This was a legal framework developed over a very long time to meet the needs of male owners of property, and it was transported to all the Australian colonies.

But a study of the history of children in nineteenth-century Western Australia uncovers a different reality. The legal category of 'child' varied, depending on gender and ethnicity, as well as on parental wealth. For some children who were orphaned, were convicts, or were classified as juvenile delinquents, the law was as much an instrument of control and punishment as it was of protection. As far as the Aborigines Protection Act of 1886 was concerned, for example, the word 'protection' was a deliberate misnomer, since the Act was designed to introduce a system of controls over child labour, and the movement of Aboriginal people, that suited the economic needs of the pastoralists.

Those who counted the population seemed to suggest that 'childhood', implying some dependence on adults, ended at the age of either 14 or 15 years. However, the first colonists, when referring to young children in their correspondence, did not exempt them from regular employment. Far from having a growing-up period free from responsibility, it seems that the economic survival of the colony often depended on the labour of children. The education of young colonists until the age of 14 years was not compulsory in law before 1871 and was not really enforced before the last decade of the century. The law was silent about the education of Aboriginal children until 1886, when the Aborigines Protection Act declared that this task was the responsibility of the newly created Aborigines Protection Board. In practice, most Aboriginal children in contact with the colonists worked alongside their parents on farming or pastoral properties or as divers on pearling boats.

A few contemporary observers who were critical of the exploitation of Aboriginal children referred to their employment as a system of slavery. This implied that these children were often taken by force from their parents and coerced into undertaking various tasks for which they were not paid wages, or that they were bound until 21 years of age by apprenticeship agreements over which they had no control. In the nineteenth century, the word 'slavery' summoned up images of the plantation system in the southern states of America. It is now widely used to refer to social systems that identify some groups as permanently inferior in status, and make this the basis of various forms of exploitation. Some contemporary observers identified the treatment of Aboriginal people as slavery and some modern historians also use the term in this context.[4]

The voices of the children of the past are generally muted in the historical records, as are the voices of working-class adults. But it is possible to learn about the lives of children by examining the ways adults treated them. The governments of the time made laws concerning children and they set up institutions for children, including schools of various kinds. The settlers talked a great deal about children: sometimes in order to justify their behaviour towards them, sometimes in discussion about their special needs, and sometimes in anger at their treatment.

The early period of settler capitalism in the Swan River Colony was the product of quite specific socio-economic changes in Great Britain connected with the enclosure of land, the beginnings of industrialization, and the growth of a rural and urban proletariat. These changes had already provided some of the impetus for the colonization of other parts of Australia. In the period following the end of the Napoleonic Wars in Europe, and the outlawing of the slave trade to the New World, various experiments in colonization tried new combinations of capital, land and labour. Both the Swan River Colony, established in 1829, and South Australia, founded in 1836, were originally designed as colonies of free settlers without convict labour. The free colonists who owned capital planned a variety of stratagems to acquire cheap land, to solve their labour problems, and to maximize their independence from Colonial Office control. In 1850, Western Australians finally argued in favour of accepting a convict work force, which gradually transformed the ailing economy.[5]

The voluminous records of the first twenty years of the Swan River Colony deal predominantly with the lives of these settler capitalists, who came to the colony to improve or consolidate their social standing and to create a society with the structures and values of early nineteenth-century Britain.[6] Men with capital resources made claims for land on behalf of themselves and their wives and children.[7] They adopted attitudes of patronage and paternalism towards their indentured labourers, who were obliged to sign agreements committing themselves and their families to periods of labour without wages, in return for free passages.[8] Most of these early capitalists experienced little disquiet as they dispossessed the Aborigines of their land.

This book considers a number of laws that helped construct different kinds of 'childhood'. For several decades after settlement, the laws of England were deemed to apply in the colony, unless specifically altered by the Governor in Council, with these changes approved by the Colonial Office. However, in 1870, Governor Weld introduced a Bill into the Legislative Council of Western Australia to establish representative government, which became law in June of that year. The new legislature was to consist of eighteen members, twelve of them elected from ten electoral districts. Perth and Fremantle were each to have two representatives. Three members were to be nominated by the Governor, and three were to be office holders—the Colonial Secretary, the Surveyor General and the Attorney General. The elections were held in October–November and the first meeting of the new, partly elected Legislative Council took place in December 1870.[9]

Although new laws still had to be approved by the Colonial Office, the period after 1870 was characterized by the introduction and passage of many Bills originating from initiatives in the Western Australian community, and which reflected local knowledge. In almost all cases, this legislation referred to the European population only, unless it was specifically directed towards Aborigines. In other words, the law consisted of two separate streams. The Industrial Schools Act of 1874 was the exception, since it applied to both groups of children. Not until 1890 was responsible government (except for control over Aboriginal affairs) granted to the colony. In 1901, the powers of the Western Australian Government were again curtailed, this time because of the limitations on State power imposed by the new Commonwealth Constitution.

While ideas about how children should be treated were embedded in the culture of the European immigrants, these ideas were further shaped according to the demands of the settlers for cheap or unpaid labour. The first settler families were provided with certain acreages of land, depending on the amount of capital they brought with them. Some settlers also brought labourers, and were allowed to count them as part of their capital for the estimation of the size of their grant of land. In due course, land had to be paid for but could be acquired for a low capital investment. When settlement expanded into the North West, land could be leased for a comparatively low sum. But, for the first twenty-one years of European settlement, the immigrants were desperately short of labour. After the introduction of convicts, between 1850 and 1868, ideas about what European children should be doing began to change, and school attendance grew rapidly.

The Acts of Parliament passed after 1870 provided a legislative framework for the activities of local settlers and investors, and most of this legislation was directed towards protecting the interests of employers. Not until the passage of the Industrial and Conciliation Bill through the parliament in 1900 did the law begin to recognize that relations between employers and employees might be regulated in the interests of more than one section of the community. In the last decades of the century, a plethora of legislative provisions designed to maintain unpaid Aboriginal labour were also introduced. In doing so, the legislators had to placate certain local critics, and attempt to convince the Colonial Office in London that all was well in the pastoral and pearling industries.

The settlers in Western Australia were fundamentally racist in their attitudes, and made characteristic nineteenth-century judgments about the inferiority of people whose culture they identified as 'primitive'. The explanation for cultural difference was believed to lie in the inherited difference in ability between different breeding populations, identified as having different 'racial' characteristics. However, many of the early settlers thought that Aboriginal people could be 'civilized' and 'Christianized', not as a basis for full assimilation but as a way of training a useful labour force. The settlers justified their land seizure by claiming that the Aborigines, who had no notion of private property, had made no use of the land.

The contemporary belief in the inherent racial inferiority of Aboriginal people meant that they were never considered as citizens. This rejection found legislative expression in 1889, when the Western Australian Constitution Act denied citizenship to all Aborigines, including those of mixed descent. While the Commonwealth Constitution of Australia gave Aborigines of mixed descent the right to vote, so-called 'full-bloods' were denied the right to vote in federal elections or to be counted in the first Commonwealth Census of 1911.

In this book, the terms 'European' and 'immigrant' are used to refer to all children whose ancestry could be traced to England or Europe. Because it proved impossible to determine with any accuracy the names of Aboriginal language groups from the nineteenth-century sources, the term 'Aboriginal' is used to refer to all children whose ancestry was wholly or partly Aboriginal. At that time, children with a mixed ancestry were identified as 'half-caste' or 'quarter-caste'. The terms 'full-blood' and 'half-blood' were also sometimes used. This book does not employ these terms except when quoting the words of contemporary figures.

Part I tells the story of immigrant children in Western Australia; their story is considered first because we learn about the presence, the number and the treatment of Aboriginal people through European eyes. The first chapter concerns the number of European children in Western Australian society before 1900 as a proportion of the whole population. For the period between 1829 and 1848, only anecdotal evidence about the presence of immigrant children in the colony is available, but the first census of 1848 provides a valuable source for the historian who wishes to reflect on the changing nature of the lives of colonial children. From then on, census material provides details about the number of children of immigrant descent in Western Australia, whether they lived in the towns or the country, and whether or not they went to school.

Chapter 2 discusses the work of immigrant children in the context of family labour undertaken in order to consolidate family holdings. The evidence shows that the people responsible for planning the first decades of settlement took it for granted that very young children were to be considered part of the work force. But some immigrant children, including those sent to Western Australia by the Society for the Encouragement of Juvenile Emigration, and the boys from the Parkhurst Prison, were especially imported from England to be put to work in the colony.[10]

The third chapter describes the expansion of education services for children of immigrant parents, and the decisions about who should be educated. By the end of the century, most of these children attended school. The slow development of education services by the colonial state was determined by the slow rate of economic development and the very low revenue base. The laws about compulsory education for these children, first introduced in 1871, paralleled the gradual changes in the economy that made it possible for European parents to manage without the labour of their children.[11] Although most European children were in school by the end of the century, the colonial government failed to provide a satisfactory system of secondary education. However, there were rapid developments in secondary education in the private sector in the 1890s. The legislation establishing secular education did not specifically exclude Aboriginal children from school: it simply did not mention them.

Chapter 4 concerns the fate of European children who were abandoned or came before the law in this society, and who were 'provided for' in various kinds of institutions. At first, orphanages in Western Australia were set up by Roman Catholic and Church of England bishops for children in need. These institutions, eventually called 'industrial schools', began to grow with the development of the economy in the 1860s, and some of them also took children who had been sentenced for criminal activity or for truancy. They gradually came to rely partly on financial support from the government, which, by the end of the century, legislated to set up its own institutions. By the 1890s, convicted children were often sent to an institution for a period far in excess of their original sentence. A limited amount of education was provided, but these unfortunate children spent most of their time working in and around such establishments under adult supervision or were apprenticed out to private employers.

Part II concerns the treatment of Aboriginal children. Chapter 5 discusses the demography of the Aboriginal population in the nineteenth century. As the counting of Aboriginal people was not seriously undertaken, this chapter relies on the limited evidence available in the census records, and contemporary anecdotal evidence.

Chapter 6 identifies the efforts made in the first half of the century to train young Aboriginal children as servants for the colonists. This early attempt at removing Aboriginal children from their parents, and confining them in an institution, to be sent out each day as servants in the houses of Perth families, was ultimately a failure. It was represented at the time by the Wesleyan Mission as an exercise in 'civilizing' and 'Christianizing' these children. Other institutions in the southern half of Western Australia, including New Norcia Mission, Ellensbrook and the Anglican Swan Native and Half-caste Home, which also housed Aboriginal children, had a much longer history. This chapter concludes by examining contemporary attitudes to the education of Aboriginal children.

There is a considerable body of history dealing with the nineteenth-century farming and pastoral frontier and the pearling industry, much of which is listed in the Bibliography. Too often, however, the focus is on the settlers and their activities, with Aborigines mentioned as extras in the landscape. There is seldom any real recognition that Aboriginal people did most of the work that laid the foundation for the wealth of a few families. Chapters 7 and 8 of this book concern the work done by Aboriginal children in the pastoral and pearling industries. The end of the convict period in Western Australia coincided with the opening up of the North West. Labour was again desperately short in the new areas, and Aboriginal people were either being displaced from their homelands by pastoralists holding leases, or being absorbed into the work force on what had once been their own land. Aboriginal children worked in the pearling industry and alongside their parents on pastoral stations, usually in return for rations. Almost no Aboriginal child, including children of mixed descent, went to school in the North West until the Roman Catholic mission was established at Beagle Bay in the early 1890s.

The final chapter concentrates on the two issues that were to prove decisive for the treatment of Aboriginal children in the twentieth century. The question of what should be done about children of mixed descent began to preoccupy many commentators in the 1890s. Gradually the idea grew that these children should be separated from their mothers and put in special institutions. The issue of Aboriginal Reserves also began to be aired. These ideas eventually found legislative expression in the 1905 Aborigines Act. The history of these nineteenth-century developments provides a background for understanding the further changes in policy towards Aboriginal children in twentieth-century Western Australia.

The history of the way children were treated by adults raises important questions about the ways in which cultural norms are transmitted from one generation to the next. Most of the elite of Western Australian society in this period clearly believed in maintaining the divisions between themselves and a poor and ill-educated working class, which would reproduce itself as the workers of the future. Their attitudes towards Aboriginal people were more confused. In many parts of the world, small colonizing elites had to learn to operate inside very large societies of indigenous people who were deeply affected but not destroyed by the colonizing process. But the colonizing initiatives of the Western Australian elite, which depended on control of the land, left the relatively small population of Aboriginal people in an impossible situation. On the one hand, most people of immigrant background were contemptuous of Indigenous culture, and both government policies and private economic initiatives threatened its survival. On the other hand, no one at this time seriously envisaged or encouraged genuine cultural assimilation. The processes of accommodation between people of different cultures, a historical commonplace for people elsewhere, were seriously impeded in nineteenth-century Western Australia.

PART I

EUROPEAN CHILDREN

CHAPTER 1

Counting the European population

Demographic framework

In 1830, the year after the first settlement of the Swan River Colony in the south-west of Western Australia, more than 1,000 immigrants arrived in thirty-nine sailing ships. Those with capital brought their possessions, their children and their servants. They were optimistic about the value of the land and ignorant of the difficulties of early settlement, soon to deter many of their countrymen. By the middle of the century, some twenty years later, the immigrant population of the settlement had reached only a little more than five times that number. Children made up a considerable part of most of the groups of emigrants who arrived in the colony: some of them part of families with capital, many of them members of the working poor who came with their masters. Whether rich or poor, whole families had to work to establish the first simple dwellings in the colony and provide the basis for a settled life.[1]

The statistical records for the demography of European children are much richer for the second half of the nineteenth century than they are for the earlier period, because the government conducted censuses regularly after 1848: in 1854, 1859, 1870, 1881, 1891 and 1901. The demographic profile of the colony became more detailed over time and, from 1848 onwards, included increasingly complex information about the age of European children and the number in school. In 1881, the census provided a special section on 'the ages of the people' and another on 'the education of the people', which included figures for school attendance and non-attendance in each district by European persons under 19 years of age.[2]

Two important events had a dramatic impact on the population profile of Western Australia in the nineteenth century. The first was the decision in 1850 to implement a scheme to bring convicts to the colony to boost the work force. Under this scheme, which lasted from 1850 to 1868, 9,700 men were transported. Very few of them were ever joined by wives or other family members and very few of them married in the colony. Apart from the convicts, the British Government agreed to send an equal number of free immigrants. Although the numbers of new immigrants who arrived in this period did not in fact ever quite equal the number of convicts, there was a rapid population growth of both bond and free.[3]

The second important event was the discovery of gold in the late 1880s, followed by the gold rush of the first half of the 1890s, which brought thousands of men, some with their families, to Western Australia.[4] These two developments meant that at both the middle and near the end of the century, there were, due to historical circumstances, reductions in the female-to-male ratio within the overall population and in the number of children as a percentage of that population.

In 1850, there were slightly more than 5,000 people of European descent in the colony. That number increased five-fold over the next twenty years, but a period of slow population growth followed, lasting until the mid-1880s. The population then grew rapidly in the next twelve years from 32,958 in 1884 to 137,946 in 1896. In that year, the proportion of females in the colony was only 42.28 per cent.

Children in the colony, 1829–1850

Although children of European origin were never central figures in the contemporary records of the Swan River Colony, there are some useful sources for establishing a profile of their overall numbers, their gender, their age, and whether they lived in towns or rural areas.[5] This limited demographic evidence also helps to uncover the contemporary ideology about the value of children and about the concept of 'childhood' in the colony.

The ways in which children were enumerated in the various kinds of contemporary census material illustrates what age categories were implied by the terms 'child' and 'children' in European immigrant society. Some records show that those listed as children were normally defined in this way because they were with their parents. For example, James Drummond, who appeared in the 1830 Muster Book, had seven children in the colony whose ages ranged from 3 to 18 years. Four of the Drummond children were over 12 years of age at the time of arrival.[6] These children, then, were the descendants of particular parents, implying a legal and obligatory relationship but no age category.

The passenger lists provided for the Western Australian colonial government, usually prepared by the captains of ships, also give some information about children. They did not at first list the children separately but included them as part of family groups. The passengers aboard the *Mistrell*, for example, included Mr and Mrs Brockman and one child and Olive Clulow and four children.[7] Occasionally, the children were listed according to their full names and ages,[8] but just as often passengers, including children, appeared under the name of the settler capitalist who was paying the fare, without details about age or occupation.[9] In most of these cases, children were identified as part of a family group, with no definition of 'childhood' in terms of age.

However, the passenger lists could be very detailed, as was the case with that supplied by Thomas Brown, captain of the *Simon Taylor*. It not only provided the names of all passengers but also separated adults from children, who were defined as those passengers under 14 years of age. The children were divided into two categories, those under 7 and those from 7 to 14 years of age.[10] The *Simon Taylor*, which arrived direct from London in 1842 after 111 days at sea, carried 219 passengers.[11] The captain's report revealed that most of the immigrants on the ship were assisted by public funds and had spent some time at the Immigrant Depot in England before embarkation.[12] Most of the family of Sam and Ann Caporn, for example, which included nine children, had waited for thirty days in the depot, although two of the older children were there for only nine days.[13] Also on board the *Simon Taylor* were the first eighteen of the boys from Parkhurst Prison on the Isle of Wight, many more of whom were to be sent to Western Australia between 1842 and 1850. They were brought to the colony as indentured labourers obliged to work out their sentences for periods from three to five years.[14] Several of these boys, who were recorded separately from those of a similar age who came with families, were 14 years of age. Passenger lists, then, sometimes did provide evidence about the ages of particular children and sometimes separated children from adults in a way that suggested an acceptance of the notion that childhood ended at 14 years of age.

There were a number of other enumerations of the population that might be examined to see how 'childhood' was defined in terms of age categories.[15] The first census conducted in Western Australia, in 1832, provided the actual ages of children, who were recorded along with their parents. There were, in other words, no separate categories for children.[16] This pattern continued in the census of 1836, which included the names, actual ages, occupations and places of residence of part of the population.[17] But the 'Statistical Report of the Colony of Western Australia', drawn up in June 1837, listed those under and over 12 years of age, suggesting an attempt to separate children from adults.[18] However, as some of those under 12 years had occupations recorded against their names,[19] this early attempt to define 'children' should not be seen as implying their freedom from the need to work.

Another possible source of information might seem to be the *Blue Books*, compendiums of statistical information sent regularly to the Colonial Office in London.[20] However, an examination of the section called 'Return of the Population, and of the Marriages, Births and Deaths' for the period 1834–50 reveals that age categories were not used during this period. The only children separately enumerated in this source are those of the military establishments of 1844, 1846 and 1850 and the children of Enrolled Pensioners in 1850.[21] In 1850, there were 126 children of the families of the Enrolled Pensioner Force sent to the colony to guard the convicts, while the number of children of members of the military establishment at any one time varied between forty and eighty.

By 1848, however, the statistics suggest that a clear definition of 'childhood' had at last emerged.[22] The 'Abstract of the Population' in October 1848, published in the *Government Gazette* of the time, separated the residents of the Swan River Colony according to the categories 'urban' or 'rural' and divided them along gender lines. Within these gender categories, the age profile tells us how many children there were under 3 years of age, and how many from 3 to 14 years of age. The rest of the population was listed under the age categories of 14 to 60 years and over 60 years. These officials in 1848 perceived 'childhood' as lasting from birth to 14 years of age, although it is not clear why the division between those under 3 years and from 3 to 14 years was made.

The total European population in the Swan River Colony in 1839, after ten years of settlement, was still only 2,610 persons, of whom 852 were females. By 1848, the population had more than doubled to reach 5,534. However, the gender imbalance present from first settlement continued, with only 2,310 females in the colony.[23]

The figures have been analysed to show the extent to which the population increase depended on net migration into the colony and on net natural increase. In 1830, the year of the greatest influx of colonists, when 1,050 people arrived and remained at Swan River, there were only twenty-six births compared to seventy-seven deaths. This was not the only year in which deaths outnumbered births. With minor variations, however, the numbers born in the colony increased steadily throughout the period until reaching 189 in 1845. This was the first of three years in the middle to late 1840s when the number of people leaving Swan River was greater than the number arriving. For five years during the first two decades of settlement—in 1832, 1836, 1845, 1846 and 1847—more people left the colony than came into it. However, by 1848, the net migration figure had increased dramatically and the yearly increase from those born in the colony exceeded 200 for the first time.[24] Margaret Anderson's analysis of marriage and child-bearing patterns for the period 1842–49 reveals that by the second decade, these early settlers were producing large families, 64 per cent of which included seven children or more.[25]

The census figures for 1848 provide the first clear picture of the total number of children of European extraction under 14 years of age in the colony. They also provide evidence concerning the gender divisions and whether the children lived in towns or in the country. There were 873 boys and 849 girls living in the countryside in 1848, a total of 1,722 children out of a population of 4,622 European people in the country. The total number of children in towns, including Perth, Fremantle, Bunbury, Albany and Guildford, was less than half the number in the country. There were 765 children living in these towns, of whom 371 were boys and 394 were girls, from a total town population of 1,908. The number of children under 3 years of age in 1848, compared to those between 3 and 14, reveals a population of very young families and high fertility levels.

Orphan and convict immigrant children before 1850

Some of the European children who came to the colony were not part of a family group but were deliberately imported as cheap labour for the settler capitalists. The Agricultural Society first considered the possibility of importing child labour in 1833. During the 1830s, fifty-four children were sent to the colony by the English Society for the Encouragement of Juvenile Emigration to become 'apprentices' to local capitalists. Another sixteen arrived in 1841.[26] There were also seven consignments of Parkhurst boys sent to the Swan River Colony as indentured labourers before 1850, all with three to five year sentences. Five ships arriving between 1850 and 1861 also carried Parkhurst boys.[27]

Under the Act that was introduced to provide for the guardianship and control of the Parkhurst boys, they were referred to collectively as 'juvenile immigrants'.[28] It is clear from Paul Buddee's detailed analysis of the records that most of the boys who came to Western Australia under this scheme were *over* 14 years of age, although there were some as young as 12. Of the eighteen 'boys' who arrived on the *Simon Taylor* in 1840, for example, four were 14 years of age, five were 15 years, eight were between 16 and 18 years and one was 20 years of age.[29]

European children in the census returns, 1848–1901

The demographic history of the settler population for the last half of the century can be built up by examining the census returns. The European population more than doubled between 1848 and 1854, because of the introduction of a convict labour force and an almost equal number of new settlers. Capital in the hands of the colonial government increased because of the sale of land, while the area under cultivation doubled in this short period. Apart from this, the convict establishment was paid for by the British Government, which meant that large sums entered the colony to pay for buildings and the administration of the system. The total population increased from 4,622 in 1848, to 12,008 in 1854, of whom 7,937 were male and 4,071 were female. The Registrar General, Charles Sholl, admitted that these figures were not accurate but claimed that they were 'a very close approximation to the actual conditions of the colony'. Five years later, in his introductory comments on the 1859 Census, the Colonial Secretary, Frederick Barlee, suggested that the overall figures for 1854 were probably inflated. However, since we have no other figures to rely on, we must take them at face value.[30]

The tables concerning children in the 1854 Census were organized differently from those of the 1848 Census, which listed children from birth to 3 years and from 3 to 14 years. In 1854, the categories were birth to 12 years and 12 to 21 years. Among the convicts under 21 years, there were twenty-four holders of conditional pardons and twenty-eight holders of tickets of leave. The census claims the total number of 'free' European children in the colony under 12 years of age to be 2,718 and those from 12 to 21 years to be 1,650, which gives a total of 4,368 young people under 21 years. According to the Registrar General, less than a quarter of the population (23.19 per cent) were children under 12 years. This figure cannot be compared with the 1848 Census, which used 14 years as the cut-off point, nor with the 1859 Census, which used 15 years as the upper limit of childhood.

The disproportionate ratio of males to females in the whole population had increased by the 1859 Census,[31] when there were 9,522 males and only 5,315 females, making a total population of 14,837. This was a 26.34 per cent increase in total population from 1854. The tables concerning children were again changed, this time providing a profile of children within five-year cohorts, as shown in table 1.

Table 1: Figures taken from the 1859 Census, showing the number of European children under 15 years

Age	Male	Female	Total
Under 1	263	313	576
1–5	862	842	1,704
5–10	734	734	1,468
10–15	551	555	1,106
Total under 15	2,410	2,444	4,854

The number of 4,854 given in the table for those under 15 years—a reasonable benchmark for the end of childhood—allows us to see that children made up 32.27 per cent of the total population in 1859. An accompanying census table of the number of children in each district shows that children in Perth and Fremantle, including the children of military personnel, numbered 2,127; that is, there were still more children in the country in towns or on farms than there were in the city.

According to the census of 1870, there were 24,785 people in the colony: 15,375 males and 9,410 females. This census also used five-year cohorts for showing the number and ages of the children of European descent in Western Australia (see table 2). The total of

9,157 for those under 15 years shows that children now made up 36.94 per cent of the total population, a small percentage increase over the 1859 figure. However, the percentage of children who lived in towns or on farms outside Perth and Fremantle had increased to nearly two-thirds of the total number of children. Only 3,261 children were living in Perth and Fremantle at this time, reflecting the rapid spread of population as more and more land was opened up.[32]

Table 2: Figures taken from the 1870 Census, showing the number of European children under 15 years

Age	Male	Female	Total
Under 1	369	358	727
1–5	1,423	1,377	2,800
5–10	1,547	1,570	3,117
10–15	1,275	1,238	2,513
Total under 15	4,614	4,543	9,157

The census of 1881 was predictably more complex than any of its predecessors, with a vast wealth of detail concerning each of the fourteen regions (two more than for the previous census). This makes some comparisons difficult. By 1881, the total population was 29,708, made up of 17,062 males and 12,646 females. This represented an increase in overall population from 1870 of 19.9 per cent, whereas the increase from 1859 to 1870 had been 67 per cent. The slackening off of population growth during this period was partly due to the ending of convict immigration but also because free immigration had slowed. This period saw a rapid rise in the number of persons born in the colony (17,773 persons for the whole period of settlement). Because there are an approximately equal number of boys and girls born in any breeding population, this natural increase had begun to level off the disparities between the number of males and females, especially apparent in the lower age group. In 1870, there had been 61.2 females for every 100 males, but by 1881 the number was 74.12 females for every 100 males.

The tables in the 1881 Census showed the number of children for each year of age, while the figure for those under 15 years was still given. There were 11,412 European children in the colony under the age of 15, with an equal number of males and females under 21. The total number under 21 made up 50.61 per cent of the total population. In his introductory explanatory comments, the Registrar General claimed that 'all persons under 15 and at the age of 65 and upwards [were] considered as dependent on the others for sustenance', thus hardening the impression that a new definition of childhood as the period up to 15 years had begun to emerge.[33]

The detailed age chart of the 1891 Census showed the totals under 15. There were 17,026 children in the colony, not including those solely of Aboriginal descent but including children of mixed descent. Of this total, 8,631 were males and 8,395 were females. The overall population of 49,782 persons had increased enormously in this period, because of the gold rushes, but this did not result in a comparative rise in the number of children, since most of the new immigrants were unaccompanied males.[34]

Table 3 consolidates the census returns of the population for the second half of the nineteenth century and shows the percentage rise in each period. In regional terms, the proportion of females to males was now more complicated, since in some towns the number of females outstripped that of males, while in the mining towns males made up by far the greatest proportion of the population.

Table 3: Figures taken from the 1901 Census, showing the real number and percentage increase between each enumeration

Year	Number	% increase
1843	3,853	
1854	11,743	204.8
1859	14,837	26.5
1870	24,785	67.0
1881	29,708	19.9
1891	49,782	67.6
1901	134,755	171.0

By the turn of the century, the total European population had risen to 134,755 persons, made up of 89,964 males and 44,791 females. In other words, there were now 63 females to every 100 males—only a very slight improvement on the 1891 figures. The 1901 age tables provided new classifications of various age groups into what were referred to as 'periods of life'. Thus, infancy was the period from birth to 2 years, childhood from 2 to 7, boyhood and girlhood from 7 to 14, adolescence from 14 to 21, manhood and womanhood from 21 to 50, mature age from 50 to 65, and old age from 65 onwards. The new category of 7 to 14 years for the period of childhood again altered the way the census figures were presented, but the figures for those under 15 years were provided separately, because it was still assumed that young people needed support until this age. Table 4 shows the age ranges at this time. There were 25,426 males under 14 years and 25,098 females under 14 years, indicating that a gender imbalance existed only in the adult population over 14 years of age, due to the excessive immigration of males over females.[35]

Table 4: Ages of the European population of Western Australia under 21 years, 1891, 1901

Age	Males			Females		
	1891	1901	% increase	1891	1901	% increase
0–2	1,434	4,687	226.85	1,429	4,616	223.02
2–7	3,191	9,282	190.88	3,051	9,117	198.82
7–14	3,532	11,457	224.38	3,479	11,365	226.67
14–21	3,300	10,464	217.09	2,954	8,454	186.19

While men always outnumbered women in the nineteenth-century Western Australian immigrant population, the approximately equal numbers of boys and girls born into large families maintained the gender balance among children. The demographic records reflect considerable uncertainty about when 'childhood' could be said to end, but by 1900 the census classification into 'periods of life' implied that children under 15 years of age were entitled to adult support. This was a remarkable change from the early days of settlement, when the work of children helped to support adults.

CHAPTER 2

Family and child labour

I N the Swan River Colony, the members of the official hierarchy, many of whom came with Lieutenant Governor Stirling on the *Parmelia,* not only were representing the British Government but were also an integral part of the capitalist class. The elite of this group attempted to secure its dominance and wealth through the control of large land grants.[1] The size of several early land grants suggests that some of these ambitious men hoped to establish vast land-holdings, comparable in size with those owned by the feudal aristocracy of earlier times or with the great estates of the high gentry in the eighteenth century.[2] George Fletcher Moore, for example, explained that since his prospects at the Irish Bar were uncertain, he had been attracted to the Swan River Colony in 1828 'by the hope of obtaining possession of a good estate' as well as some official appointments.[3] Moore was one of a group of settlers who not only held public office but also established themselves on large land grants, where they exploited an Aboriginal and European labour force that worked for wages barely sufficient for survival, or for no wages at all.[4]

The labour question was indeed of overwhelming importance at the time, since the success of these rural capitalists depended on the availability of cheap labour. The question of who was to be included in the work force in the colony is therefore of considerable importance if the nature of settler capitalism in the Swan River Colony is to be understood. Although the male head of a family group was sometimes the only one identified in the historical records in terms of his occupation, there is abundant evidence to show that his wife and children were part of the work force. However, the importance of women and children as workers has not been recognized in the existing literature, a failure that has seriously distorted the historical record.[5] The broad division between capitalist settlers and their workers, however they may have been identified in the original records, is much too schematic to convey the reality of human interaction in this period. This chapter explores family and child labour in the period before 1850.[6]

The economic value of children

From the time of settlement, various laws borrowed from English practice were applied in the colony to define gender relations within the family and to determine the age of majority. The age of marriage without the approval of parent or guardian was fixed at 21 years for males and 18 years for females, but this was altered by a colonial Act in 1845 to raise the age for females to 21.[7] Within marriage, the father had almost absolute power over his children until they reached the age of majority. He had the legal right to determine their religion, their education and their right to marry. He could put them out to work and take the proceeds. The rights of the father over questions of guardianship and custody were sacrosanct in 1829. The mother had legal rights over her children only if her husband had died, and even then these could be frustrated if her husband had appointed a legal guardian.

There was considerable social legislation in the nineteenth century concerning immigrant families and children. In 1845, for example, one of the earliest Acts of the colony dealt with the plight of women and children who had been left without adequate support, a problem that the colonial state hoped to pass on to near relatives.[8]

Under this Act, relatives were made liable for the support of destitute persons, especially wives, and children under 10 years of age. Magistrates were given the power to seize the goods of husbands or near relatives who attempted to evade their responsibilities.[9] Children over 10 years of age were considered able to support themselves. One part of this legislation gave magistrates the power, with the consent of one parent if that parent was living in the colony but otherwise without consent, to indenture any child between 10 and 18 years of age. Such children could be put to work in any reputable household, with the intention that they earn their keep and not become a charge on the state.

> And be it enacted, that it shall be lawful for any two justices, with the consent of either of the parents, if living, and in the Colony, but if otherwise, then without such consent, on the application of any reputable householder, to bind by indenture any child in respect of whose maintenance any order shall have been made under this Ordinance, such child having attained the age of ten years, as an apprentice, until he or she shall attain the age of eighteen years, to any master or mistress willing to receive such in any trade, business, or employment whatsoever suitable to the child, and every such binding shall be as effectual in law to all intents and purposes as if the child had been of full age and bound himself or herself to be such apprentice.[10]

Some of the earliest documents provide evidence of the economic value of women and children. In January 1829, the British Under Secretary for the Colonies, Horace Twiss, issued the first set of regulations 'for the guidance of those who may propose to embark, as settlers, for the new Settlement on the Western Coast of New Holland'.[11] The second paragraph of these regulations stated that settlers would be granted land at the rate of 40 acres for every sum of £3 they were prepared to invest. Paragraphs 4 and 5 of the regulations stipulated the ways in which such capital might be made up. All instruments of husbandry, for example, could be included in the total invested. Every 'labouring person' brought to Western Australia by a settler would be deemed to be worth £15 in the computation of the total capital outlay. The payment of the cost of emigration for one indigent labourer, therefore, represented an additional 200 acres of land for the capitalist.

The applications for land to the Colonial Secretary in the Swan River Colony began by listing the name of the settler applicant and all those people, including his own family and other individual servants or whole families, who had been brought to Western Australia at his expense. It is instructive, therefore, to consider the relative value of members of each labouring family according to age. These first regulations stated that women, and children above 10 years, were included in the class of 'labouring persons', and therefore each represented an addition of 200 acres to the land entitlement of the settler. In a revised set of regulations issued by the British Colonial Office on 3 February 1829, the value of children between 3 and 10 years of age was set out in the following terms:

> With respect to the Children of Labouring people under that Age i.e. 10 yrs, it is proposed to allow 40 Acres for every such Child, above 3 years old, 80 Acres for every such Child above 6 years old, and 120 for every such Child, above 9, and under 10 years old.[12]

While we cannot assume that children of such tender years were perceived as immediately valuable in the work force, this clause was clearly designed to encourage settler capitalists to pay for whole families to emigrate to the Swan River Colony. The same clause also foreshadowed subsequent legislation to make the settler capitalists responsible for the future maintenance of all such persons 'should they from infirmity or any other cause become unable to maintain themselves there'.

Two applications for grants of land in 1829 and 1830 illustrate the way in which these regulations worked. In January 1830, William Locke Brockman arrived via the *Mistrell* with his wife, Fanny, and their two-year-old son, Edmund.[13] His letter applying for a land grant described the applicant's 'family' including, apart from these three, one carpenter, one bricklayer, one servant and three labourers, one of whom had a wife. The report of the valuation of Brockman's claim indicates that he was allowed £105 for the labourers he had brought to the colony: a claim of £15 for each person, including the labourer's wife. This sum represented 1,400 acres of land as part of his grant. The total value of his capital, which also included 'instruments of husbandry', was estimated to be £1,512 4s 11d, for which he was granted 20,160 acres.

An application for land in September 1829 by Robert Antell Partridge was based on his claim that he had brought with him three adult labourers and two children, as well as instruments of husbandry. For his servants and their children, he was allowed £54 in the computation of his capital, indicating that the two children, of 4 years and 7 years, were between them worth 120 acres of land.[14] Thus, both women and children were specifically taken into account as part of the potential work force for the new colony. Both at the time of their arrival and in terms of their future capacity to reproduce the labour force, they were essential to the colony's survival. However, the intention to make those with property, the settler capitalists, responsible for any workers who should prove unable to maintain themselves reflects the current perception in Britain that indigent people could be a heavy burden on the state.

The so-called 'empty lands' of the colonies were touted by the advocates of colonization as a way of employing the surplus population of Britain, while at the same time reproducing the class structure to be found at home. The end of the old Poor Law, first introduced in Elizabeth's reign, did not come until 1834, but Poor Law assistance had been gradually reduced from 1780, exacerbating the plight of a growing section of the population. Many contemporary social theorists, who wrote tracts about the social problems of the later eighteenth and early nineteenth centuries, cast the debate in terms of 'overpopulation' and 'surplus labour', the solution to which was emigration.[15] In the Swan River Colony, the size of land grants, tied partly to the employment of labour, was such that the new settler capitalists could be assumed to have the resources to prevent the development of an indigent class that would otherwise become a burden on the colonial state.

A close analysis of other documents from the early period provides an opportunity to consider how childhood was defined, and reveals much about the contemporary attitude towards the value of children, and what work might be expected from them. Labourers' children under 3 years of age were disregarded in the question of land entitlement. Yet their mothers were counted and were therefore considered important in the process of production and reproduction. The age of 10 years was the point at which 'children' were to be regarded as *persons* and given adult work status, as suggested by their inclusion in the regulations as part of the general category of 'labouring persons'. This is underlined by a letter written in January 1829 by Under Secretary Twiss to Thomas Peel, who had begun to plan his scheme designed to win him a grant of 250,000 acres of land in the Swan River Colony:[16]

> I am told your impression is that your stipulation was only to take out 400 souls, and that under that denominator you might include children of tender ages. If you will turn to the Correspondence, you will find that my expression has always been not *souls* but *persons*, the object of the large grant to you being to secure persons capable of all the work necessary for a new settlement. The four hundred, therefore, whom you are to land, must be persons of more than ten years of age, although you have an allowance for children below that age, according to the rate explained to you in my letter of the 21st of the present month.[17]

The letter of 21 January, to which Twiss alluded, simply set out the allowance for children of various ages in terms of land allotment, as previously listed in the land regulations.[18] It seems, then, that children over 10 years of age, regardless of gender, were considered to be 'persons capable of all the work necessary for a new settlement'.

Eight years after the first settlement of the Swan River Colony, Governor Stirling sent a dispatch to Lord Glenelg, including a table 'illustrative of the combinations which take place between land, capital and labour, in the several occupations of colonial life in this country'. The table was accompanied by comments on the principles lying behind its framing, a discussion of the effects of the occupations of the people on their social and moral condition, and, finally, Stirling's comments on the 'principal objects to be attended to in framing regulations relating to land'.[19] Although this dispatch was designed to promote particular land policies, it also reveals much about the real nature of family labour in the Swan River Colony.

The table itself contains a column describing the labour required for certain kinds of occupations and the wages that would have to be paid. Whereas stock keeping involving fifty head of cattle on 2,000 acres of pasture needed only one herdsman, 600 head of sheep on 3,000 acres was said to require a herdsman's family consisting of three people. Mixed farming, involving the planting of some crops and the keeping of sheep, horses and cattle, altogether requiring 7,500 acres of land, was envisaged as needing a large work force consisting of one superintendent, three shepherds, three ploughmen and eight boys and women. Other sections dealing with tillage and with whaling have similar entries indicating the numbers and kinds of persons required as labourers. The working of arable and pasture land 'in proper proportions' on a farm of 5,000 acres, for example, was estimated to require a superintendent and a work force of 'ploughmen, shepherds, women and boys, twenty nine in number'.

Stirling said that this dispatch was 'guided by attention to the State of things *as they exist at present in this settlement*' (my emphasis). It suggests that while there were some occupations, particularly small-scale stock herding and whaling, that were being carried out by adult males, most of the activities in the colony depended on family labour. Stirling argued that his evidence suggested that supermedial tillage and supermedial stock keeping (that is, those arrangements employing the greatest number of people) would produce the most rapid accumulation of capital. However, he believed that the colony should support the smaller establishments, since they offered 'steady and constant employment to boys and women, and even children, and tend thereby to keep families together under parental superintendence'. Since well over half the children of European origin lived in the countryside in the Swan River Colony, Stirling's table is invaluable evidence of the importance of family labour, including the labour of children.

Contemporary attitudes to the employment of children

Further evidence of contemporary attitudes to servants and labourers, many of whom were children, comes from the diaries and letters of early settlers. They assumed that they had the right to profit from the work of the poor, including children, and from the exploitation of Aboriginal land. Some colonists were explicit in their advocacy of child labour. William Tanner, a Wiltshire landowner, emigrated in 1831 with his family and servants, including one Jeremiah Cook, his wife and ten children.[20] Tanner was granted 35,000 acres of land, selected in the Swan district and the Avon Valley. He had not been long in the colony when he wrote to his mother and sisters, complaining of the costs of servants and outlining the arrangements in his own household:

> I allude to the scarcity of female servants which of course causes the wages of those that are to be got to be high. £36 a year is the present highest wages, girls of 16 or 18 get £10 or £12 a year, below 14 years old is to find them in clothes and give them no wages. Two of the little Cooks, (of Kenneth) we have spared in this way, Phoebe and Sarah. Betsy we have as a nurse maid, Jane is our cook to whom we give £10 a year as she is a good girl (she is bound to me at no wages, but now her father is dead I should have to find her in raiment which would have cost her £6 a year. She is to have £12 a year next half year).[21]

Tanner's letters, like those of other settlers, were partly designed to provide useful advice and information for friends and acquaintances, some of whom were themselves contemplating emigration to the new colony. He referred in 1831 to the memorial sent to the Colonial Secretary in London requesting that labourers' families be sent out, commenting that 'people learn to do almost entirely without women servants by employing boys and men in cooking and various other things they don't often do with you'.[22] He instructed his mother concerning the indenture system, particularly in regard to the emigration of children:

> I would advise any lady coming out here to bring one or two girls from the age of 9 to 13, if they leave England at the former age they will be able to do something by the time they arrive, if they be above the latter they will probably be soon married which will annul the engagement with you. A written engagement or rather *an indenture of apprenticeship*, signed by themselves and possibly by their guardians or parent, is absolutely necessary, a common *indenture* of apprenticeship is *by far* the best for any persons under age. [original emphasis]

As Tanner indicates, capitalists could find themselves without female servants, in spite of having paid their fares, if they were not indentured, since these female immigrants could command high wages in the early days of the settlement. In any case, marriage annulled all former work agreements. Tanner suggested that the girls be apprenticed at an age that was young enough to guarantee a reasonable length of service before marriage. This early correspondence from the Swan River Colony suggests that, for some settlers, children were regarded as the most desirable emigrants for the labour force because they could be more readily controlled and, in a period of labour shortage, commanded much lower incomes. Tanner continued:

> Perhaps boys between 14 and 16 are the next best persons to bring, indeed I should prefer them to men for most purposes (they of course won't do as good mecanics [sic], not having had the necessary experience) only that it is most desirable to have females. Have those under age

bound for 7 years, tho' when they are 21 they become free. I would not contract to give a minor any wages...[23]

The Tanner family, which had been granted 35,000 acres of land, lived in Perth and depended on their servants for domestic and farm labour.[24] William Tanner's resources and energies were such that he was able to establish the Western Australian Bank with John Septimus Roe in 1840 and keep part ownership of the *Inquirer* newspaper. He acted as a director of the Perth Agricultural Society for a period in the 1840s, and accepted appointment to the Legislative Council.

Thomas Brown and his wife, Eliza, left England for the colony in 1840 and took up the estate of 'Grass Dale', 11 square miles in extent, about 4 miles from York, and later also a large pastoral grant called 'Glengarry' near Champion Bay. In 1851, Thomas Brown was appointed to the Legislative Council by the Governor and then as a Police Magistrate, first at Perth and later at Fremantle. In spite of their large land-holdings, it is clear from Eliza Brown's letters that her husband was both a contractor and a working farmer for much of the 1840s in order to keep up his mortgage payments. Her picture of a working 'household' includes immediate family members, Aborigines and hired children. One Aboriginal boy called Corell worked for a long period with the family, exchanging some of the domestic chores with their son, Thomas, who was sharing the household tasks at 7 years of age. Eliza Brown also had the assistance in 1845 of a Parkhurst 'boy'. She explained to her father that this juvenile emigrant was bound to her for five years and that she had contracted to feed and clothe him and 'pay the Government about £3 a year for his services'. A few months later, she told her father that she had had only one female domestic servant for more than twelve months, 'quite a little girl'.[25] Adults and children, both Aboriginal and European, worked side by side in this society. Distinctions of class and colour may have been disregarded while the work was being done, but they are revealed with great clarity when the wage structures are analysed. Aborigines received no monetary payment at all, and the prevailing shortage of female labour led to the employment of children for their keep or for a pittance in wages.

In outlying regions, the shortage of labour and the problem of finding servants were even more acute. John Ramsden Wollaston, for example, tried desperately to maintain servants in his small household first at Picton and then at Albany. It gradually becomes clear, as he recounts the details of his daily life, that his wife, Mary, was constantly involved in household chores, and that the few servants they were able to employ were either not satisfactory or not permanent. In April 1842, the *Diadem* arrived with a boatload of working emigrants and Wollaston hired a man and his wife

> and a very nice lad belonging to another family. The two former for £30 a year and the lad for what I please… I have taken this step as an act of necessity and I hope and pray that I may be able to pay and feed them by a providential increase of our means.

This first couple proving unsatisfactory, he then employed 'a man and his wife, two boys and a little girl'. He remarked in his diary that

> the boys are very useful; the little girl too young to do anything. Wages for the whole party—£50 a year and board. This is a fearful undertaking, but we were drawn to it from necessity, for Mary and I could not continue to work as we have done without wearing ourselves out.[26]

During this period, Wollaston was living off his private means and constructing his own house, as well as a local church where he hoped to conduct regular services with a stipend from the government. His journal gives an account of how the members of the family, and those servants and Aborigines dependent on the family, were engaged. There were clearly divisions on the basis of class and ethnicity. The servants lived in the old hut and did not eat with the Wollaston family; the Aborigines were provided with flour and some of the meat they killed in lieu of wages, and were not provided with any dwelling. The servants could leave if they found they could make better arrangements, and they could be dismissed at any time. The Aborigines arrived and left again on a fairly irregular basis. In spite of these elements of fluidity, we can see that this 'household' was jointly engaged in an enterprise not unlike the family economy of the European peasantry, one that interlocked occasionally with the market economy. Yet the Wollaston family had the pretensions and ideology of the English gentry class and had come to the colony in the hope that they would be able to provide for their large family accordingly. Both John and Mary Wollaston were in their fiftieth year when they determined to leave his curacy at Wickham and follow their son to the Swan River Colony. They arrived with two daughters and three of their sons. Wollaston was finally provided with a stipend by the Governor and in 1849 became the first archdeacon of the Swan River Colony. But before he was able to re-establish himself as a clergyman, he had been forced to try to live off the land, like many families in the first twenty years of settlement.

This excerpt from Wollaston's diary illuminates the pattern of family labour, common in all the settled districts:

> Our outdoor labours are progressing. John is finishing his boat, which answers very well. Our whale boat is sunk in the river and must be hauled up and repaired. William and George are trussing barley straw to save for the cattle and sifting the little grain that we have saved. Teddy is going tonight to sleep in the bush to hunt at daybreak tomorrow. My man Moore and his boys are clearing and burning for next year's crops. Mary and the girls are attempting to mend holes in stockings, as big as a fist. Lastly, I have been doing odd jobs and helping here and there...[27]

The letters and diaries of the early settlers suggest that the children of the labouring class, many of them with parents who had considerable trade skills, were absorbed very early into a work force that also included the children of their masters and itinerant Aborigines, both adults and children. This was the characteristic pattern in the countryside until 1850, during which time the labour necessary for clearing land, building houses, caring for flocks and herds, and undertaking domestic service was in very short supply.

Education was provided for some immigrant children, at first by religious institutions and, after 1846, by the colonial state. However, attendance was not high and did not rule out both regular and irregular participation in the labour force.

Encouraging family emigration

The idea of 'family' or 'household' labour remained as one of the colony's working assumptions in confronting the very real economic problems before 1850. In 1838, the shortage of labour was such that the Governor in Council agreed to a sum of £1,000 being made available 'for the purpose of encouraging the introduction into the Colony of Labouring Persons'.[28] At the same time, it was agreed that local settler capitalists could have 'an abatement from the price at which Crown land may be purchased to the extent of £20 for every married labourer and his family'. This was followed in 1840 with an arrangement whereby intending settlers leaving England could obtain extra land on arrival if they undertook to pay for the emigration of labouring families:

> Purchasers or depositors are to be entitled to claim bounty on emigrants introduced by them, if coming within the description presently to be specified, at the rate of one adult person of 15 years and upwards, two children between 7 and 15, or three children between 1 and 7, for every 20 which they pay.[29]

It is clear from a later set of instructions to the Land and Emigration Commissioner from Lord John Russell that the choice of family groups was made because the encumbrance of children encouraged people to see the advantages of emigration.[30] The presence of children also made it more difficult for immigrants to change their minds or to move around once they arrived in the colony. In 1842, the desire to maintain a stable labour force in steady employment led to the introduction of legislation aimed at controlling the movement of workers. Any person 'employed in any manner howsoever, either as a manual or a home servant or in any other capacity', who left that employment could be brought before two justices of the peace, who were also usually landowners, and condemned to three months' hard labour.[31]

Orphans as a labour force

The children who are most visible in the colonial records are the juvenile immigrants, the first of whom came to the colony from England as labourers in 1834 under the auspices of the Society for the Encouragement of Juvenile Emigration.[32] The records reveal that the most eligible children, in terms of their potential for apprenticeship, were those between 9 and 14 years of age.

In July 1833, the colonists became aware that a new society had been set up in London 'for the permanent support of Orphan and Destitute Children by means of Apprenticeship in the Colonies'. The provisional committee of this body wanted to know whether healthy boys and girls between 12 and 15 years of age were required for service in the colonies and, if so, how many of each sex were needed. The society also sought advice on whether a system of apprenticeship could be instituted for these children, or whether there was some other way of shifting responsibility for them to some authority in the colonies, 'the children being without parents or other legal guardians'.[33]

In 1833, the Agricultural Society in the Swan River Colony took up the question of the economic advantages of importing child labour under such a scheme, and its possible implementation was discussed in the press:

> There are but few families in the Colony, who have not experienced considerable inconvenience, from the dearth of servants, or sacrifice, where they could be procured, from the enormous wages which are expected, and obtained, for services of a very *mediocre grade*. We have little doubt there are many families would readily give security for the employment of certain descriptions of

servants, suited to their avocations, at a specified rate, which would fully reimburse the society, for their primary outlay, and effect a saving to the colonists in the first year of half the expense attending their conveyance hither. The number and description of apprentices by this means would easily be arrived at, and evince our disposition to offer every assistance in the furtherance of so benevolent an object.[34] [original emphasis]

Debate ensued concerning the possible setting up of a colonial committee to arrange the dispatch of such children, and the appointment of a colonial agent who would receive them and place them as apprentices with 'settlers of good character'.[35] In September 1834, the regulations were hurriedly put in place for apprenticing the boys and girls from Britain already 'arrived in the colony from the Society for the Encouragement of Juvenile Emigration'.[36] The boys were to be indentured until 21 years of age and the girls until 18, and each was to receive clothing and wages of between 1s 6d and 3s a month, according to age. The fee returnable to the society for each boy or girl was to be £12, to be paid as the committee determined. The speed with which these arrangements were made was due to the fact that the first group of these children had already arrived on the *James Pattison*, under the care of Governor Stirling, who was returning to the colony from England. They were then placed in employment under the new terms of apprenticeship, which were reported to be 'highly liberal, and advantageous to those settlers requiring additional cheap labour'.[37]

The two problems of destitute children and the need for labour and population in the colonies had long been associated. The Philanthropic Society set up in 1788, and incorporated by Act of Parliament in 1806, took pauper boys and girls into schools that provided training in certain skills and then found them places in 'service'—sometimes in England, sometimes overseas. Those initiatives came originally from the setting up of the Society for the Suppression of Juvenile Vagrancy, later called the Children's Friend Society, which operated for only three years under that name because of the outcry about the treatment of emigrant children in South Africa.[38]

An Act of George I had embodied the notion of giving those 'who contracted to transport convicts a property and interest in their services', and juveniles were included in those sentenced to transportation.[39] Earlier legislation presupposed an organized traffic for the transportation of children for commercial profit.[40] The Poor Law Amendment Act of 1834 empowered parishes to assist in the emigration of the poor, including children who were destitute or orphaned. An amendment to the Act in 1850 sought to control such emigration by requiring that these children indicate their agreement before a justice of the Petty Sessions. It required that Poor Law Boards satisfy themselves concerning the provision for the welfare of such children, both on ships and overseas. These precautions were inserted as the result of a debate about the fate of more than 4,000 girls between the ages of 14 and 18 years who had emigrated from Ireland to various parts of Australia.[41]

The Parkhurst children: The first convict labour force

The belief that children were a valuable part of the work force was further reflected in the decision to bring boys from the Parkhurst Prison, to be apprenticed as cheap labour to local landowners and businessmen.[42] Legislation was passed in 1842 to provide for the management of this scheme in the colony and to outline the rights and responsibilities of these children. The Governor had the power to appoint a legal guardian for the Parkhurst boys, whose ages ranged from 12 to 21 years.[43] As discussed in chapter 1, this Act raises the question of the legal definition of childhood, since the ages of these 'juveniles' covered such a wide spectrum. The guardian had the power to apprentice the boys to any approved master or mistress for two to five years, and he retained the right of access to them.

The Parkhurst children were the subjects of a special law because they were technically prisoners, and must therefore be seen as the first convicts to come to the Swan River Colony.[44] The restraints on their freedom might be seen as stemming from this cause. But such constraints also made it possible for local settlers to exploit their labour for minimum wages, at a time when wages in the free labour market were being driven up by a shortage of workers. Part of the first clause of the Act, which stated that the immigrants who were subject to the Act were to be named in the *Government Gazette*, was reworded in 1844 and amended in 1849 to cover groups of children other than those specifically mentioned in the previous Act.[45] The extension of these controls over all immigrant apprentices reveals the paradox that all such persons, whether or not they were prisoners, were particularly vulnerable to exploitation because of their juvenile status. Far from protecting these 'infants', as the law defined them elsewhere, it singled them out for special duties and obligations and for special punishments.

According to the historian Paul Buddee:

> one can commiserate with the early settlers in Western Australia when few, if any of them, had yet adjusted fully to the hardships of the new country and its remote situation, suddenly to find themselves with hundreds of Artful Dodgers thrust upon them. Yet they tackled this new challenge, determined to make the boys trustworthy workers for them, and in most cases succeeding.[46]

However, these children were *not* 'thrust upon' the people of the Swan River Colony: their emigration was eagerly awaited by the settler capitalists, who wanted cheap labour.

A special prison, to which a farm was attached, had been established at Parkhurst on the Isle of Wight in 1838.[47] This prison was designed to take boys over 14 years of age for a period of preparation and training before they were sent overseas. However, it seems unlikely that any of those transported learned any skills, since few worked on the farm before 1849, by which time the last group had left for Western Australia. Between 1838 and 1853, 1,498 children were sent to Australia and New Zealand. They were permitted to emigrate as ticket-of-leave prisoners, which meant that they were free, with a conditional pardon, at the end of an apprenticeship. In that period, 334 boys were sent to Western Australia to be indentured as servants or apprentices of local settlers.[48] The establishment of Parkhurst has been seen by some historians as an essentially benevolent solution, found by English society, for reforming and educating juvenile criminals, with a view to their ultimate absorption into colonial society as free men.[49] But, since it acted as a juvenile emigration agency for colonial settlers, it was also one of the moves by which property owners in the colonies were able to benefit from the revenue provided by the British Government for the original incarceration and supposed training of these children.

The first group of boys from Parkhurst Prison arrived on the *Simon Taylor* in good health on 20 August 1842, and were kept in the Immigration Depot until they could be allotted to prospective employers. In September, the Act that allowed for the appointment of a guardian and set out the conditions under which the boys were to be apprenticed was passed in the Legislative Council.[50] The children, at least in law if not in practice, had some redress against neglect or ill-usage in the right of appeal to a justice of the peace. Employers were responsible for 'the moral, religious and technical instruction, the health, comfort and general treatment' of their apprentices. But they also had the power to bring recalcitrant apprentices before a justice of the peace. The punishment for 'misdemeanor, misconduct or ill behaviour' was

> commitment to any Home of Correction or Common Gaol with hard labour for any term not exceeding three calendar months, and the Court may fine such offender to the extent of all or any part of any annual allowance then due to him; and in case of a second or further conviction may order (in addition to such fine and imprisonment with hard labour) that such offender shall undergo a whipping not exceeding three dozen lashes.[51]

These clauses followed closely the earlier breach of contract legislation and put a great deal of power in the hands of employers of child labour—especially as the courts were presided over by justices of the peace, who were also landowners. Nor did the apprentices have any recourse to legal counsel. In January 1843, Jonathon Schoales, who was a private speculator in immigrant labour and who had been appointed Guardian of Juvenile Immigrants under this Act, reported to the Governor concerning the fate of the first eighteen boys. Some people were reluctant to have them as apprentices, partly because there were local children who were seeking apprenticeships. But Schoales also reported that some potential employers objected because the boys were 'so very small...and delicate in appearance'.[52]

This initial reluctance was soon overcome, and all the boys were apprenticed.[53] After barely six months had elapsed, Schoales was able to report that he already had fourteen applications for apprentices from any future juvenile emigrants brought to the colony. Only two complaints had been received about the behaviour of the children and, in each case, he had been able to 'induce the masters to receive the boys back again'.[54] Schoales, their guardian, reported in detail on each boy, indicating that many of them were able to adapt well to their new circumstances and had received excellent reports from their employers. Such reports dwelt mainly on their usefulness or otherwise to their employers. Parkhurst boy No. 17, for example, was unusually fortunate in having his indentures cancelled 'and the remainder of the time given to him as a reward for his good conduct; and on account of his age, was now employed boating on the Swan River'.

But some boys were unable to accept their new situations with equanimity, sometimes because their indenture period extended beyond the expiry of their original sentence. Parkhurst boy No. 12, a shepherd, was 'removed from his former master on complaints by both parties. I think the lad's temper is ruffled by having to serve so long over the period of his sentence'.[55] Some boys were declared unsatisfactory for some reason or were regularly punished. Parkhurst boy No. 32, for example, was 'incorrigible; in constant punishment', while No. 34 was removed from his former mistress for being 'too small and weak'. The identification numbers were those given by Schoales, who regularly prepared a report for the Governor.[56] According to the 1845 report, forty-six of these boys were 'first class' and had not been reported for any fault during the previous year. Only two boys were classified as incorrigible. Jonathon Schoales believed that very little misconduct was 'concealed' from him.

There was increased demand for Parkhurst boys in 1845 with the improvement in the colony's economy, which led to a new labour shortage. These immigrant boys were taken into the households of European settlers, both in Perth and in outlying districts. Altogether, seven consignments of Parkhurst boys were sent to Western Australia before 1852. The boys were indentured for periods of two to five years, and their experiences as family servants, apprentices and farm workers varied greatly.

In 1845, Schoales addressed a number of difficult questions that had arisen during the three years of experimentation with the immigration of juveniles from Parkhurst Prison.[57] While some of the apprentices claimed that their indentures actually extended their sentence period, others seemed to be shortening their sentences considerably if, in fact, they were to be regarded as 'free' at the end of their indenture period. Another issue of great interest concerned the pattern of behaviour after their indenture period was completed. At this time, there were only four apprentices who had completed their time and two of them, or possibly three, had chosen to remain in the colony as skilled workmen.

But probably the most important issue concerned the need identified by both the guardian and the Governor to separate the hardened and incorrigible offenders from those who gave satisfactory service. The Governor at first claimed that the plan of government juvenile immigration, which aimed at permanent reform, would not achieve its greatest possible success unless the Governor had the power 'to make a sudden and terrible example'.[58] The threat he proposed for a lad who repeatedly misbehaved was that of banishment, which implied a transfer of the offender to Van Diemen's Land. In his report, Schoales was less arbitrary and more inclined to suggest comparatively reasonable remedies for the incorrigibles. He no longer wanted the cost and responsibility of keeping them at the Immigration Depot. He suggested that the depot be removed from Perth to 'complete isolation', where he could put the incorrigible boys to useful work and keep them separated from others who might be contaminated by their example. He denied that he wanted a prison, and yet his words do not sustain his denial. 'I would have neither bolt nor bar, *except so far as requisite to afford due separation, classification, and, above all, some degree of solitary confinement* [my emphasis].'[59]

The settler ideology, which rationalized the employment of other people's children, emerges most clearly in the documents written for the Colonial Office. The colonial Governors and their appointees were either justifying action already taken, or urging changes of policy, which had to be supported by persuasive arguments. But the evidence is overwhelming that all sections of the settler elite supported the use of child labour. The indefatigable Jonathon Schoales sent a circular to fifty-three employers of the Parkhurst boys in 1845.[60] Almost all of these members of the colonial elite, including members of the Legislative Council, justices of the peace, clergymen, surgeons, merchants and land-holders, replied to the circular and agreed that the benefits of the system counter-balanced its evils. They also agreed that more boys were needed, and that their presence would not 'contaminate' the children of the free settlers. Everywhere in the Swan River Colony, 'family' labour was supplemented by the work of the Parkhurst children and by Aborigines, both adults and children, who were gradually being absorbed into a clearly defined working class. Both groups were regarded as especially valuable because they could be employed for their keep without any regular wage, they could be readily controlled and instructed, and they could be expected to reproduce a compliant working class within a generation.

The punitive attitudes of these adult males against adolescent boys is revealing of the nature of this colonial venture. The colony was undercapitalized and its success depended on the land being made productive. The settlers had come with the intention of re-creating the class structure already existing in Great Britain, whereby rural and merchant capitalists maintained themselves at the expense of an impoverished work force. Yet here the shortage of labour, which had driven up the price that labourers could command, had limited the profitability of their capital investments in land. There were no already established crops that could be expropriated, as in other parts of the British Empire; there were no really quick profits to be made out of trade of any kind, even though some trading ventures had soon been established.

Ending the importation of unaccompanied children

The importation of unaccompanied children as child labour ceased
in the second half of the nineteenth century because of the arrival of
adult convicts after 1850, which led to the gradual transformation of
the Swan River Colony's economy. By 1868, 9,700 men had worked
on government projects and as ticket-of-leave prisoners on private
holdings. They were responsible for the construction of many public
buildings including the Fremantle Gaol, Government House, the
Perth Town Hall, the Supreme Court building, the Pensioner Barracks
and the Governor's Residence on Rottnest, as well as smaller
buildings in regional areas. Their labour also consolidated the
economic position of the rural and commercial capitalist class in the
southern regions of the colony. The arrangement with the British
Government in 1850, which saw the arrival of the convicts, also
stipulated that an equal number of free emigrants should come to
Western Australia as long as convicts were dispatched. The number
of these immigrants who were young women, especially requested
by the colonists as servant girls, reveals that some kinds of labour
shortages persisted.

The shortage of servants led to an unsuccessful attempt in
1885 to revive the idea of importing children as future workers. A
scheme was envisaged whereby the Immigration Board would foster
the emigration of girls between the ages of 10 and 11 years from
England, so that they might become inmates of a special Training
Home for Girls in the colony, with the object of supplying the
demand for female servants. Miss Ellen Barlee, who first put the
proposal to the Crown Agent in London, envisaged a receiving home
in England where parents could leave their children until they were
shipped overseas. Like most earlier and later schemes to provide
child labour, the whole exercise was rationalized in terms of child-
saving.

> Now if West Australia, for instance, would open a training
> Home for 50 children to commence with, well selected, in
> a few years they would go out into families and act as
> leaven in the field of service, while a constant supply

would follow; and so on in most of the colonies. England would thus be saved the sin of letting them remain, as at present, wild and wicked. Few who have not tried it know how useful a well-trained child of 12 or 14 is in a home, and how easily moulded to its employer's requirements...I am convinced, were this scheme set on foot and aided by State Emigration, most of our colonies would adopt it for both boys and girls, in preference to adult emigration, and 3 or 4000 children might, as the scheme progressed, be yearly shipped and saved from ruin. Privately Miss Rye and Miss McPherson are doing this— but it is needed on a larger scale, and in most Colonial Towns surely ladies could be found to organize such Homes, and work them under Government supervision.

While the idea apparently appealed to M. F. Ommanney, Crown Agent for the Colonies, the Western Australian Immigration Board did not follow it up.[61] The Colonial Secretary brought the matter before the Legislative Council in 1885, but the scheme received little support. Maitland Brown, the elected Member for Gascoyne, said that while the scheme was characterized by philanthropic intentions, the cost to the colony of training children from 6 years of age until they could be employed at 14 would be tremendous. He thought it desirable that children be kept in institutions in England until they reached 14 years and then sent to the colony.[62] The plan had some things in common with earlier schemes to provide cheap labour, but is more clearly a forerunner of the twentieth-century importation of thousands of unaccompanied children under the Fairbridge scheme, and the Christian Brothers' emigration scheme.[63]

The gradual proliferation of schools during the convict period is evidence that some of the European settlers had become able to manage without the assistance of their own children. However, European children continued to work with their families for the rest of the century, often at the expense of attending school.

CHAPTER 3

Parsimony and discrimination
in education

NINETEENTH-CENTURY legislation on education is commonly interpreted as evidence of the gradually increasing commitment to the importance of education. However, there were committed educationalists in the colony from its earliest days, many of whom struggled throughout their lifetimes to improve educational opportunities, even though some were only interested in education for a small elite. There were also landowners and other capitalists in this new society who were reluctant to lose the labour services of very young people, even if they were their own children. Compulsory elementary education was not developed until the settlers were well established and had an alternative supply of labour. Even then, they had to be forced by law to send their children to school and, in the North West, pearlers and pastoralists continued to use child labour well into the twentieth century.

Elementary education for European children

While it is clear that European child labour was commonplace for several decades after settlement, some European children were being educated during this period.[1] Many of the first schools in the Swan

River Colony were 'private venture schools' established by individuals for private profit. They could be day, evening or boarding schools. A total of seventy-six such schools were established in the Swan River Colony before 1871, thirty-one of them in Perth and forty-five in the country. Although some of them lasted for only a short period, between them they provided either 'a patchwork of education provisions over enormous distances', when no government-supported services were available, or an alternative to the government secular schools.[2] One of the most successful religious schools was that set up at the Convent of Mercy in St Georges Terrace by six sisters of the church who arrived with the Catholic Bishop, Dr John Brady, in 1846. The school, which opened in 1849, immediately began to teach children beyond primary school age, and can thus be seen as the first secondary school in Western Australia. Two-thirds of the sixty girls who first attended this school were from Protestant families.[3]

Two government-funded schools, the Perth Boys' School and the Perth Girls' School, were established as a combined school in 1846; they were separated in the following year. The first pupils attended the combined school, also known as the Colonial School, in the courthouse. These schools were open to all religious denominations 'at a scale of payment so low as to admit the children of all but the most destitute. The latter are admitted to learn reading, writing and arithmetic free of any charge'.[4] Government-funded schools were also set up at Fremantle, York and Albany.

In 1847, Governor Irwin appointed a Committee for the Management of Colonial Schools, which was almost immediately transformed into a General Board of Education, with considerable responsibilities for directing the establishment of a school system to cater for children of any denomination.[5] The General Board of Education wanted government schools 'to be regarded as the common source of sound secular knowledge, moral habits, intellectual training, and general religious principles'.[6] In 1848, there were eighty-three pupils in colonial government schools, and by 1849 the number had risen to 166. By 1848, the board could claim that it had established 'a general system of education' by providing salaries for schoolmasters who taught in secular schools.[7]

In 1849, the total number of reported enrolments for all schools was 427. As there were 2,487 children in the colony at the end of 1848, an estimated two-thirds of whom were of school-going age, it is apparent that only approximately one-quarter of the children eligible to attend school were actually being taught at primary school level.[8] This outcome reflects the reluctance of the colonists to invest public money in education, as well as an assumption on the part of many educated people that the working poor did not need to be educated. This view was characteristic of settler societies that were dependent for their wealth on rural activities based on a combination of cheap land and cheap labour.

While it is not possible to determine the accuracy of these early enrolment figures, nor what they represented in terms of regular attendance, the figures do indicate that the colonial government established more schools for boys than for girls. The schools at Murray, Guildford and York, for example, were called boys' schools, although the first two appear to have enrolled a few girls in 1849. The York school enrolled only thirty boys. Until 1850, most children in the country had no access to education, and boys made up the greatest number of pupils in government secular schools.

It is clear, then, that by the middle of the century there was some sort of institutional recognition of 'childhood' as a fixed period that ended at 14 years of age, but no widespread acceptance of a necessary connection between childhood and education. The children of town dwellers, especially boys, had the greatest opportunity to attend secular schools. The 1850 'Return of Government Schools for the Colonial Office' stated that colonial government schools were

> free to pupils of any denomination whose parents may be unable or unwilling to pay; but in the case of those whose circumstances may be so good as to render their gratuitous education unjust to others, it is intended as a discouragement to such class to limit the amount of instruction. No such case, however, has as yet occurred and generally speaking the parents prefer paying.

The report stated that schools were confined to secular instruction: doctrinal teaching was carefully avoided and religious instruction left to parents. The colonial Governor, Charles Fitzgerald, claimed in his dispatch to the Colonial Office in connection with the 1854 Census that 'education had had the deepest consideration', but that his views on the importance of education had met some opposition

> from many who think the cost of education much too high for the classes that usually attend government schools more particularly in the Australian colonies, where they are not permitted to remain at school beyond the age of fourteen or fifteen at the utmost, before being called upon to follow some occupation. The sum appropriated for the service has also been thought excessive looking at the limited resources of the colony. I am bound to record my concurrence in the present scheme as a matter of experiment which, if it fail, is easy of discontinuance.[9]

In its first report, the General Board of Education set out the ambitious principles it believed should underlie the education system of the colony. One was that education given at government schools 'should ultimately be limited only by our own means of obtaining instructors'. Boys' education was to be that which obtained at a good English grammar school, and for girls 'such a one as a respectable middle class person would endeavour to secure for his daughter in England'. The board claimed that it was not possible to educate boys and girls separately, as would be the case in a large community. However, it felt that the colony should provide cheap education for the children of middle-class parents, and education for working-class children, some of whom it believed would eventually become members of 'the governing body'.[10]

The 1854 report of the General Board of Education provided details about the number of schools and enrolment figures. Four new schools had opened in the previous year—at Fremantle (for girls), at Pinjarra, at Vasse and at Port Gregory. The York school had been placed with Fremantle on the 'permanent list', achieved when a population grew to a particular size, and the Perth and Fremantle Boys' Schools had occupied new premises. A new schoolhouse had been built at Toodyay, where the local school committee had been very active. The Guildford school was 'more satisfactory than last year', but there were not yet enough teachers for the Fremantle Girls' School and the Fremantle Infant School. In fact, the main problems identified in the report seemed to be the number and standard of the available teachers. There were by that time thirteen government schools in all, enrolments having increased from 444 in 1853 to 644 in 1854, 132 of which were in new schools. Excluded from this figure was the number attending school in Albany, which had failed to provide a return. This means that there were some 650–700 children attending government schools out of a population of 12,005 people.

In its 1854 report, the board set out the rules governing the administration of the school system. All schools receiving aid from colonial funds through the board were to be open for inspection at all hours and provide at least five hours' secular education each day. Anyone wishing to establish a school had to communicate with the secretary of the General Board of Education, stating the number of children likely to attend, the names of three respectable persons who could form a school committee, the proposed school's distance from the nearest established school and the nature of the accommodation to be provided. The government would provide assistance at the rate of £20 per year for twelve pupils and £35 per year for twenty-five pupils. The salary of the teacher would be recommended by the board once the school was established. School fees were to be charged, but free books would be available for the first three grades. School holidays were to occupy one month every year.[11]

In a letter to the chairman of the York District Education Committee in June 1850, the General Board of Education stated its belief that conflicts over religious issues had been largely resolved. Schools were 'now designed for Protestants only', the Roman Catholics having applied for and obtained a separate grant of public money for their own exclusive system. Catholics were welcome but no concessions would be made for them. All doctrinal teaching was to be avoided, and no minister of a church could teach religion in a government school.[12] The board also clarified a problem arising in the York area over a particular teacher, explaining that the system of education was limited to primary school teaching:

> Mr Teede receives his allowance from Government not for offering a finished education to the wealthy classes, who cannot properly be made an object of general taxation, but for such tuition in the ordinary branches of general education as is required for the class of yeomen, shopkeepers, and the like; anything beyond this being made a matter of private arrangement between the parents and teacher.

Mr Teede could not claim part of his salary for any pupils he taught in the higher branches of learning, including Greek, Latin and Mathematics.

The letters of the board at this time reveal the ways in which the system of education operated and the kinds of problems it faced. New schools could not be established without local community participation, and the board had great difficulty finding suitable persons to act as teachers. In its 1854 report to the Colonial Secretary, it stated that there were only two qualified and regularly trained schoolmasters and one trained schoolmistress in the schools. Salaries depended on the number of pupils attending, while teachers also received a part of the fees paid by parents. The teachers constantly asked for increased salaries, but the board was limited in its response by the low level of government funding.[13] In 1855, the board wrote to the Colonial Secretary, explaining why the very poorest children were not being taught beyond third grade. It stated that the board had always tried to avoid

> any distinction in education or treatment founded on the mere influence of social rank, their object being that all classes should as far as possible be educated alike and together. The only exception to this principle has been in the case of such pupils as may be altogether exempted from payment of any kind whose education it has been suggested should be confined to the three lowest forms—

This was certainly not done for the purpose of punishing parents but with the wish of stimulating the parents to make proper and needful sacrifice for the education of their children—it being thought that inability to pay would be improperly pleaded, if no penalty at all were attached to such a position. The Board however are not so strongly in favour of this exception as to wish to retain it should his excellency consider it objectionable.[14]

In this letter, the board made it clear that it was opposed to the continuation of state aid to Catholic schools, and saw itself as ideally the sole provider of education services. It stated, in response to queries and objections, that for no great additional expense, the present schools in Perth could cater for higher grades (all classes) if enough teachers could be found. This would make education cheaper for the upper classes, who were not necessarily the wealthy portion of society. It did not support the suggestion that scholars be divided into three categories according to their ability to pay fees.

The growth of schools and levels of literacy

The 1859 Census showed that there were then fourteen schools in the colony, with 641 enrolments. This census also included a table showing the levels of literacy in the colony generally. The number of those over 5 years who could read and write was 6,946, about half the population, while the number who could neither read nor write was 3,011. The same table in the 1870 Census indicated that 13,326 people over 5 years of age (or three-quarters of the adult population) could read and write, and the number who could do neither was 3,945. The total population at this time was 24,785.

There were forty-six schools in Western Australia in 1868, twenty-one of them funded by the government and twenty-five receiving grants-in-aid. Fees were charged to pay for books and furniture. All teachers in the secular schools were appointed and dismissed by the General Board of Education, subject to the approval of the Governor. There was no standard qualification for teachers but the Board employs three trained and certificated English masters, and two trained and certificated mistresses. Whenever practicable, a competitive examination of candidates for the office of male and female teachers is required.

There was no system of teacher training in the colony, but pupil teachers were appointed at the age of 13 years and were supposed to have an apprenticeship of five years. Schools were inspected annually 'for the most part' by the headmaster of Perth Boys' School.[15] They were kept open as long as there were twelve students attending, and that attendance had to be at least 100 times a year for the teacher to receive a capitation grant.[16]

Table 5 shows that the number of schools and the overall attendance numbers did not begin to increase until the early 1860s. This suggests that it took ten years for the impact of the convict

Table 5: Development of schools, 1856–69

Period	No. of schools	Enrolment	% attendance
1856	11	429	
1857	12	513	
1858	13	643	
1859	14	742	69.4
1860	16	874	65.8
1861	20	897	67.7
1862	23	1,037	68.4
1863	28	1,247	67.7
1864	32	1,454	70.0
1865	36	1,568	69.4
1866	41	1,803	70.8
1867	42	1,946	70.0
1868	48	2,054	70.0
1869	55	2,188	71.7

Source: WA Census, 1870.

labour force to be widely felt in the colonial economy. In the period from 1863 to 1873, the second decade after the provision of convict labour, the number of primary schools increased from twenty-eight to sixty-one. However, although the number of children enrolled in schools increased rapidly in this decade, the poor attendance records remained much the same. A table in the 1870 Census shows that most government schools were mixed in gender terms, although there were schools specifically for boys or girls in Perth and Fremantle, and at Geraldton, Guildford and York.

No attempt was made in the 1870 Census to record the number of children in private schools. The Catholic Church, which set up education services in small, privately run schools from the 1830s, controlled the largest group of schools outside the secular system. The Church of England also established schools from the earliest days of settlement, when J. B. Wittenoom, Colonial Chaplain, with the help of small subsidies, set up schools in Perth for 'respectable families'.[17] However, throughout the nineteenth century, the Catholic Church was the only substantial alternative provider of education at the primary level.

The General Board of Education remained responsible for the coordination of all local initiatives until 1871, when the colonial government, following the passage of the 1870 Education Act in England, passed the Elementary Education Act. This Act signalled a new level of state intervention in the provision of education, since it divided most of the schools into two categories—government and assisted—thus resolving, in their favour, a long dispute over funding for church schools. Some unfunded private schools also continued to exist outside these two categories.

This has since been seen as the most important piece of legislation in this field in the nineteenth century, since it was designed to establish a government-funded system of elementary secular education. In introducing it into the Legislative Council, the Colonial Secretary, Frederick Barlee, noted the existence of 'conflicting opinion' and 'rancorous party feeling' surrounding the issues raised by this Bill. He claimed that the Bill, based on the Irish education system, would allow all denominations to avail themselves of schools 'without fear of meeting anything offensive to their religious views'. However, part of the objection to the Bill was the fear that private schools would lose government financial assistance.

According to Barlee, the original Bill did indeed aim to limit government spending to what was required for government-funded secular schools, as well as setting up a Central Board of Education and district boards to exercise direct public control over these institutions.[18] However, when the Bill became law on 17 August 1871, the Elementary Education Act made provision for some continued financial assistance to private schools, with the same distinction in nomenclature between so-called 'government schools' and 'assisted schools'.[19] However, no grant-in-aid for assisted schools could be obtained for building purposes, and those schools wanting to claim government assistance had to provide considerable detail about their operations. With minor alterations, this system of grants lasted until 1895.[20]

The Act set out fairly stringent controls over the operations of the government schools through a system of district boards and a scheme of regular school inspection.[21] This was a consolidation of the system that had been in operation for more than fifteen years. The Act made attendance compulsory and provided the most unequivocal definition of the term 'childhood', because it required

> parents of children of such age, not less than six years nor more than fourteen years to cause such children (unless there is some reasonable excuse) to attend school, which children do not reside three miles from a Government school.[22]

This Act was amended in 1874 to increase the provision of funds for both government and assisted schools,[23] and again in 1877 to make administrative changes with respect to the level of financial support for both kinds of schools.[24] William Atkinson, who had been headmaster of Perth Boys' School from 1862, was appointed Inspector of Schools in 1871 and had to visit seventy widely dispersed schools.

The 1881 Census contained tables, more detailed than in previous censuses, providing a full profile of the education services in the colony, showing the four different kinds of environment in which 6,327 children were being educated (see table 6). Figures of the number of children being educated at home show how difficult it was for the government to provide services over the sparsely populated areas.

Table 6: Profile of education services, 1881

Type	No. of children	%
Government schools	2,777	43.89
Assisted schools	1,323	20.91
Private schools	748	11.82
Educated at home	1,479	23.38

The percentage of children between 4 and 16 years attending school varied from place to place, with Perth (79.18 per cent) and Fremantle (78.24 per cent) recording the highest enrolments. The attendance at Williams, for example, was only 52.01 per cent, while that at York was not much better at 59.18 per cent. A comparison of the tables for the percentage of enrolments for 4–16 years with that for 4–14 years shows that children also left school earlier in Williams and York, for example, than in Perth and Fremantle.[25]

By the time of the 1891 Census, the levels of literacy had risen, with 79.93 per cent of the total population over 5 years of age able to read and write. Females were marginally more likely to be literate than the males of the community. There were 17,026 children under 15 years of age in Western Australia, and the return of school enrolments for children between 4 and 16 years showed the numbers in country districts and the numbers in the towns separately (see table 7). The census indicated that 92.5 per cent of children between 6 and 14 were receiving education. In terms of overall numbers, the state system educated about two-thirds of the total number of children, with denominational schools educating about one-fifth of them. More boys attended state schools than girls, but more girls stayed at school after 14 years of age. There were more girls than boys at the private and denominational schools and receiving education at home. Very few children stayed on after 14 years of age, but a greater percentage of children at denominational and private schools than at government schools continued their education beyond 14 years.

Table 7: Profile of education services, 1891

Type	Number of children	
	Country districts	**Twenty towns**
State schools	4,452	2,986
Private schools	1,793	1,405
At home	1,880	422
Not instructed	4,106	1,516

Although attendance at assisted schools was not itemized in the census, the figures show that the number of children 'not instructed' in the towns was high, given that schools were within reach of most children. The figures support other evidence that little effort had been made to enforce school attendance. The numbers 'not instructed' in the country districts, on the other hand, might seem to be explained by the gold rush of the period, which saw the movement of the population into areas with no facilities at all, let alone established schools.[26] This was partly true, although the population statistics of the gold rush period suggest that most of the diggers at first were unaccompanied males. While many of the children not attending school were on farms that were still outside the reach of education services, there were many others along the new railway line and in the goldfields who, from the 1890s, were only gradually provided with schools. The settlers along the railway line, which was built to service the goldmining areas, were entitled to apply for a government school when they could claim to have ten or more school-aged children in their community. The Public Works Department erected timber-framed transportable classrooms with kalsomined canvas walls, known as tent schools. The accommodation for the teacher was the responsibility of the parents.[27]

Compulsory attendance

The issue of school attendance was a difficult one in a society where so many people still depended on the work of children. For two decades, the Central Board grappled with the issue, explaining to the district boards that they should appoint an officer to serve notices on the parents of children who were not attending school. The Central Board supplied a pamphlet setting out a guide as to how the local by-laws about compulsory education should be explained. The attendance officer, who was paid a small fee by the Central Board, had the power to take proceedings against parents in the police court.[28] However, in practice, the board advocated leniency. For example, in June 1874, the Central Board wrote to the District Board of Vasse, in response to a query, stating that

> employment at home cannot be made a valid excuse for
> non-attendance at school; however, as it is imagined that
> in this instance it will not take a very long time to plough
> Mr C. Moriarty's land, the Central Board see no objection
> to the District Board permitting his son to be absent from
> school for that purpose.

But most of the official responses of the Central Board reiterated that education was compulsory for all children, including those who attended Catholic schools. Nonetheless, it was difficult to be draconian about the application of the law when so many children remained outside the reach of any school, and when the establishment of a school depended on local initiative. The report of the Central Board of Education for 1882 referred to the failure of parents to realize the value of education to their children. However, it observed that 'perhaps it is as well that they do not do so, as the revenue at our command would not have admitted of the establishment of any more schools'. The Central Board may have comprised keen educationalists, but the government was parsimonious with funds and parents were evading the compulsory education requirement.[29]

In 1880, the Central Board of Education urged the government to alter the Elementary Education Act 'to enable magistrates to punish those children who wilfully keep away from school…with a whipping or confinement on bread and water'.[30] Two years later, the board saw the question of the cooperation of parents over the issue of attendance as its most difficult problem:

> Expenses would be reduced…if parents could only be induced to cooperate with the District Boards, in a determination to see that all children of a school age are not allowed to be absent from school; [there is] a growing desire to have schools open, and apparently a sincere wish to have the children educated on the part of the parents; but the vain attempt to accomplish two things at one time, viz, to make use of them at home one day, and send them to school another, has had on some schools a ruinous effect. It has in some instances been found difficult to maintain an average attendance of 12, with 20 or 25 on the rolls, from this cause, and it forms one of the great difficulties we have to contend with.[31]

By 1884, the report of the Central Board showed that there were thirteen persons employed by the board and paid small stipends to try to enforce attendance. However, the 1885 report indicated that although some new schools had been opened, others had closed. This was reportedly due to the removal of families from particular neighbourhoods, the depression in local industry and the 'apathy of parents'. But parents may sometimes have doubted the value of the education being provided. The Central Board's 1884 report describes some of the schools and refers to the standards of education being achieved. At Chapman, for example:

> the school is held in a small and inconvenient room of a dwelling house, but has the advantage of being centrally situated…The attainments of scholars are low. The school was closed from the commencement of the second quarter to the beginning of the last quarter of the year.

The situation at Cossack was no better. There the school was held in a large room 'which serves all public purposes in Cossack' and was reported to be 'thoroughly disorganized and has been neglected by the late master'. On the other hand, the school at Dongara, where discipline was good, was an excellent stone building 'suitable for a school and in good order'.[32]

By 1886, the yearly report declared that the compulsion clause of the 1871 Act was a failure, since school attendance had actually declined in that year. Whooping cough in the southern regions partially explained this but did not account for the overall decline. This report also included further descriptions of the hopelessly inadequate school buildings and the poor standards achieved. At Boyanup, for example, the school was held in a wattle and daub building, while at Kelmscott the Church of England place of worship was also the schoolhouse. In both places, progress was reportedly poor.[33]

Changes in primary school education in the 1890s

The Shearer Commission, which reported to the Governor in 1888, was set up to inquire into elementary education in Western Australia. It made detailed recommendations about the inspection of schools, the keeping of attendance registers, and the conduct of examinations, as well as about the promotion of students from one grade to the next. The commissioners argued that the scope of education should be broadened by the addition of new subjects thought to be useful in the colony, including Domestic Economy, History, Bookkeeping and Agriculture.[34] A number of changes were introduced as a result of the Shearer Commission. In its report in 1888, the Central Board of Education raised the question of abolishing school fees altogether and pointed out that there were twenty-five private schools in the colony over which it could exercise no control. It also provided details of the examination for the Teaching Certificate of Efficiency.[35] The Shearer Commission inquiry signalled the beginning of a change in the education system that would flow through to the 1890s, at a time when the population was increasing rapidly.

The original 1871 Act was twice amended in the 1890s. The Act of 1893, introduced three years after the establishment of responsible government, made significant changes to the administrative structure of the state system in that the powers of the existing Central Board of Education were passed to a government minister, and a Department of Education was established.[36] District boards were now to be elected by a limited franchise, details of which were set out in the Act. It also set out conditions under which religious instruction could be provided in colonial schools. The Governor was entitled to make regulations concerning many aspects of school administration including inspection, discipline, the treatment of children suffering from infectious diseases, the payment of teachers, the scale of grants to schools and the election of district boards. In other words, the Minister of Education in Cabinet could now make most of the important decisions about the provision of education services in the colony.[37]

After the 1893 Amendment Act, the amount of the grant per head for children attending government schools was increased from £3 10s to £4 10s. This increase was necessary partly because of the improved scale of teachers' salaries, planned under the new regulations, which abolished payment by results. A new scale of fixed salaries was introduced, calculated partly on attendance, along with the classification of schools, and the requirement that teachers be certificated. In the same year, a new teaching program was introduced to permit children who had completed Grade 7 to remain at school to continue their education. This decision, while not really offering a satisfactory solution, at least recognized the increased demand for secondary education. It was called the 'ex-seventh program'.[38] Another curious change was that henceforth girls were to take the same Arithmetic lessons as boys but were to be given 'separate and easier questions in the exams'![39]

An Act again amending the 1871 Act, and which became law in November 1894, dealt entirely with the question of compulsory school attendance for children between 6 and 14 years. Some exemptions were allowed under clauses 4 and 5 on the grounds of distance from the nearest school or because of sickness, but parents who neglected to send their children to school were liable to be fined.[40] Cyril Jackson identified many of the problems within the primary school education system soon after he became Inspector General of Education in the new department, set up in 1893. Jackson visited city and country schools and commented on the poor buildings, the uneven quality of the teaching, the pupil teacher system of training, the inadequate curriculum and the poor attendance record.[41]

However, the economic growth of the 1890s meant a rapid increase in the demand for new schools. In 1892, there were sixteen requests, in 1893 there were twelve, and by 1894 the number had risen to twenty-seven, of which nineteen were approved. One of these was the first school in the goldfields, which was opened at Coolgardie. The table provided in the 1894 report (see table 8) shows the rapid growth in the number of schools from 1885 to 1894, even though the percentage attendance figures actually declined over the whole period.

Table 8: Increase in the number of primary schools, 1885–94

Year	No. of schools	Enrolment	Average attendance	% attendance
1885	94	4,479	3,349	75
1886	89	4,508	3,346	74
1887	90	4,673	3,600	77
1888	93	4,679	3,659	78
1889	94	4,744	3,625	76
1890	101	5,014	3,818	76
1891	104	5,345	3,910	73
1892	117	5,973	4,324	72
1893	127	6,338	4,625	73
1894	137	7,418	5,367	72

The new regulations introduced under the 1893 Act actually came into operation at the beginning of 1895. 'Compulsory officers' were appointed in that year in fifteen education districts, and the

Education Department suggested that the police might enforce attendance, as was done in Victoria and New South Wales. However, the department was still acting gently over the issue of attendance by first warning offending parents of future consequences if they continued to disregard the Act. As late as 1896, it was not attempting to enforce the compulsion clause in the goldfields, for example, because of the difficulty of finding sufficient accommodation in the schools there.

The Public Education Act of 1899 implied that many children under 14 were still often a regular part of the work force when it forbade the employment of children who were not exempt from school attendance. A new element of compulsion was underscored by the appointment of special officers to secure regular attendance. Under the same Act, all fees previously paid for children under 14 years of age were abolished. However, school fees were still to be paid by the parents of children who attended school beyond Grade 7. Finally, this Act introduced a specific ban on the employment of children under 14 years of age, with the exception that under clause 12 'the Minister may, at his discretion, give special exemption for children between the ages of 12 and 14, in cases of poverty or sickness of parents'.[42] If a child under 14 years was beyond the control of the parent, a justice could commit such a child to an industrial school, with the parent obliged to pay maintenance.[43]

By 1901, the number of children between the ages of 6 and 14 years who were attending school had risen to a total of 26,335, made up of 13,214 boys and 13,121 girls. The census of this year provided a detailed profile of literacy levels, and of the newly created State's education options, including the numbers attending school in terms of age and gender. It indicated that 92.5 per cent of children between 6 and 14 were receiving education. The census figures regularly included the number of students educated in denominational schools. This number reached 4,700 by 1901, approximately one-fifth of the total school population. The so-called 'dual system' set up in 1871, whereby the government funded both secular and denominational (assisted) schools, came to an end in 1895, following another period of intense debate about the future of non-government education in Western Australia.[44] Under the

Assisted Schools Abolition Act of that year, all grants-in-aid to schools 'not belonging to the Government' were cancelled, and a sum of £15,000 was set aside out of government revenue to provide for grants every second year to those schools that had previously been 'assisted'.[45]

Secondary schools in Western Australia

The first secondary school in Western Australia, opened by the Sisters of Mercy in Perth in 1849 for both Catholic and Protestant girls, had enrolled 279 girls by 1853.[46] The first Church of England Bishop, Mathew Blagden Hale, was the prime mover in a scheme to provide secondary education for the sons of the wealthy settlers. A grammar school was opened in 1858, and five years later it moved into 'The Cloisters', especially built for the purpose.[47] A Bill incorporating the governors of this collegiate school was passed in 1865, but the school struggled with low attendance and financial problems until it finally closed in 1872.[48]

The Bishop's School was kept alive for many years by injections of money from Bishop Hale's personal income in the face of constant staffing and financial problems. In 1863, by an ordinance of the Legislative Council, the school was placed under the control of a Body Corporate consisting of the Anglican bishop, dean and archdeacon, who hoped between them to rescue the school. In 1885, an Act was passed to dissolve this corporation, because it had not been able to carry out the objects for which it was incorporated, and to try to resolve the financial difficulties attendant on this failure.[49] Eleven years later, a private Act of Parliament gave the trustees greater freedom to rent or sell the school properties and reinvest the proceeds as they saw fit.[50] The actual demise of the school in 1872 came about at a time of debate on the question of government support for denominational schools, which had led to the introduction of financial support for so-called 'assisted' schools in the 1871 Elementary Education Act.

In the 1870s and early 1880s, the Anglican Church made three further attempts to establish secondary schools. The Perth High

School, sometimes seen as the continuation of Bishop Hale's Church of England Collegiate School, opened in 1878.

An Act was passed in 1876 to make provision for the higher education of boys 'similar to that given in the Grammar and advanced schools in the other Australasian Colonies'. The substance of the Act dealt with the appointment of a board of governors who would be responsible for the establishment of the Perth High School, which would receive a subsidy from the government.[51] In a letter to the Secretary of State, Governor Robinson outlined the intention of the government in supporting the establishment of such a school, while also explaining the basis of Roman Catholic objections to it:[52]

> The object in proposing to establish the High School on a purely secular basis was, obviously, that its advantages should be available for the children of all denominations—that no one denomination should be favoured to the exclusion of another, as would undoubtedly have been the case had the school been established as an assisted denominational one; and certainly it appears to me to have acted on any other principle than the one which has been adopted would have been manifestly unjust and improper. That the Roman Catholics (who number, according to the Census of 1870, 6,674 out of a total population at that date of 23,351) are prevented by conscientious scruples from sending their boys to a school where the system of instruction is secular, but which is nevertheless open to them as to others if they choose to take advantage of it, seems to me no reason why the rest of the community should suffer.[53]

The opposition from the Catholic Church was based partly on the perception that this was really a move designed to support the Anglican establishment.

An amending Act was necessary in 1883 to allow the school governors to raise money on mortgage.[54] The Perth High School Act was again amended in 1892 to reduce the number of school governors and allow for their appointment by the Governor with the advice of the Legislative Council, instead of solely by the Legislative Council, as had been done formerly. The rights and duties of the governors were further clarified.[55]

Although the Perth High School had some government funding, it was run as a private school by a board of governors, most of whom were indeed Anglicans. The children came largely from fee-paying Church of England families, although the teaching was secular. The annual reports provided very little detail about the school, but we learn that the original inadequate building had been enlarged by 1883, allowing for a better arrangement of lessons and more room for the boarders. There were between fifty and sixty boys at the school until 1890, when the numbers dropped to twenty-five, apparently due partly to staffing problems. In 1892, as many as 104 children had attended at some time during the year, but the numbers from then until 1900 remained in the sixties. The report of 1890 lists the subjects being taught. These included Latin, Greek and French, as well as various kinds of classes concerning the English language. Mathematics was taught through a combination of six separate topics including Euclid and Mensuration. The curriculum also covered Surveying, History, Geography, Bookkeeping, Drawing and Music.[56]

In 1897, the High School Act 1876 Amendment Act was passed. The object of this legislation was to increase the subsidy given by the government to the Perth High School from £500 to £1,000. The debate on this Bill revealed deep dissatisfaction with the high school, which, according to Alexander Forrest, Member for West Kimberley, 'had become a by-word in the Colony'.[57] Parents were sending their children overseas or to schools in other Australian colonies for their high school education. Several speakers said that the government should increase the grant beyond the amount requested, referring in some cases to the teachers' very low rate of pay.

The other two secondary schools involving the Anglican Church were the Bishop's Girls' School, which was founded in 1877 and lasted for ten years, and the Fremantle Grammar School for Boys, which opened in 1882. Henry Briggs, who was the headmaster of the latter, had the support of St John's Anglican Church. The

Fremantle Grammar School had no financial subsidy from the government but received a grant of land for the school.[58]

The absence of a fully funded and developed government secondary school system for both boys and girls reflected the failure of governments to put sufficient revenue into education. Not until 1910, when Perth Modern School was established as the first fully funded State high school, did the government begin to accept responsibility for the provision of secondary education. The increased demand for education beyond elementary school level had led, in 1893, not to a properly funded secondary school but only to the 'ex-seventh program', which was introduced in six of the largest government primary schools and four small ones.[59]

However, there were private schools offering secondary education by the last decade of the nineteenth century, including the Perth Grammar School, which operated from 1889 to 1895, and the Perth Commercial Academy, which had opened its doors in 1872 and lasted until 1899.[60] The late 1800s also saw the establishment of several church schools that ultimately were to provide many of the secondary education services in the twentieth century.[61] In 1895, the Irish Catholic Brothers opened a school for boys in St Georges Terrace.[62] In the same year, another school for boys was opened by Charles Harper, and was subsequently taken over by the Church of England to become Guildford Grammar School. Scotch College for boys was opened in 1897 in Perth and then moved to Claremont. In 1901, the Church of England Community of the Sisters of the Church began a school for girls in Perth known as Perth College. These were all elite schools with relatively high fees.[63]

The opening of so many private secondary schools reflected the rapid changes in the economy and the increase in the size of the population, largely due to the discovery of gold. Other changes in the field of education pointed to some readiness on the part of the government to put more revenue into the provision of education services. A system of teacher training was introduced, and Claremont Teachers' Training College was opened in 1902. Technical education, which had begun in a variety of small institutions in the nineteenth century, was consolidated when the Perth Technical School opened in 1900.[64] The payment of teachers by results came to an end, and in

1899 fees were abolished in all state elementary schools. The first steps in the development of special education for the handicapped also appeared at this time with the beginnings in 1896 of both the Western Australian Deaf and Dumb Institute and the Victoria Institute and Industrial School for the Blind.[65]

By the end of the nineteenth century, almost all children of European descent were enrolled in schools, although their attendance was often episodic. However, the government was still trying to establish the first primary schools in outlying areas, especially in the newly populated goldmining and railway settlements. Since there were still very few schools in the North West, children in outlying areas had to be educated at home or sent to Perth. The establishment of the Perth Technical School in 1900 reflected the shift from a largely agricultural economy to one depending crucially on goldmining. By this time, the economic growth of the last three decades of the century had created a wealthy elite supporting a number of fee-paying private schools, which offered both primary and secondary education. However, the government did not provide a fully funded State secondary school until 1910 and, even then, most children had to rely on the 'ex-seventh program' if they wished to extend their education beyond primary school.

CHAPTER 4

Paupers, bastards, delinquents and larrikins

IN the second half of the nineteenth century, a legal and institutional framework was gradually erected to take account of the increasing number of children who were abandoned, neglected or brought before the courts. The history of the treatment of these children reveals that there were contradictory forces at work. On the one hand, there were the disciplinarians who thought in terms of punishment and the virtue of hard labour. On the other hand, there were a few humanitarian people with a genuine concern for the children's future, who wanted to find rational solutions to their problems.[1]

'Bastard' children

In the early years of settlement, the problem arose as to what to do with 'deserted wives and children and other destitute persons' who, due to 'death, sickness or other casualties, as well as by desertion or neglect of husbands, parents, or other near relatives', had no visible means of support. In 1845, an Ordinance was passed to try to transfer the responsibility for such persons to their relatives so that they would not become a charge on the colonial state (see p. 25).[2]

By the end of the 1860s, there were four orphanages established in Perth, all of them caring for neglected children and all of them needing financial assistance. An Act was passed in 1871 to try to compel putative fathers to maintain their children.[3] If a justice could be persuaded as to a father's identity, this person was obliged by law to pay a sum of money weekly for the maintenance of the child until 14 years of age or until the mother married. This Act was superseded by that of 1875, which removed the clause about the marriage of the mother and allowed the court to extend the period of maintenance to 16 years.[4] The father was responsible for the financial support of the child, and the mother for its care and well-being, on pain of being punished as a rogue and a vagabond. This Act also gave power to the managers of orphanages and other institutions to collect maintenance for any 'bastard' child who was committed to their care by the government:

> When a bastard child becomes a burden on the public funds or upon any public or municipal body, or shall have passed under the actual care or custody of the certified manager of any certified school, orphanage or other institution, so that such certified manager shall have acquired all the powers and privileges of a father over and in respect to such child, or shall be deemed to be the lawful guardian of such child, the officer in charge of the poor house in the one case, or the recognised officer of such public or municipal body in the second case, or the certified manager of such certified school, orphanage or other institution in the third case, may apply to two Justices in Petty Session, and thereupon such Justices may summon the man alleged to be the father of the child to appear before any two Justices to show cause why an order should not be made upon him to contribute towards the relief of the child.[5]

In 1896, the Bastardy Laws Act 1875 Amendment Act increased the maximum amount that a justice of the peace might award as a weekly payment to the mother of a 'bastard' child, from 5s to a sum not exceeding 12s 6d. Under the original Act, 'this payment was to provide for the education, maintenance and bringing up of the child until it arrives at the age of 14 years'.[6] Under this new amendment, the age of dependence, as defined by legislation concerning maintenance, had risen from 14 to 16 years, although children were permitted to leave school at 14 years.

Orphanages for pauper children

The Perth Poor House had its modest beginnings in the early 1860s, but not until 1882 was a Poor Relief Department established by the government to supervise its activities as a place for adults and children who had no families to support them. The first practical response to the evidence of a growing number of neglected and pauper children came from various religious bodies, when orphanages were established from the late 1860s. Matthew Gibney, a priest in the Roman Catholic Church who arrived in Perth in 1863, was instrumental in setting up the St Vincent de Paul Society in Perth two years later. In 1868, as chaplain of this society, Gibney led a delegation to the Governor requesting that the Catholic female orphans at the Poor House be removed to the care of the nuns at the Convent of Mercy. When the Governor agreed to this proposal, eleven girls between the ages of 4 and 10 years were moved to the Convent of Mercy, the Governor agreeing to a payment of 8d a day for the upkeep of each child. When a new building was erected for the Sisters of Mercy in 1871, the old building became the St Joseph's Girls' Orphanage, Perth.[7]

In 1872, nine Catholic boys were also taken from the Poor House to a monastery in Subiaco, which had been completed for the Benedictines in 1859. These monks had moved to join their brethren at New Norcia, and Father Gibney, Vicar General of the Roman Catholic Church from 1870, became the manager of this orphanage. The children were only subsidized at the rate of 6d a day from 1874, but the orphanage also accepted boarders, who were obliged to pay £25 per year for their keep, with a promise of a good elementary education. A primary school teacher was employed and a printing press was installed, which produced the *Catholic Record* newspaper.

This St Vincent's Boys' Orphanage, as it was called, also had 25 acres of olives and vineyards, which provided an opportunity to teach the boys horticultural skills. In 1876, after an outcry about the treatment of a child at the orphanage, the Sisters of Mercy took charge of the establishment under Sister M. Francis Goold. St Vincent's also took children who had been convicted of criminal offences, and both it and St Joseph's Girls' Orphanage took children who had only one parent who could not care for them. In some cases, children were maintained at the orphanage by a parent. In 1897, St Vincent's Boys' Orphanage was taken over by the Christian Brothers, who had arrived in Perth in 1894. They built a new orphanage at Clontarf, which they occupied in 1901, at which time the girls were transferred from Perth to the Subiaco establishment, which was under the control, at this time, of Mother M. Benedict Murphy.[8]

The Swan Protestant Orphanage was opened near the Causeway in 1868 in a small group of cottages, after a successful appeal for funds from the Church of England hierarchy. Its first enrolment consisted of seven girls and one boy. The set of rules, which were drawn up almost immediately, declared that the orphanage took children between the ages of 2 and 9 years until they were between 12 and 14, and that all of them would normally come from the government relief list.[9] They were to be chosen on the basis of need 'without reference to the religious tenets of their parents' and were to be permitted to attend 'that place of Worship to which their parents may have been attached'.[10]

Twelve months later, a boys' orphanage was added. According to the *Inquirer*, the second annual report stated that these institutions were 'not simply designed as a happy home and a moral refuge for orphaned or destitute children, but as a nursery for cheerful, hard-working servants'.[11] The boys' orphanage, which was moved to Middle Swan in 1876, was founded by Archdeacon Brown, who was also its manager for many years. At first, these institutions also received a government subsidy of 8d per day for each child, reduced in 1874 to 6d. The boys' orphanage received a grant of land at Middle Swan so that the boys could be taught farming.

Children were frequently sent first of all to the Perth Poor House depot at Mount Eliza and then transferred to one of these four orphanages.

The Industrial Schools Act of 1874

Legislative controls over pauper and delinquent children, whether of European or Aboriginal origin, were introduced in 1874, apparently to make it easier for institutions to retain control of children even up to 21 years of age and to use their labour. The wide-ranging Industrial Schools Act set out to direct the lives of needy children and juvenile offenders under the age of 21 years, within the framework of the existing orphanages. These were to have certificates of approval from the Governor as industrial schools.[12] In introducing the Bill, the Colonial Secretary, Frederick Barlee, stated that

> its object is to promote the efficiency of schools, orphanages and other kindred charitable institutions that have been founded for the purpose of providing for and educating orphan and necessitous children, by giving greater powers over such children to the directors and managers of these institutions. At present these authorities were powerless to retain in custody any child voluntarily surrendered to their charge, and the object of the Bill before the House was to grant them such power as would enable them to do so, and to stand 'in loco parentis' towards the children placed under their management. *It was too often the case now that when children had received a sufficient training at these institutions to render their services useful, they were quietly removed from the custody of the managers, and all the civilizing and Christianizing influences brought to bear in their training were thrown away.* [my emphasis]

Apart from these orphans and 'necessitous children', juvenile offenders were particularly singled out in this Act, which stated that it was 'highly expedient' for such institutions to be used as reformatories for offending children. The effect of this Act was to extend the sentences of juveniles, handed down by the courts, and to create a precedent for incarcerating children in institutions for long periods, regardless of the court's findings. It gave the government the right to intervene in the running of charitable institutions, and allowed it to use such institutions to house juvenile offenders who would otherwise have to be sent to adult prisons.

The 1874 Industrial Schools Act was amended three years later because one of the orphanage managers had been overzealous in apprenticing a boy as soon as he arrived at the institution; it appeared as if he were operating an employment agency. This amending Act, according to the Hon. O'Grady Lefroy, acting Colonial Secretary, had been brought in to remedy a weakness in the existing Act:

> The Bill proposed that no child voluntarily surrendered or taken in accordance with the 5th section of the existing Act, into any school, orphanage, or other institution certified under the Act, shall be deemed to be in the custody of the certified manager—nor shall the manager acquire the powers of a guardian over such child—unless such infant shall either be an actual inmate of the institution, or, being over 12 years of age, shall have been educated as an inmate of such institution for a period of at least three years. The Bill further provides that no indenture of apprenticeship shall be of any force or validity unless the infant is a party to the same, and the Resident Magistrate of the district in which the proposed master lives signifies his approval of the same.

A debate followed about limiting the powers of the managers of these institutions, and also about whether Aborigines should be exempted, because, otherwise, the Bill would strike a blow at the missions. It was moved to exempt Aborigines but this motion was defeated.[13]

The amending Act as passed attempted to prevent some of the worst possible abuses, in that children under 12 years of age could not immediately be put to work, and children had to be 'party' to the agreements made. However, it is doubtful whether this Act made much difference in practice. Many of these children were powerless against adults because they had no help from parents, while the magistrates were often themselves employers of cheap labour.[14]

The Larrikin Act of 1880

Another Act put on the statute books in 1880 was designed to deal with the 'troublesome disease' of larrikinism, which, according to the Attorney General, had broken out in Perth and Fremantle. This was the first Act dealing with 'disorderly conduct', an offence that would remain in one statute or another from then on. Under this Act, any person convicted of disorderly conduct 'in a street, public thoroughfare, or public place in the Colony, or in any passenger boat or vehicle', could either be fined a sum not exceeding £10 or be sentenced to 'such fine with or without imprisonment, with or without hard labour, for any term not exceeding six calendar months'.[15] Convictions of young persons under this Act added to the number of juveniles in industrial schools. The report of the Superintendent of Police for 1881 referred to the growing larrikinism in the colony:

> Although the class of offences bearing the generic name of 'larrikinism' has not been developed to any great extent amongst us, it is certainly beginning to show its ugly head. One of its worst features is a practice that is becoming prevalent in certain towns for knots of young lads to collect in different places, and insult passing females by offensive language.
>
> These young blackguards owe immunity from punishment they richly deserve to the disinclination of those insulted to come to court to prosecute.
>
> The best deterrent of such conduct would be a sound flogging administered in public; but in the absence of so

drastic a remedy, it is to be hoped magistrates will, in all cases brought to their notice, put in force the powers they possess in no hesitating manner.

Another kind of 'larrikinism' was described by a correspondent to the *West Australian* newspaper in 1883. He referred to

the intolerable nuisance occasioned by troops of young larrikins perambulating the town, rigged out as a sort of mock musical band, with penny whistles, concertinas, drums etc making night hideous with their horrible din.

Apparently, this had occurred both at Fremantle and in East Perth, 'somewhere in the neighbourhood of the Convent schools'. The writer was anxious to know whether the police had any power to act against these young offenders.[16] The report on gaols and prisons for the year 1886 indicates that sixteen juveniles had been punished under the Larrikin Act.[17]

The regular reports of the Superintendent of Poor Houses provided details about the number of children in the established orphanages in the 1880s, during which time numbers remained fairly stable (see table 9). These figures show that there were more girls than boys living in orphanages throughout the 1880s, that the number of Catholic children was greater than the number of Protestants, and that the numbers were at their highest in 1887–88. These four establishments, originally referred to as 'orphanages', began to be discussed under the nomenclature of 'industrial schools' after the 1874 legislation was introduced to make sure that children earned their keep in various ways.

Table 9: Total number of destitute children maintained in orphanages by the government, 1883–90

Year	Swan Protestant Orphanage, Middle Swan (boys)	Swan Protestant Orphanage, Perth (girls)	St Vincent's Boys' Orphanage, Subiaco (Catholic)	St Joseph's Girls' Orphanage, Perth (Catholic)
1883	32	25	52	59
1884	22	22	50	57
1885	18	27	49	59
1886	25	32	51	59
1887	25	41	49	61
1888	24	39	43	64
1889	22	37	44	50
1890	20	32	42	59

Source: Reports of the Superintendent of Poor Houses, published each year in the WA Legislative Council Votes and Proceedings.

Rottnest Reformatory and the Industrial Schools Amendment Act of 1882

The site for the Rottnest Reformatory was chosen in 1879 and the building was opened in 1881. Inside a 6-foot high stone wall were a superintendent's house, a workshop, a kitchen, two large dormitories, a schoolroom and four small cells for refractory boys.[18] When it opened, the young prisoners were under the supervision of a warder who was a tradesman, so that they might be taught some useful skills.[19]

Before the opening of the reformatory, children under 14 years of age who had broken the law were sent to various places. Some went to the Perth Gaol, where it was difficult to keep them separated from the adult prisoners. Others were placed in one of the several orphanages. The issue of whether juvenile offenders should be placed in institutions with non-offenders was taken up by an amendment to the Industrial Schools Act in 1882. In his introduction to the Bill, which passed with little debate, Attorney General A. C. Onslow made it clear that not all of the orphanages were prepared to accept offenders. He pointed out that, under the existing Act, the Governor was empowered to direct that

> juvenile offenders, who were considered too young to be sent to prison, might be sent to any institution certified under that Act (such as orphanages) if the managers were willing to receive such offenders into their establishment. But, for obvious reasons, the directors of these charitable institutions were often unwilling to receive these black sheep into their fold, and it therefore became necessary to appoint an institution for the reception of these juvenile criminals, to which they might be sent without the consent required under the present Act. It appeared to the Government that no place would answer this purpose better than the Rottnest Reformatory, and all the present Bill proposed doing was to enact that that establishment should be constituted an institution within the meaning of the Industrial Schools Act, and that the person in charge of the Reformatory shall be the 'manager' thereof, for all the purposes required by the said Act.[20]

Boys between 11 and 16 years of age who were convicted were sent to Rottnest Reformatory from 1881. According to official reports, this reformatory had a schoolmaster and the boys were also taught gardening and carpentry.[21] The report for the first year, which explained the improved behaviour of these juvenile offenders as being due to 'the severe birching which some of them have received at the Gaol', suggests that reformation through education was combined with physical punishment.[22] Far from restraining such a policy, the government passed an Act in 1884 to regulate punishment by whipping, giving great power to the controllers of gaols. Clause 5 stated that 'every such sentence of whipping in the case of a person under the age of fourteen years, summarily convicted, shall be inflicted privately'.[23]

From the first year, the Colonial Sheriff, James Roe, argued in favour of ignoring the actual length of the sentences handed down by the courts. He suggested that

> longer sentences (say three or four years) be given, so that they could not only forget their old associates, but have the chance of acquiring some knowledge of a trade which would enable them to get their own living when discharged.[24]

In practice, the sentences imposed by the courts of law were often disregarded.

The superintendent of the Rottnest Reformatory, W. D. Jackson, also advocated that these young boys be kept in the reformatory until they had learned a trade, regardless of their sentences. In his report for 1882, Jackson provided a table concerning the boys in the reformatory, indicating that their ages ranged from 8 years to 17 years, and that six of them were already 14 years or over. He recommended that boys who were reconvicted be given sentences long enough for them to learn a trade—'say 17 or 18 years of age'.[25] This issue was taken up by the Colonial Secretary, who wrote to the Governor as follows:

> In future it would be well for all magistrates who sentence boys below the age of 14 years to imprisonment to report at the same time to the Governor whether they recommend their retention for a longer period, in order that Your Excellency in Executive Council may issue instructions for them to be further detained in an Industrial School until 14 years old, the limit given by the Industrial Schools Act.
>
> If the recommendation to keep the boys until 17 or 18 years of age is considered the right course, the Act would require amending, but this proposal to my mind is excessive; 14 years is ample. On the whole the report is

not unsatisfactory, if the class from which these boys have sprung is remembered, and the dissolute nature of the parents, in some instances borne in mind.[26]

In the same year, George Shenton, Legislative Council Member for Toodyay, expressed much the same sentiment when he asked the Colonial Secretary in the Legislative Council whether it was the government's intention to send youthful male offenders to Rottnest. He said that under the Industrial Schools Act

> it is competent for the Governor, whenever any youthful offender is convicted and sentenced to be imprisoned *for a longer time than three days*, to direct such offender to be sent to any of the institutions registered under the Act, *for a period of not less than two, and not more than five years*; and he thought it would be very desirable that the Reformatory at Rottnest should be available for the reception of this class of offenders, rather than that they should be sent to gaol to mix with confirmed thieves.[27]
> [my emphasis]

From 1886, the reports concerning the Aboriginal prison on Rottnest sometimes included figures for the reformatory as well. The table for the year 1888, for example, indicates that the government was indeed following the policy of keeping children in the reformatory until they were 14 years of age, regardless of their sentences.

Delinquent and neglected children and the Industrial and Reformatory Schools Act of 1893

The Industrial and Reformatory Schools Act was passed in 1893 in order to deal with the increasing number of children before the courts.[28] This Act was a direct response to complaints about the number of children who were not attending school, especially in the Fremantle area. Although its short title invites the conclusion that it was an extension of the 1874 Industrial Schools Act, which had been passed nineteen years earlier, this later Act reveals the intention of the government to intervene more actively in the provision of institutionalized care for children. Whereas the 1874 Act sought to regulate the existing charitable institutions, the 1893 Act envisaged the provision of additional reformatories and industrial schools by the government. This was clearly a response to the chaotic economic circumstances of the 1890s.[29] Under the new legislation, a child could be declared 'neglected' and retained in an industrial school, while a child who had committed a felony could be sent to a reformatory in lieu of prison. Clause 10 allowed for children in gaols to be transferred to reformatory schools.[30]

Clauses 2 and 3 of the Act empowered the Governor to set up reformatory or industrial schools and to conduct, manage and supervise such schools, as well as to control the appointment of staff. Under this Act, a boy or girl under the age of 16 was deemed to be a child, and a 'neglected' child was defined as fitting one of the following descriptions:

> 1. Any child found begging or receiving alms, or being in any street or public place for the purpose of begging or receiving alms.

> 2. Any child who shall be found wandering about or frequenting any street, thoroughfare, public house, or place of public resort, or sleeping in the open air, or who shall not have any house or settled place of abode or any visible means of subsistence.

> 3. Any child who shall reside in any brothel or associate or dwell with any person known or reputed to be a thief, prostitute, or drunkard, or with any person convicted of vagrancy under any Act now or hereafter to be in force.

> 4. Any child who, having committed an offence punishable by imprisonment or some less punishment, ought nevertheless, in the opinion of the Justices, regard being had to the age of such child and the circumstances of the case, to be sent to an industrial school.

5. Any child whose parent [sic] represents that he wishes
such child to be sent to an Industrial School and gives
security, to the satisfaction of the Justices before whom
such child may be brought, for the payment of the maintenance of such child in such School.

6. Any child under fourteen years of age certified in
writing by the Chairman of a District Board of Education
to be habitually absent from school, and to be beyond the
control of his parents.

The sixth definition of a 'neglected' child under the 1893 Act,
which concerned children who were truants from school, was
effectively superseded by section 13 of the 1899 Public Education
Act, which also dealt with the question of truancy. Section 13
stated that

[i]f a Justice is satisfied by the parent or guardian that he
has used all reasonable efforts to cause the child to attend
school, but that the child is beyond his control, the Justice
may, without inflicting a penalty, order the child to be
sent to a certified Industrial School till the age of 14; the
parent or other person for the time being legally liable to
maintain the child, and shall, if of sufficient ability, contribute to his maintenance and training therein, a sum not
exceeding ten shillings a week, the exact amount to be
assessed by the Justice at the time of the committal of
such child.[31]

There *were* similarities between the 1874 Industrial Schools
Act and the 1893 Act, not the least of which was the power given to
the managers of industrial schools to determine the punishment of
children convicted of an offence. The Act stated that

in lieu of *any sentence* that might but for this act be
passed as a punishment [the courts could] direct that such
child be sent forthwith to any reformatory school, to be

there detained for not less than two years nor more than seven years and no child not so convicted shall be sent or maintained in any Reformatory School.[32] [my emphasis]

The last part of this clause meant that children under the age of 16 years, who were in need of care for any reason other than the commission of a felony, were to be kept separate from those who had been convicted. In spite of this clause, the distinctions between children who were in institutions because they had been abandoned, and those who were there as a result of a conviction, became increasingly blurred. The government Industrial School for Boys and Girls at Subiaco was established in 1894 under the new Act, in order to meet the increasing demand for places for European children who were in need of assistance or were before the courts.[33] The other new institution for children was St Kevin's Industrial and Reformatory School for Roman Catholic Boys, at Glendalough, which was opened in 1897. Older children were now sent to these new industrial schools or to the Rottnest Reformatory, while the four longer established institutions took children under 10 years of age.

The police were largely responsible for apprehending the children who ended up in these institutions. They delivered them first of all to the 'lock-up', where they mixed with adult prisoners, before being brought before a magistrate. Many of these children were simply declared to be truants or 'neglected' and were sent to an industrial school. Those who were sentenced and committed to an institution under section 9 of the Industrial and Reformatory Schools Act were sent to Rottnest or to St Kevin's Industrial and Reformatory School.

By the 1890s, Rottnest Reformatory, which had been established to receive children who had been sentenced by the courts, was receiving some children who had not been convicted. In 1894, the Superintendent of Prisons on Rottnest, E. F. Angelo, complained that the reformatory was overcrowded because children committed to an industrial school without a criminal conviction were being sent to Rottnest, in spite of the fact that the Subiaco Industrial School had been established in Perth by the government. Angelo thought it 'most undesirable that these neglected waifs should be condemned to association with young criminals'. However, he was also concerned at the extra cost to the reformatory, funds for which had just recently been granted as a separate item from that of the prison for Aborigines. He concluded his comments with the information that certain 'incorrigibles' had been returned to gaol on the mainland.[34]

From the late 1880s, according to these yearly reports, the number of juvenile prisoners had begun to rise. Although the figures are not always easy to unravel, it appears that the number reached thirty-five in 1893, most of whom were sent to the Rottnest Reformatory. However, the numbers for all prisoners in Fremantle Gaol were tabulated according to age after 1894, indicating that a few juveniles also remained there or had been returned there from Rottnest as 'incorrigibles'.[35] The 1898 Commission of Inquiry into the Penal System in Western Australia, which reported in 1899, stated that there were at that time 'about a dozen youths, whose ages range from seventeen to twenty-one years' in Fremantle Gaol.[36]

The Rottnest Reformatory was enlarged in 1895 to cope with the influx of juvenile criminals and neglected children sent to the island because of overcrowding in the industrial schools.[37] By the end of the century, the figures provided in the police reports reveal that there was a considerable increase in the number of juveniles charged with various offences, but mostly with larceny and being neglected and uncontrolled. In 1896, the reformatory building on Rottnest was extended.[38]

The pattern of convictions

Until the late 1880s, most of the convictions against children were for relatively short periods. In 1888, for example, four boys were given sentences from one to three months in the Rottnest Reformatory, each for being 'a rogue and a vagabond', and seven boys received sentences from fourteen days to three months for larceny. One boy was committed for three years for 'unlawful possession of housebreaking instruments'. Two of the 'rogues' also received a birching. But these were not the actual periods the boys would spend in the reformatory. All of them were kept until they were 14 years of age, by order of the Governor in the Executive Council. Without details of their ages, it is not usually possible to determine how much this extended their sentences. But the comments in the year's 'Report on Gaols and Prisons' alongside the name of one of the 'rogues', William Vantell, states, 'By order of Council to be kept for five years, but not beyond the age of 14'. In other words, a sentence of fourteen days could be extended by as much as five years, depending on the age of the child.[39]

By 1895, the length of sentences had begun to increase dramatically, while some children were simply committed to a reformatory until 16 years without any actual sentence. In March 1896, for example, 13-year-old James Morris received a conviction of five years for the larceny of one duck, while in October 14-year-old George Wored, who was convicted of stealing a silver watch, was sentenced to seven years. Four children who were defined as 'neglected', 'destitute' or 'habitually absent from school' were sentenced to a reformatory until they reached 16 years of age.[40] The number of children committed was rising at this time. In 1899, for example, forty-eight were committed as neglected children, ten were convicted of an offence, and five were committed under the Public Education Act for truancy. The contemporary 'Reports on Gaols and Prisons' reveal that there was a problem about what to do with convicted girls, who were at that stage only sent to the government industrial school at Subiaco. The total cost of maintaining these institutions in 1900 was almost £9,000.

The records reveal that some of the magistrates had clearly accepted the arguments of various people that children should be convicted for long periods so that they would stay in an industrial school long enough to learn a trade. However, children were also used as cheap labour on various government projects. James Longmore, Superintendent of Industrial Schools and Reformatories, stressed the importance of an extended period in these institutions as the best way of helping children:

> It cannot be too strongly emphasised that all children
> requiring the discipline of an Industrial School should be

committed for the full period allowed, not for the purpose of actually retaining them in the institution, but simply in order to exercise control over them. Magistrates are inclined to look upon these institutions too much as prisons, where children are sent for a month or two as punishment, instead of considering them more as homes for children who are homeless, or who are being neglected by their parents, or are in some other way thrown on the State for succour and support.[41]

But Longmore's arguments also made it clear that the children could be 'licensed out' of these institutions to work in the community. He believed that there should be a better system of licensing out, so that the children could earn some money and demonstrate their maturity. The system was still controlled by the Governor, and Longmore wanted the managers to have greater control. The Governor decided which boys could be licensed out, according to section 15 of the 1893 Industrial and Reformatory Schools Act. Under this process, children could be placed in a work situation and allowed to live outside the institution, an arrangement enabling people to make use of them and to pay them very little. Young children especially could also be boarded out in family homes, although Longmore observed that

it must not be forgotten that people do not take children for the love of them, and no system requires so much care and systematic inspection as boarding out. Continuous vigilance is necessary to prevent abuse.[42]

Examples of the children who were 'released into domestic service' sometimes appeared in the yearly reformatory reports. In November 1896, for example, Albert Wirth, a neglected child of only 13 years, was released to Mrs Shearer, Perth, to work out his five-year sentence. Fourteen-year-old William Barrett, who was in the reformatory for five years 'for obtaining goods by false pretences', was released into the care of Captain de Burgh, Fremantle.[43]

William Dale, Inspector of Institutions, was critical of these procedures. He thought more attention should be given to the future of the children. In his 1897 report on the Swan Protestant Orphanage, he stated:

> I think the Orphanage authorities make a mistake in sending them [the boys] to situations on reaching the age of 14 years, being the period when the Govt. subsidy ceases. I would like to recommend that on attaining that age, they should be kept to work on the farm for at least twelve months, they might be allowed a certain sum monthly in addition to board, lodging and clothes, which should be placed in the Savings Bank in trust for them. It would be of great service to them when leaving the institution.[44]

Reporting on the institutions for children

Some examples of the ways in which the colonial state responded to the needs of the destitute show the detailed nature of the administration of this small society. The parsimonious nature of the responses of its officials was partly due to the small revenue base from which they operated. In December 1880, for example, the Resident Magistrate of Fremantle wrote to the Colonial Secretary concerning the family of a convict, Thomas Casely, who had been imprisoned for six months for stealing. The family of four children, the eldest only 7 years of age, were starving, and the Resident Magistrate suggested that the two eldest children be put in an orphanage so that the mother had a chance of supporting herself and the youngest ones.[45] William Dale, at that time Superintendent of Poor Houses, was consulted, and he suggested that the children not be sent to an orphanage but rather that the family be given rations, half the cost of which could be passed on to the Imperial Government, through its financial responsibility for the convict establishment in Western Australia. This solution was accepted.[46]

A different solution was found in 1881 in the case of the five Lampey children, who were between the ages of 3.5 and 11 years.

William Dale wrote a memorandum to the Colonial Secretary explaining why he had asked the Resident Magistrate in Fremantle to locate these children and to send them by steamer to the Poor House:

> Permission was given on 19th February for Mrs Lampey and their admission into the Perth Poor House. They were received on that date, Lampey having been sent to Prison by the Resident Magistrate, Fremantle. Mrs Lampey was a few days after committed an in-patient in the Colonial Hospital and is there still. On her husband's discharge from Perth Prison he removed the children from the Home to Fremantle. I beg to state he is a notorious drunkard and not a fit person to have the care of his children in their mother's absence. Should she soon be well enough to leave the Hospital, there is no hope of her again being able to look after her children, her illness and her present state having been caused by her husband's cruelty to her. If the children could be placed in the Protestant Orphanage, away from the father's influence and evil example, it would be a good thing, and I would respectfully recommend the same for the favoured consideration of His Excellency the Governor.[47]

The regular reports on these institutions, prepared by the managers, do not tell us much about the personal experiences of the children. However, they explain that they were all expected to attend school and were kept busy in other ways, as well. The Orphanage and Industrial School for Roman Catholic Girls in Hay Street, East Perth (also called St Joseph's Girls' Orphanage), established in 1868, was reported on favourably in 1900. The children, who numbered between seventy-eight and ninety-four for that year, attended St Joseph's School and were taught along with the other scholars. It was reported that they passed a good examination in all subjects except Arithmetic.

> In this institution the girls have an excellent industrial training; one only requires to visit the school to ascertain

that. The senior girls are now being taught to cut out their own dresses and work the sewing machine, two additional ones having recently been added. The training in domestic work is very thorough; what with baking, cooking, laundry and needlework, the girls are kept busily employed, and are turned out well equipped to earn their living.[48]

There were between seventy-eight and eighty-seven boys on the roll at St Vincent's Orphanage in Subiaco during 1900. Here the boys were reported to be variously employed: some had been taught printing, since the orphanage had its own printing press; some were engaged on the farm, where they were taught to milk and look after stock; a few were being taught shoe-making and carpentry. The boys baked their own bread. The reports from the lower-school classes were 'exceedingly creditable', but the higher classes had not done well 'partly owing to the fact that three hours per day are devoted to school work, the rest of the time being spent in manual training'. The children at these two Catholic institutions included orphans and 'delinquent' children sent to the orphanage in lieu of a gaol sentence, but both institutions also admitted some children who were on a 'private list'—often children whose parent or parents could not care for them and agreed to pay for their keep.

The smaller orphanage and industrial school for Protestant girls in Adelaide Terrace, also established in 1868, which had between forty-nine and sixty inmates in 1900, was reportedly improving in several ways. The children were taught at the school and the teaching staff had been 'entirely re-arranged'. Additional furniture had been provided and an improvement in school results was expected in the following year. Here, the industrial training included laundry work, and an adjoining building had been fitted out for this purpose. This arrangement was to provide training for the girls, and it was hoped to derive some income from their work.

According to the 1900 report, the boys at the Swan Orphanage and Industrial School for Protestant Boys in Middle Swan were well looked after and were learning to be farmers:

Attention is mostly centred, and rightly so, on agriculture,
being a training most suitable for the boys and also for the
requirements of the State. The 'Boys' Farm' is progressing
rapidly, and a considerable acreage is now under cultivation. The boys have cows, sheep, goats, and horses to
tend. They are acquiring knowledge of farming, gardening, fruit growing, butchering, tailoring, boot repairing,
carpentering, and blacksmithing. It will be seen from the
list of occupations now being carried on at the farm, that
the boys are receiving a much improved training than
they formerly received.

However, the report on the educational results for this orphanage
suggested that there were not enough staff, especially for the
younger children, and that the facilities were inadequate.

These four institutions had all begun as Christian orphanages
and been in operation for about thirty years. They had been
controlled by legislation from 1874, when the first Industrial Schools
Act was introduced, and had been incorporated into the state system.
The number of destitute, abandoned or delinquent children in these
orphanages began to rise, especially from 1894, reaching a total of
277 by 1900—a very large number for such a small population.[49]
This rise was connected with the huge increase in population in the
1890s because of the discovery of gold. Many families failed to
establish themselves in the goldfields, and a large settlement of
people with no visible means of support grew up in East Perth.
However, the rise in the numbers of children in these institutions
was also the result of the introduction of the Larrikin Act in 1880, the
much more draconian Industrial and Reformatory Schools Act of
1893 and the Public Education Act of 1899, which were partly a
response to the growing social problems of the period.

The other three institutions—Rottnest Reformatory, the
Subiaco Industrial School for Boys and Girls and St Kevin's Industrial
and Reformatory School for Roman Catholic Boys—had a very
different history. The new Subiaco Industrial School, established in
1893, gradually became a receiving house for older children, many of
them truants or neglected children.[50] In 1900, for example, it housed

seventeen neglected children, three convicted children, six detained for truancy under the Public Education Act, and one destitute child. Shoemaking and carpentry were taught to some of the boys, and the girls had 'a good training in household duties and laundry work, as well as being trained to make their own clothes and use a sewing machine'. The account of school work indicated that many children were in classes lower than appropriate for their age and some had not been advanced to the next grade. The report of the Super-intendent of Industrial Schools and Reformatories suggests that this institution was in some sort of turmoil. The building was not originally intended for both boys and girls and, as the situation of the building was not adequate for a boys' home, it would 'more and more be used as a receiving depot for the temporary reception of inmates prior to their transfer elsewhere'.[51]

St Kevin's Industrial and Reformatory School for Roman Catholic Boys, which was opened in 1897 by Sir John Forrest, was the other institution established in the last decade of the century.[52] This three-storey school was erected by the Oblate Fathers of Mary Immaculate, and was surrounded by 300 acres of land provided by Bishop Gibney.[53] The clearing of scrub around the school had not at that time been completed and fencing was still going on. There were children as young as 4 years of age and as old as 14 in this institution, run by Father O'Ryan and four lay brothers. Some of the children were orphans, some had one parent living and some had both parents living. There were thirty-nine boys resident at the end of 1899 and another twenty-seven were admitted during 1900. The children were taught elementary and technical education, but only three hours per day were devoted to schooling for the older boys, while five and a half hours were spent in industrial training. Physical exercise was emphasized, and the children at Glendalough were reported to be busy with carpentry, tailoring, farming, gardening, shoemaking, baking and bee-keeping.

> A valuable lathe has recently been erected in the carpenter's shop, which is now well stocked with chisels, planes, and other necessary tools. The boys have prepared the posts, rails, and gates for the fences. Some of

the boys are learning to plough, and look after horses and cows. Sheep are kept and slaughtered when required. All the bread required for inmates and staff is baked on the premises. Bee-hives have recently been introduced, and this industry promises to be successful.[54]

There are obvious contradictions in interpreting this pattern of state intervention. On the one hand, it could be argued that the colonial government and religious bodies were responding to the obvious needs of a very vulnerable section of the population. On the other, such a response must be seen in class terms. In the absence of any welfare provisions, a system grew up that confronted the problem of poverty by disciplining the children of the working class, a solution for which, whenever possible, the parents them-selves would pay. The children could be trained to be usefully and cheaply employed inside these institutions but also employed under arrangement with local landowners and businessmen.

The 1898 commission of inquiry

In 1894, the *West Australian* newspaper expressed the concern of some of the critics of the reformatory system, referring to delinquent children as 'more offended against than offending'. The paper advocated a different system of dealing with juvenile delinquents, especially girls, by 'placing the children in the care of good and respectable people, and giving them all the advantages of the surroundings of home', for which such people would be paid 'a sufficient fee'.[55] This pattern of 'boarding out', widely used in New South Wales at that time, was a cheaper option but one that could also lead to exploitation. The perception that there were insufficient places in the existing system for the growing number of delinquent children finally led to an official investigation.

The 1898 Commission of Inquiry into the Penal System was set up largely because of the criticisms levelled at the government by F. C. B. Vosper, journalist and editor of the *Coolgardie Miner*, con-cerning the unsatisfactory treatment of young prisoners in Fremantle

Gaol.[56] The commission reported that these boys could not be profitably employed, that they had only one hour's schooling a week, and that the building was ill adapted to the reception of young prisoners, who spent most of the day in their cells.

> There are some cases where, from the nature of the crime, it may be necessary that these youthful prisoners should be kept in close confinement: but in the majority of instances your Commission are of the opinion that the interests of society would be best served and adequately protected by releasing the youths altogether, and placing them under a species of police supervision, such as is contemplated in the 'Prevention of Crimes Act, 1898'.

The commission directed particular attention to two young brothers in gaol for seven and ten years, respectively, for a crime that in England would be punished by a sentence of two years with hard labour. It pointed out that taxpayers were supporting 'two young fellows' who, prior to their incarceration, were earning excellent wages and supporting a widowed mother and younger siblings.[57] It recommended that no boy under the age of 16 and no girl under 18 years of age be in gaol.[58]

The commissioners took evidence, all of which appeared in the final report, about the government-run Subiaco Industrial School for Boys and Girls and Rottnest Reformatory. They provided figures from the Inspector of Charitable Institutions for the number of children in these two places and the cost of their maintenance. These figures were important in connection with a proposal, made by Commandant Booth of the Salvation Army, that the government close its own institutions and allow the Salvation Army to care for these children. The Salvation Army wanted government funding of 7s 10½d per week for each industrial school child, and 10s 6d per week for each Rottnest child. Commandant Booth spoke of the work done by the Salvation Army in other Australian colonies and pointed out that his organization had already been granted 15,000 acres of land at Collie and was seeking another 5,000 acres.

> We would put both boys and girls on the Collie land,
> and we only ask to be paid for the time that they are with
> us. We would expect free rail passes for our officers. Our
> agents would know the parents throughout the Colony
> who were best fitted to be entrusted with the care of the
> children after they left us.[59]

This was a proposal for a system of 'boarding out' some of the
children by the Salvation Army. It was not clear how many of
the children would remain in the Collie establishment, but, under
the Industrial Schools Act, the managers of institutions had the power
to employ children in any way they wished, after consultation with
their parents.

Evidence was also taken from F. J. Fowler, superintendent of
the Subiaco Industrial School, from John Watson, superintendent
of the Rottnest Reformatory, and from James Longmore, Inspector of
Charitable Institutions. Fowler gave some details about the establishment of the school in 1894 and of the cost of salaries for staff. He
said that 'neglected, destitute and uncontrollable boys' were sent to
Subiaco from all over the colony by police magistrates. But the
school did not take convicted children. He explained that boys
occasionally absconded (there were twelve cases in 1897) and, when
caught, were then sent to Rottnest, a policy he did not endorse
because the boys were not convicted criminals.

Most of the twenty-six boys and twenty-one girls in the
institution at that time, some as young as 6 years, came from parents
who were immigrants from other colonies, and the parents were
obliged to support the children if they could afford to do so. The
number of children in this institution attested to the family disloca-
tion resulting from the gold rush and the economic depression.
Superintendent Fowler explained that children received three hours'
schooling a day and the rest of the time was spent on mending and
making clothes and doing the cooking. The children were sometimes
birched if they misbehaved and there was a special cell for refractory
children. It was not a dark cell and it was not used at night.[60]

James Longmore claimed that out of the seven institutions
under his department, Rottnest, Subiaco Industrial School and

St Kevin's Industrial and Reformatory School all dealt especially with children who had committed offences. This difference from Fowler's report suggests that Longmore considered all children sent to these institutions by magistrates as 'offenders', even though they had not been given a sentence. He spoke with approval of a 'boarding out' system, although he did not think the colony was 'sufficiently settled' for its introduction. He reiterated the need for longer periods in detention for children who had been convicted.

> At present some of the children go to Rottnest for absurdly short sentences [six months or so] and when they come out we lose all control of them. The best thing would be to send all the children to an Industrial School, and there should be power to commit them, as in England, for detention up to 18 years of age. In the case of short sentences, it is impossible to teach a boy a trade properly.

He also advocated a special court for children or sittings on special days.[61]

John Watson's evidence revealed that he had boys at Rottnest with sentences of up to five years, most of whom behaved well, 'but we have had one or two vicious ones'. He claimed that the children had three hours' schooling a day, and seventeen boys had obtained certificates at the previous year's examination. He described the boys' activities as painting, carpentry and gardening. Watson had been at Rottnest for eighteen years and was apparently proud of what he claimed were the achievements of the boys.[62]

His evidence, however, must be contrasted with information provided to the Premier by the then Governor just two years earlier. In 1897, the Governor of Western Australia, Sir Gerard Smith, who had a residence on Rottnest Island, began to take an interest in the reformatory. He wrote in protest to the Premier concerning the dual purpose of the reformatory, which was providing for both juvenile criminals and neglected children. But he had also observed the treatment of the boys first hand and described their activities in this letter:

As to the employment of these boys at Rottnest, and their education, what Colonel Angelo calls 'remunerative' employment consists, as I can vouch for with my own eyes, in breaking stone with heavy hammers, and without any protection for the eyes, in burning lime which causes bleeding from the eyes and ears, and in pushing about heavy ballast trucks filled with sand and rubble for the construction of some railway or tramway, quite unneeded and which I believe is not approved for construction by any authority whatever. I believe such employment, fitted only for strong men, to be distinctly illegal and I trust Ministers will put a peremptory stop to it. In any case, whether illegal or not, it is dangerous and inhuman and is quite worthless for the purposes we must all have in view in reforming or educating the young people of the Colony. The education given is two hours daily, of a very limited character.[63]

Governor Gerard Smith told the Premier that he would refrain from making suggestions for change because he believed that the education question was under consideration. But he also wrote to Colonel Edward Angelo, who had overall responsibility for the reformatory, to ask a number of questions about its operations. Angelo replied that the institution operated under the Industrial and Reformatory Schools Act of 1893, that there were printed regulations governing its operations, a copy of which he supplied, and that the children had lessons between 3 and 5 o'clock every afternoon, after the normal school day for the local children ended. He, too, deplored the presence of both criminal and neglected children in this one institution, since he believed that the latter should be in an industrial school in Perth.

In the final report of the Commission of Inquiry into the Penal System, the possibility of the government accepting the offer of the Salvation Army to undertake the whole task of providing for the kinds of children currently sent to Subiaco and Rottnest was kept open. The commissioners made eight recommendations regarding the custody of the children in the event that the government rejected this solution:

1. That the Government Industrial School at Subiaco be, in future, used as a receiving house for all boys and a detention house for all girls.

2. The Reformatory at Rottnest to be done away with, and an Industrial School established at Rottnest, for all male juvenile offenders.

3. From Subiaco the male children will be drafted off to Rottnest institution, where they will be classified by the Superintendent or other Governing authority.

4. That the Commitment order of the magistrate shall, in all cases, be for an indeterminate period, up to a maximum of sixteen years, for boys, and eighteen years for girls, but not less than twelve months shall be spent under strict discipline.

5. After twelve months the Superintendent of the Industrial School may recommend for apprenticeship any children who, in his opinion, appear to be sufficiently reformed. In all cases of apprenticeship the children must go to persons residing in the country districts only, and not in or near Perth.

6. The Superintendent or other Governing authority should, from time to time, notify the Resident Magistrates in the various rural districts that certain boys are open to engagement or apprenticeship under the statutory conditions. Under no circumstances are any boys to be sent to persons of whom the Resident Magistrate does not approve.

7. During detention at Rottnest all boys should be put to work improving the land, gardening, and outdoor industrial occupations generally.

8. Under no circumstances should boys under the age of sixteen be committed to prison; no girls under the age of eighteen.[64]

Partly as a result of these recommendations, Rottnest Reformatory was closed in 1901. In that year, the Salvation Army established two senior industrial schools for Protestant children at Collie—one for boys and one for girls—and, in 1902, a junior industrial school for Protestant boys. The Subiaco Industrial School became a receiving depot for boys and girls, while St Kevin's Industrial and Reformatory School at Glendalough continued as before, as did the other Roman Catholic and Anglican establishments.[65]

Consolidation of laws regarding children

During the nineteenth century, two currents of thought existed in some contradiction to one another. On the one hand, the courts reflected a growing leniency about the age at which European children should be deemed 'responsible' for criminal activity, and there was an increasing reluctance to imprison them along with adult criminals. On the other hand, they were often committed to institutions for periods much exceeding the period of punishment appropriate for their crime under the law.

The law was consolidated in 1902 in the Criminal Code.[66] This was undertaken partly because many of the statutes used in the colony had been adopted from English law and had never been written down in detail as Australian law. The earlier pattern of regarding a child of 7 years as responsible for his (sic) criminal acts was retained in the new law but was now qualified:

> A person under the age of seven years is not criminally responsible for any act or omission. A person under the age of fourteen years is not criminally responsible for any act or omission, unless it is proved that at the time of doing the act or making the omission he had the capacity to know that he ought not do the act or make the omission. A male person under the age of fourteen years is presumed to be incapable of having carnal knowledge.[67]

This meant that the court was obliged to show that the accused child demonstrated adult comprehension of the nature of the crime, thus reducing the likelihood of the conviction of a very young child and encouraging leniency in the courts.

Two short sections near the end of the code referred to the fate of children who were convicted of crimes. Unless he (sic) had committed treason, murder or manslaughter, a child under 12 years could not be imprisoned for more than one month, could not be fined more than 40s, and could only be whipped under specific circumstances with six strokes of the cane. A child who was over 12 but under 16 years could be sent to gaol for three months, fined £10, whipped (if a male) and might be called upon to make restitution.

However, the sting in the tail of these limitations on the ways in which a child might be punished lay in the threat of an extended period in a reformatory or industrial school, which was an alternative option for the judge. If the child over 12 years had a previous conviction, his sentence in such an institution could be extended to three years. This was a continuation of the policy that had first taken shape thirty years before in allowing the Governor in Council to commit children to long periods in institutions, regardless of the length of their sentences. There had been, in other words, an increasing tendency to rely on sending children to so-called reforming institutions, which really provided alternative forms of imprisonment.

PART II

ABORIGINAL CHILDREN

CHAPTER 5

Estimating the Aboriginal population

THE demography of Aboriginal people grew in complexity during the nineteenth century, although the census material was unreliable and local reports of the size of the total Aboriginal population were full of contradictions. The 1881 Census required European people 'to state on their schedules full particulars as to each Aboriginal in their employ', while 'each Resident or Police Magistrate is desired to obtain, if possible, the number of Aborigines, in his district, who were not depending on the settlers for their subsistence'.[1] However, although Aboriginal people who were employed by Europeans were enumerated in these census reports, no attempt was made before 1891 to estimate the entire Aboriginal population.[2] The only details appearing in the 1881 Census were the figures for Aborigines in service districts and towns, a total of 2,346. No real attempt was made at this time to count the growing number of Aborigines working in the pearling and pastoral industries in the North West.

The superintendent of the 1891 Census claimed that, because the 1889 Constitution Act 'makes distinct reference to the population of Western Australia "exclusive of Aborigines", it would not have been possible to add them to our numbers on this present occasion'.[3] However, chapter 13 of the 1891 Census dealt with 'The Half-Caste Aborigines' in three pages, providing an age profile and details about religion and occupation. There was also a special chapter, with an appendix of four pages, dealing with 'Aborigines', including tables showing birthplace, age, occupation, education and religion. Thus, the counting of the Aboriginal people began in earnest in 1891, even though the information was kept separate from that concerning Europeans, and was still of doubtful accuracy.

Aboriginal children before 1850

The history of European settlement in the Swan River Colony between 1828 and 1850 tells the story of the gradual spread of land-holdings and of early conflict with the original inhabitants. The destruction of Aboriginal society, at this time especially in the southern regions of the colony, might encourage the belief that in this early period the growing European population, who wanted access to large tracts of land, simply wished to rid the colony of Aboriginal people. However, there is considerable evidence that, even before 1850, the colonists of the south viewed Aboriginal people, both adults and children, as a potential source of valuable labour.

Although the settlers who had capital brought servants and other skilled and unskilled labourers to the colony, often in family groups, they complained constantly throughout this period that they could not get an adequate supply of labour. To supplement their work force, they attempted to absorb and 'settle' Aboriginal groups so that the adults could be gradually integrated as workers into the community, and so that Aboriginal children could be trained.[4] In 1850, the labour situation changed radically with the arrival of the first consignment of convicts to the Swan River Colony, and the colony began to expand more rapidly. The period between 1829 and 1850 is therefore the first phase of Aboriginal–settler relations, during which time they contended for control of the land.

It is not possible to know the number of Aboriginal children who were in contact with European settlers before 1850. However,

the attempt to estimate the total Aboriginal population of the Swan
River Colony from the time of settlement has a long history.[5] A
number of social groups, known collectively as Nyungar, lived near
the places of first settlement in the south-west corner of the
continent. After nearly a decade of observing the local Aboriginal
population, Governor James Stirling concluded that they lived in
tribes of about 120 persons, and that their population numbers had
'long been stationary at their present amount'. He believed that this
was because of their food-gathering habits, their absence of 'fixed
habitation' and their failure to develop techniques to increase their
food supply. It was impossible, he claimed, to give an accurate
estimate of their total numbers, but he thought that, during that ten-
year period, some 750 Aboriginal people had visited Perth from the
surrounding districts 'to the extent of forty miles each way'. He was
prepared, however, to give the estimate of 'one native to each
portion of ground of two square miles'.[6]

In 1837, Francis Armstrong, who as Protector of Aborigines
travelled widely in the colony and had a considerable knowledge of
Aboriginal languages and customs, drew up a specific list of names
of Aboriginal people from the Moore River to the Murray River and
inland to the Avon River. He also listed groups west of the Avon
River in 1838–39. But his lists, although probably intended as an
addition to the 1837 Census, did not indicate ages. His successor as
Protector of Aborigines, Charles Symmons, again listed the local
Swan groups in 1840, adding one that Armstrong had omitted. But
these lists were limited in the area they covered and were not
exhaustive.[7] Other contemporary observers, including George
Fletcher Moore, Sir George Grey and Bishop Rosendo Salvado, made
estimates of the size of the Aboriginal population, although most of
them did not believe that such estimates could be very accurate.[8]
Bishop Salvado, for example, writing in 1851, observed that

> [many writers] have tried to make approximate calculations
> for the square mile, but they differ so much between
> themselves that there is little to be gained from such
> estimates. In any case, how could one succeed in fixing the
> number of inhabitants in a country which is for the greater

part unknown, and when the people are unevenly scat-
tered, and wander from one place to another *ad infinitum*?[9]

Similar doubts had been expressed in a publication twelve years
earlier by Nathaniel Ogle.[10]

As the Swan River Colony expanded and acts of violence
became more commonplace, the new settlers developed a great
interest in the size of the Aboriginal population and whether it was
increasing or declining. The men who were appointed as Protectors
of Aborigines (or of Natives) in the period, particularly those who
had responsibilities in outlying districts, were those most likely to be
able to provide information on these issues. Peter Barrow, appointed
as Protector of Aborigines 'for the hilly country' of Western Australia
in 1840, wrote as follows in his report of 1841:

> I have visited every part of my field of labour, from the
> most northern to the most southern settlements, namely
> from Toodyay to King George's Sound, and have seen
> many of the natives; my knowledge, however, of their
> number is but scanty, nor is it easily acquired. I am
> endeavouring to make a census of the black population,
> but this must of necessity be the work of much time.[11]

The contemporary interest in the possible decline of the
Aboriginal population could be more readily satisfied by anecdotal
evidence. Charles Symmons, Protector of Natives in 1844, stated in
his yearly report:

> The question having been frequently mooted as to the
> numerical increase or decrease of the population since the
> settlement of this Colony by Europeans, I have lately
> endeavoured to procure such authentic information on
> the subject as circumstances and the scattered nature of
> the aboriginal population would permit.
>
> From the result of these inquiries I am induced to
> believe, that, whatever numerical fluctuations may have
> occurred in certain districts, yet that the aggregate

numbers are much as they were fifteen years since. From the salubrity of the climate, the absence of all contagious diseases, and the now rare occurrence of fatal hostilities among themselves, it might reasonably be inferred that a population under such favorable circumstances must rapidly increase. Such, however, is certainly not the case. But I shall not attempt to analyze this seeming anomaly further than by remarking, that the women seldom rear (even if they produce) more than one or two children; a fact possibly to be attributed to their ever roving habits, and consequent fatigue, their exposure to the hardships of the bush, and to the circumstance that the ceremony of weaning is usually postponed until the child has attained 4 or 5 years of age.

Such being some of the natural checks to a rapid increase of population, it may be easy to infer that the mortality occasioned by old age, casualties, or the ravages (as in 1843) of the influenza, or other local disease, must naturally tend to equalize the proportion of births and deaths amongst the aboriginal tribes.[12]

The reader of the reports of the Protectors of Aborigines is bound to conclude that the settlers were being provided to some extent with the kind of information they hoped to hear. Thus, Thomas Yule, acting Protector of Natives in the York district in 1845, congratulated himself on the fact that 'between Beverley and Tood-yay, about one hundred miles in extent, and containing about five hundred natives, who are constantly mingling with us, the number of delinquencies has been so small'. He reported that the appearance of the Aboriginal population had improved since an earlier visit, but disagreed with Barrow's report of the previous years in which he claimed that their numbers were declining.[13]

The 1848 Census of the total population of the Swan River Colony listed those Aboriginal men and women who were employed by Europeans, along with 'an estimate of their numbers in the located districts'.[14] In the report of this census, the administrator stated that there was an immediate practical purpose behind the enumeration of Aborigines: it would make possible a more accurate estimate of the consumption of flour in the colony. He also claimed that knowledge of 'the names of individuals belonging to the several tribes...with a degree of certainty' would allow useful estimates of their numbers.[15] The census total of 1,960 Aborigines included 541 in employment, of whom 418 were men and 123 were women. These figures, however, give us no information about the presence of Aboriginal children near the centres of European settlement.

Recent interest in the size of the Aboriginal population in colonial Western Australia has focused on the related issues of the size of that population at the time of European settlement and on the changes in the demographic patterns for the ensuing decades.[16] Hallam's exploration of this issue concentrates on the region most densely populated by Europeans

> centred around the area where the Helena enters, stretching to the sea on the west, thirty two kilometres into the hills to the east, north towards Lennard's Brook, south to Mundijong (rather under two thousand square miles).[17]

Hallam's calculation gives a minimum of 440 persons for this region, or twenty-three persons per 100 square miles. She refers to Salvado's contemporary estimate of 555 Aborigines for about 2,800 square miles: a density of twenty people per 100 square miles.[18] According to both Paul Hasluck, writing in 1942,[19] and Lois Tilbrook, in a more recent analysis,[20] the figures were probably higher than this. Hasluck claimed that his examination of contemporary evidence and later estimates suggested that the European and Aboriginal populations were about equal in 1842, when there were 3,000 European immigrants in the Swan River Colony.[21]

Even if we accept Hasluck's estimate for 1842, Aboriginal families were undoubtedly smaller than European families at this time. While a great many families of considerable size had arrived from England, and European fertility levels in the colony were high, there is evidence that fertility levels were very low in Aboriginal society. Gillian Cowlishaw argues that 'low physiological fertility, rather than high infanticide and infant mortality accounts for the low birth rates which are reported for pre-contact Aboriginal populations'.[22] Cowlishaw's summary of the figures collected on Aboriginal fertility rates in Australia reveals general agreement on an unusually high proportion of childless women and very low estimates of the average number of live births per woman. Hallam's analysis of the evidence collected by contemporary observers suggests that no more than two children commonly resided with their parents in the Swan River Colony.[23]

While low physiological fertility may have resulted from the blockage of fallopian tubes as a result of infection after abortion, fertility levels were apparently also affected by a variety of factors including spontaneous abortion, low levels of male fertility, longevity of breastfeeding and coital infrequency. However, Cowlishaw puts the greatest emphasis on the likely infrequency of ovulation, due to absence of body fat and to the maintenance of high levels of prolactin due to breastfeeding. A full explanation for this phenomenon in Aboriginal society would involve a careful analysis of food-gathering patterns, food taboos and breastfeeding patterns.

These claims received some support from the account of Bishop Salvado concerning child rearing and breastfeeding, although he also referred to the pattern of infanticide for children who were crippled or deformed, as well as for third and subsequent daughters:

> I have never met a crippled or deformed person, male or female, among the natives, and I have heard it said that a baby suffering from any abnormality is put to death as soon as it is born...A third daughter has the terrible fate of being put to death by her own mother. The reason they give is that it is not good to let the women become too numerous...When a woman shows that she intends to kill her daughter, one of the other women will sometimes prevent her by taking the child herself. The mother of Benedict Upumera is one such woman and 'Kookina', of whom I speak elsewhere, is one of the girls.[24]

These practices, if carried out, may have reflected an acute recognition of the importance of children in Aboriginal society, since undue protection of weak children, or the presence of too many children, would have threatened the survival of the whole community. However, the greater number of surviving males in the Aboriginal community may also have been due to the frequent death of mothers in childbirth.[25] Salvado observed that the tenderness of parents for their children 'goes to excessive lengths'.[26] He referred to the close relationships between children and parents, which meant that parents were reluctant to hand over their children to European men for purposes of education, unless these men had 'gained their affection'.[27]

The 1829 settlement in Western Australia disrupted the economy of the Aboriginal people. The granting of huge tracts of land to settler capitalists, and the settlement of small-holders around waterholes, combined to deny Aboriginal people access to their traditional land. A combination of fencing, land clearing and killing of game had the effect of reducing the availability of food supplies. In particular, the expropriation of the best arable soil drastically reduced the supplies of reed rhizomes and yam tubers, which provided the major carbohydrates in the Aboriginal diet. By 1850, those who no longer had access to their 'traditional' lands were increasingly attaching themselves to the centres of European settlement, and thereby giving an inflated idea of their overall numbers.

Bishop Salvado records in his memoirs that upon his arrival in 1846, 'there was plenty of opportunity for meeting the many natives roaming about the town'.[28] Many were forced to rely on what they could earn from farm or domestic labour, or on handouts from the European population. The 541 Aborigines listed as employed in the 1848 Census included both men and women. The contemporary records also provide substantial evidence that children of Aboriginal descent were increasingly regarded as members of the work force.

Aboriginal children in census returns, 1848–1901

In 1858, Bishop Salvado collected and printed what was called the *Census of 1858*, which was held in the archives at New Norcia. It was reprinted by Sylvia Hallam in 1989 as an appendix to a publication of a dictionary about New Norcia for the Bicentennial year of 1989.[29] This census consisted of 'lists of known Aborigines for a group of nine localities north of Perth'.[30] While this meticulous recording provides valuable evidence about marriage and child rearing patterns in the region, it does not offer much demographic information about the whole Aboriginal population in the south of the colony.

The counting of Aboriginal children was simply ignored in the early census returns of Western Australia. In the 1891 Census, they received some attention, but the details about children of mixed descent, then labelled 'half-castes', were presented separately from the rest of the population. There were 318 children under 16 years of age, out of a total of 575 persons of mixed parentage, while the figures claim that seventeen males and twenty-six females were 'scholars'. This information is included in a table on 'Occupations of Half-Castes', which also gives a figure of sixty-two male and sixty-one female infants and children at the top of the 'Occupations' column. These figures suggest that young children worked with their parents in family groups, although the figures are so small that they are difficult to interpret.[31]

In the section on Aboriginal people in 1891, the Super-intendent of Census, Walter Gale, explained that no attempt had been made to count the 'uncivilized Aborigines', but that there were three groups enumerated: those employed by Europeans, those living near towns, and those 'roving from one station to another'.[32] The total number of Aborigines apparently in some sort of contact with European society was estimated at 5,670 persons (see table 10). The census tables indicating ages showed that there were few very young children: only forty-six under 1 year, 336 between 1 and 10 years, and 796 between 10 and 20 years.[33] The small number of children under 1 year suggested to Gale that the Aborigines were dying out.[34]

Under the column indicating 'Occupations', 307 of the total number were classified as scholars and infants, but 'only sixteen of the Aborigines were returned upon the schedules as being able to read and write'. The census table showed estimated ages for the Aboriginal group in contact with Europeans in 1891, although it was admitted that the figures were unreliable. The only clearly identified

Table 10: Age of Aborigines, 1891

Age	Males	Females	Total
Under 1	21	25	46
1–10	182	154	336
10–20	520	276	796
20–30	570	436	1,006
30–40	393	340	733
40–50	281	215	496
50–60	153	97	250
Over 60	85	60	145
	2,205	1,603	3,808
Age not stated	1,018	844	1,862
Total	3,223	2,447	5,670

Aboriginal children in another table showing the occupations of Aborigines by districts were 307 'infants'. This table of occupations is quite detailed and it must be presumed that many of the working Aborigines were children who were employed along with their parents.

The figure in the census of 1891 of 1,579 station and farm servants suggests that some Aborigines in the North West might have been included, although the number is clearly too low to be accurate. Nor do the categories seem flexible enough to account for all Aboriginal workers. According to one observer of life in the North West:

> [t]hey were the white settler's best friend and those of us who were there in the 'seventies and 'eighties appreciated their work and treated them accordingly. They shepherded sheep, fenced in the paddocks, did all the shearing for thirty or forty years and did it well. They tackled all kinds of station work, they were reliable bullock drovers and horse

teamsters and they worked cheerfully and solidly. At the
De Grey in my time there were 400 natives. They shore
between 50,000 and 60,000 sheep each year and scoured
all the wool. Our job in those times would have been more
back-breaking and more heart-breaking than most men
could endure but for the black men.[35]

This contemporary account of the value of Aborigines as
workers in the North West includes fencers, shearers and wool
scourers, yet none of these occupations was mentioned in the 1891
Census list.[36] The census statistics are apparently a very poor guide to
the contribution made to the overall economy by Aboriginal people;
they tell us little about children's activities, and little about how much
the settler capitalists of the North West depended on Aboriginal
people for their economic survival. As far as population statistics are
concerned, according to an attachment to the 1896 report of the
Aborigines Protection Board, no one knew with any certainty how
many Aborigines lived in the colony's North West:

The number of Aboriginal natives in the Kimberley
District can be only vaguely guessed at, since a large
portion of the district has not been travelled by whites at
all, and even in some places where whites have travelled
for several years, no idea of the number of natives can be
obtained, since their resorts are inaccessible to white men,
and no dependence can be placed in the reports of this or
other colonies, where numbers are concerned.[37]

The author of this report on the Kimberley district, George Marsden,
claimed that 5,000 natives 'could be taken to be the outside'. Another
appendix to this report, this one by C. A. Bailey on the Southern and
Eastern Goldfields, claimed that there were about 300 Aboriginal
males in the goldfields area.[38]

Other claims about the number of Aboriginal people, made in
the last years of the nineteenth century, indicate how little was really
known about their overall numbers. In the 1888 debate on the
Aborigines Bill, Septimus Burt suggested that the Aborigines in the

south had almost died out.[39] However, in the same debate, the Colonial Secretary, Sir Malcolm Fraser, claimed that there were 'far more natives in the Colony than we have ever seen or come in contact with'. In the debate on clause 70 of the Constitution Bill in 1889, 'to promote the preservation and well-being of the Aborigines', the question of the number of Aborigines in the colony and whether or not they were dying out was an issue of some importance. This Bill was designed to appropriate £5,000 per annum out of revenue for the Aborigines Protection Board, or 1 per cent of total revenue when it exceeded £500,000. Several speakers opposed the clause, partly on the grounds that Aborigines were likely to gradually decrease in number, thus requiring less and less financial support. But Sir Malcolm Fraser reiterated his view 'that natives probably existed in thousands, if not tens of thousands, in the unsettled and unexplored portions of the Colony'.

John Forrest, at this time Commissioner of Crown Lands, also claimed that there were 'thousands upon thousands of natives in the interior of our territory, who have never seen a white man' and that three-quarters of the territory was still unknown.[40] However, in 1892, when he was Premier of Western Australia, he made a distinction between the settled districts and the interior. He sent a memorandum to the British Colonial Secretary, claiming that there were misconceptions about the Aboriginal population. As part of his argument in favour of abolishing the Aborigines Protection Board, he said that

> the paucity of aborigines within the settled districts is not realized. In the south-west corner of the colony, with the exception of a few score scattered about here and there, they have entirely disappeared, while within what is called the settled portions of the colony the natives work on the sheep stations, and the police visit the stations and protect their interests when necessary.[41]

In the same decade, in May 1896, the Lieutenant Governor, Sir Gerard Smith, referred in correspondence with the Secretary of State for the Colonies to the '15,000 or more natives still left among us', but at the same time revealed his belief that they were part of a dying race.[42] This was also the view of the chairman of the Aborigines Protection Board, who stated that 'although there is no doubt that the number of natives is gradually decreasing, the number dependent on the Board is on the increase'.[43] In 1899, on the other hand, Henry Prinsep, Chief Inspector of Aborigines after the establishment of the Aborigines Department in 1897, estimated that there were 30,000 Aborigines in the colony. His figures included 4,749 who were employed, 743 who were on relief provided by the government, and 6,691 who were self-supporting. The rest were 'wild natives' who were not generally in contact with Europeans because they lived in the Kimberley or in the far interior.[44]

This wild conjecture about the size of the Aboriginal population was possible because there had been no detailed treatment of the Aboriginal population in census returns. However, the 1901 Census in Western Australia, undertaken after the establishment of the Commonwealth, had to conform to Commonwealth requirements. The issue of the counting of Aboriginal and 'half-caste' people received attention in the superintendent's report. A note at the top of the first census table stated that it had been intended to exclude all Aboriginal people, whether 'full blooded or half caste', from the census; however, the Commonwealth Attorney General had given an opinion that

> in reckoning the population of the Commonwealth, 'half castes' are not Aboriginal natives within the meaning of section 127 of the Commonwealth of Australia Constitution Act, and should therefore be included.
>
> In order therefore to avoid the creation of two sets of population figures it has been decided to include half-caste aboriginals with the general population, and a column relating to these has consequently been introduced in the following pages in tables dealing with population, the number of half-castes being in each case included in the grand total.[45]

In spite of this rather confusing explanation about 'half castes' being counted with Europeans, a small separate section concerning 'half castes' appeared in the census, as well as a larger section on 'Aboriginal people', which also included 'half castes'.

The census included figures for the Aboriginal population for the period dating from as early as 1848, although some of these had never been included in the published census details before 1891. It is possible to conclude that the coming of convicts in 1850 drastically reduced the number of Aborigines in employment, the figures for which began to rise dramatically again after 1870, two years after the convict era ended. The 1891 and 1901 returns suggest that at the end of the century, Aborigines were an integrated work force and an essential part of the Western Australian economy. The 1901 figures show 6,212 Aborigines, including 'half castes', in Western Australia, while according to the 'Occupations' table, 412 'half castes' and 3,766 'full blooded' Aborigines were in work. There were 546 'half caste' children and 790 'full blooded' children under 15 years of age. It is worth noting that the terminology was now quite explicitly racist in its identification of these people according to the so-called absence or presence of European 'blood'. This 1901 Census was the last conducted by the Western Australian Government.

The first national census, after the creation of the Commonwealth of Australia in 1901, was undertaken in 1911 according to the regulations set out in the Commonwealth Census and Statistics Act of 1905. Now all so-called 'full blood' Aboriginal persons were deliberately excluded from the count. This was made very explicit in the first volume of the *Census of the Commonwealth of Australia*, 3 April 1911:

> For all general tabulations, including those relating to non-European races, the cards relating to full blood Aboriginal Australians were eliminated, owing to the provision of Section 127 of the Commonwealth Constitution, that 'in reckoning the number of people of the Commonwealth, Aboriginal natives will not be counted.' In this matter an opinion has been given by the Commonwealth Attorney-General's Department that persons of the half blood are not 'Aboriginal natives' for the purposes of the Constitution, and *a fortiori* that persons of less than

half Aboriginal blood are not Aboriginal natives. In the results dealt with in this chapter, half caste Aboriginal natives have been included, those having Aboriginal blood to a less degree than one half, and European blood to a greater degree than one half, being included for tabulation as European.

The result of this decision was paradoxical because those who prepared the census tables for publication referred at the top of every table to the absence of figures concerning 'full blood' Aboriginal people. For example, in the tables concerning the kinds of dwellings occupied in Australia, the heading includes a reminder that the table is 'exclusive of dwellings occupied solely by full blood Aboriginals'. Therefore, although the so-called 'full blood' Aboriginal people of Australia were not counted in the 1911 Census, we are reminded of their presence by attention being drawn to their absence.

There were more Aboriginal people than European immigrants in Western Australia between 1829 and 1850, when the convict period began. They were displaced from occupations by convicts but made up a large part of the work force in Western Australia by the 1880s, especially in the North West. European observers concluded that Aboriginal families were small in comparison to immigrant families in the first few decades of settlement, but there is no reliable evidence about children in nineteenth-century census returns. Neither the much expanded Western Australian 1901 Census nor the first Commonwealth Census of 1911 provides any significant evidence about Aboriginal children, because only Aboriginal people of mixed descent were included.

CHAPTER 6

Institutions for Aboriginal children in the south

The value of Aboriginal labour

During the nineteenth century, European people commonly explained the differences between their own 'civilization' and the 'savagery' of the indigenous people of their colonies as due to racial difference, which implied, in this case, that Aboriginal people could never be fully assimilated.[1] But some of the early settlers in Western Australia were optimistic that Aboriginal people could be sufficiently trained to interact positively with the immigrant population. Alexander Collie, for example, writing to his brother in 1831, said that

> there is here an excellent field for the missionary. Young boys could easily be accustomed to value the comforts of civilized life and thereby [have] our moral and religious habits instilled into them. Even the older might, I think, be readily educated.[2]

The gradual employment of adult Aborigines by European settlers, in return for food, also suggested the value of educating and 'civilizing' the children, who would presumably grow up better able than their parents to adapt to European culture.[3] Governor Hutt believed that Aborigines could become a useful part of the work force. In 1841, two years after his arrival, he claimed, in a long dispatch to Lord John Russell, that the separation of European and Aboriginal people was not necessary in the Swan River Colony, since all opposition between the two races was fast disappearing:

> The best proofs, perhaps, which I can bring forward in support of this statement are, that they are on terms of the freest and most unconstrained intercourse with us; that they flee to us when needful for protection; that they have no hesitation in leaving their wives and children within the sanctuary of our shelter; that, owing to the scarcity of European labourers, many are employed in different parts of the colony as menial servants in the houses, or on the farms; that the native and white children may be seen daily amusing themselves together at our games in the streets.

Hutt argued against the separation of the Aboriginal people on mission stations and also against the establishment of reserves. He wanted to see the Aboriginal people encouraged 'to mingle among us, and to frequent our dwellings...to receive the wages and rewards of hire'.[4] These were only 'preliminary' steps to the real experiment, which was that of 'training up the children, and of imparting to them the first elements of useful knowledge'. In instructions issued to the Protector of Aborigines in 1840, Hutt declared that

> perseverance in any industrial pursuit is hardly yet understood among them, but you may encourage them to perform occasional service for hire and reward; and you will discourage, as far as you can, the exercise of gratuitous charity. A savage is always a beggar, and neither he, nor any other man, will work if bread can be procured by mere asking and importunity.[5]

Charles Symmons, Protector of Natives, also convinced of the value of Aboriginal labour, wrote in 1841 that

> [t]he conduct of the natives has been uniformly correct and peaceful; and, in the present dearth of white labour, their usefulness to the settler, either in domestic drudgery, or in the rural occupations of the farms, is daily becoming more apparent, and consequently more readily recognized.[6]

He reported that the monthly distribution of flour at the rate of 1 pound to each male and female adult was impatiently awaited by tribes far removed from Perth and had 'answered the end proposed', which was to attach the Aboriginal population to the settled districts.

In 1842, Governor Hutt explained to Lord Stanley, Secretary of State for the Colonies, that his 'earnest endeavours had been directed to dislodging the Aborigines from the woods, and encouraging them to frequent our town sites and farming locations'.[7] His policy had met with some success. The 1844 Population Return stated that the enumeration did not include 'the civilized portion of the Aboriginal race who are daily employed by the Europeans as servants and labourers—the number employed cannot be less than 200'.[8] But the more specific 1848 Census recorded a total of 541 Aborigines in employment at the end of the second decade, a considerable number in light of the small European population of 6,530 people, over one-third of whom were children under 14 years of age.

The idea that the Aboriginal workers might become part of settler households was expressed by the Protector of Natives, Charles Symmons, in 1841:

> No plan would appear better devised for eventually breaking down the barrier which at present intervenes between the settler and the Aborigines. Once prevail upon the adult savage to domiciliate himself for a length-ened period under our roofs, a gradual appreciation of the comforts and luxuries of our civilization will naturally creep upon him, together with a consequent disgust of,

and inability to return to his former precarious and desultory mode of life.[9]

Special bounties in the form of a remission in the purchase price of land were devised for those settlers who could show that they had provided steady employment for Aboriginal people, male or female, and had taught them appropriate skills over a period of two years.

The Wesleyan Mission School

An attempt to establish an Anglican mission school for Aborigines was made by Dr Louis Guistiniani and his two catechists, Friedrich Waldeck and Abraham Jones, who came to the Swan River Colony in 1836 for the Church Missionary Society. This attempt, which did not involve the children in daily labour, failed when Guistiniani was attacked in the columns of the *Perth Gazette*, and lost the support of the local population, because of his championing of the rights of the Aboriginal people. A later attempt by Abraham Jones was also unsuccessful, partly because many of the Aboriginal children under his care died during an influenza epidemic.[10]

However, the Wesleyan Mission School, set up in 1840, did not attract similar opposition from the settlers because it operated on a different basis. It began as part of a plan to train Aboriginal children as servants and labourers for the business and farming community.[11] The children worked in Perth households for most of the day, but also spent two hours each afternoon at lessons provided by the Wesleyan master, Reverend John Smithies, and an interpreter, Francis Armstrong.[12] In 1841, Charles Symmons stated in his report to the Governor that 'the native children of both sexes domiciliated with the inhabitants of Perth continue to give general satisfaction, and their usefulness increases in proportion to their length of service'.[13]

By 1841, there were, on average, twenty-five Aboriginal children at the Wesleyan Mission School, half the cost of which came from public revenue, and the rest from money raised from the local population. The management committee of the mission school included John and Joseph Hardey, who had selected more than 16,000 acres in the Swan and Avon districts; two builders, Henry Trigg and George Lazenby, who were also property owners; and George Shenton, who established himself as the first chemist in Perth and extended his activities into the general merchandise and agency business.[14]

In December 1840, Charles Symmons referred to the peaceful relations between the Aborigines and settlers in the Swan River Colony. He believed that this was due to some extent to the appointment of a police constable

> whose sole duty was to patrol the streets of Perth, and prevent the occurrence of those frequent outrages, and petty annoyances, which had previously been a source of serious complaint and inconvenience to the inhabitants of the town.[15]

Importance was also attached to the apparent successes achieved in introducing Aboriginal children to 'civilized life':

> One striking, and most important feature of improvement in the rising aboriginal population, is the success which has attended the experiment of domiciling some fifteen or twenty boys and girls with the inhabitants of Perth, where they are clothed, fed, and gradually initiated in the (to them) mysteries of civilised life. It is most gratifying to state that they give general satisfaction to their employers, while their daily attendance at the school under the superintendance of the Rev Mr Smithies, the Wesleyan Minister, and the instruction of the Native Interpreter, Mr Armstrong, ensures that *surveillance* over their moral conduct which promises future most beneficial results.[16] [original emphasis]

This report referred also to the code of regulations drawn up by Mr Armstrong for the guidance of the 'native children' and their employers.[17] The rules of the school provided that

on week days many of the children whose age will admit
of it, are dispersed as servants among the inhabitants of
Perth; that for two hours, from one till three every afternoon, they attend the school, and that they spend their
evenings and sleep at Mr Armstrong's house, where also
they pass the whole of the Sunday, and are present at the
morning and evening services of the Wesleyan Chapel.[18]

For 'recreation and encouragement', the children were allowed one
day's holiday every two months. In the event that the control and
surveillance exercised over these children should seem too severe,
Symmons explained that

it is this change and variety of scene in their employ-
ments, or daily lessons, and practice of civilization, by
which, as it seems to me, they are reconciled to what
would otherwise be to them irksome confinement. They
are not tied down for any great number of hours to one
work, or to one place; and that they are contented with
their new situation in life is shown, by the general satisfaction they give to their families, and from the very
few instances in which they have attempted to quit their
service.[19]

It is clear that Francis Armstrong was a key figure in an
arrangement that saw Aboriginal children spending their evenings
under surveillance, reporting for work in European households in
the early morning, and attending school for two hours daily. Much
emphasis was placed on the evils of loitering, which could be readily
observed by the local citizens.

Francis Armstrong had arrived with his father in the colony in
1829, aged 16 years, and had been appointed 'Interpreter to the
Natives' in 1835. He and Mary Anne Mews, both Wesleyans, were
married in 1836 and took over the aptly named 'Institution House'
as the centre for a Wesleyan mission directed at converting the
Aborigines. The children were employed according to the regulations
drawn up by Armstrong, and the colonial government provided 'for

the clothing, lodging and Sunday board of a considerable number of native children of both sexes'. Charles Symmons believed that 'the altered appearance and respectful demeanour of the late denizens of the bush, must bear ample testimony of the valuable interest to which the Government funds have been applied'.[20] Many of the Aboriginal parents could be persuaded to leave their children with Armstrong because they were clothed and fed in return for their labour.

The numbers at the mission increased when it expanded to the farming establishment at Galilalup. It is clear from the words of Francis Armstrong that its ultimate purpose was to provide satisfactory labour for the European settlers:

> Should the children not suit their employers, or misconduct themselves, any complaint will be immediately looked into by the Committee; and if, *after being threatened, and repeatedly punished*, they appear to be incorrigible, they may be sent back, and others, if disengaged, will be provided in their stead.[21] [my emphasis]

The 1843 report of Charles Symmons, Protector of Natives, to the Colonial Secretary contains an account of the examinations given to twenty-eight Aboriginal children at the Perth Wesleyan Mission School, suggesting that they were indeed rapid learners:

> The elder boys and girls read alternately verses from the New Testament with much fluency and gave intelligent answers to questions…relative to the subject they have been reading. They spelt with general correctness words of 2, 3 or even 4 syllables, and enumerated with rapidity from one to one hundred. Very creditable specimens of the boys' writing on slates were then exhibited, as also of the needlework of the girls, by whom not only their own frocks, but the tunics of the boys had been made. They evinced equal proficiency in their answers to queries from Watt's Catechism, and in repeating the Lord's Prayer, Creed and Decalogue.[22]

The Governor, John Hutt, was present at the examination of the Aboriginal children and soon afterwards received the second annual report of the committee of the Wesleyan Mission School. It contained a request for more funds to be provided so that the school could increase its number of children, whom it intended to obtain from 'distant tribes'.[23] This claim supports earlier suggestions by Charles Symmons that there were not enough children for all those who wanted Aboriginal servants in Perth. The annual report speaks of the number of buildings being increased and of the children being 'regimented' in order to make good use of their labour:

> The advantage of the union of children and labor is already felt; for, in addition to the former hours of instruction, the youngest boys and girls, not in situations, are now instructed every forenoon, and at other times are employed in picking wool etc.
>
> The afternoon service is from 2 to 4, the evening from 7 to 9 o'clock, at which all the elder children are instructed in writing and figures, committing to memory various portions of scripture catechism, and at 9 o'clock the day is closed with reading a portion of scripture, singing a hymn and concluded with prayer.[24]

At the end of his fourth year as Protector of Natives, Charles Symmons reported the withdrawal of the government stipend from an Aboriginal school at Guildford, although he claimed that advances continued to be made at the Wesleyan Mission School. The Wesleyan experiment was said to be successful, with the pupils now subjected to 'more constant supervision than before':

> Their meals are taken in the presence of the Wesleyan minister and his family, and a greater order and decorum thereby enforced. Dormitories and other necessary apartments have been erected by subscription, and other arrangements are in process of organization, all tending to a further gradual perfection of this interesting experiment.[25]

By the first half of 1844, Charles Symmons was reporting that

> the most hazardous, and yet the most interesting period of
> our experiment is fast approaching, now that many of the
> pupils have attained the age when the passions are more
> fully developed, and the desire of emancipation from
> control begins to assume the mastery.[26]

The Protector referred obliquely in this passage to the fact that it was
proving difficult to keep the young women in school, or as servants
in Perth households, when the Aboriginal elders were demanding
their return to their own society. A few months later, because of the
local demand for labour, an Act was introduced 'to prevent the
enticing away of girls of the Aboriginal race from school, or from any
service in which they are employed',[27] with fines of £2 for the first
such offence and £5 for a second offence. There was also growing
anxiety about the behaviour of the older children at the mission.
Symmons hoped that the marriage of these young people could
provide the solution:

> To endeavour to obviate this difficulty, it is proposed
> forthwith to marry the eldest of the pupils, making the
> best arrangements our position will permit to ensure them
> a comfortable subsistence, and thus deprive them as much
> as possible of any inclination to return to their brethren of
> the bush; while on such as are of a somewhat less
> advanced age, we expect that the ceremony of betroth-
> ing them to each other will act not only as a check to
> misconduct, but as a stimulus to future wellbeing.[28]

In the following year, he was less sanguine about the success
of these marriage arrangements, although he believed that some of
them would have to be accelerated, presumably because the
Aboriginal girls were pregnant. There is a note of warning and of
exasperation in his comment that 'impatience of control on the part
of the lads, and the necessity for the most watchful supervision of the
girls, are daily becoming more apparent'.[29] His enthusiasm was now

reserved for the introduction of the infant school system of instruction for the youngest children.

Doubt about the long-term success of the 'civilizing' work carried out with Aboriginal children began to appear five years after the Wesleyan Mission School was first established, when it became clear that it would prove difficult to prevent these children returning to Aboriginal society. In 1846, Charles Symmons revealed that quite fundamental changes had recently occurred in the functioning of the school, which had previously operated entirely from the premises of the Wesleyan Mission in Perth. In August 1845, the pupils had been removed from the old site, and from their daily employment, to live on 60 acres of land about 11 miles north of Perth, near Alder Lake. The females returned to Perth for the winter months, but the rest of the children remained there on a permanent basis.

Symmons rationalized this change in two ways. He said that 'it was found requisite to open a wider field to test the capabilities and enlarge the sphere of usefulness of the pupils'. He also referred to the deaths of several of the pupils and the ill-health of many others, attributable to their 'change of diet and their artificial and confined mode of life'.[30] It is clear from this report that the 'civilizing' experiment, which had combined work and school, was proving a failure, and a costly one in terms of the survival and health of the children concerned. The illness of the children was later attributed to tuberculosis, possibly contracted from the dairy cows kept by the mission.[31]

Symmons found it difficult to write openly and directly about the changing nature of Aboriginal–European relations, perhaps because he did not wish to accept an element of failure in his own role as Protector of Natives. By 1847, his January report was full of internal contradictions, and revealed the existence of considerable problems. He wrote, for example, about the 'undisturbed tranquillity' of Mr Turner's settlement at Augusta, 60 miles from the next station, but then claimed the 'absolute necessity' for an additional police force to be stationed in this district. Concerning the education of Aboriginal children, he stated that

> it would however be not only deceptive, but, as it were,
> underrating whatever small success may have hitherto

attended our efforts, were I to disguise the discourage-
ments and difficulties that are continually besetting our
attempts to civilize the youthful native population; years
of residence beneath our roofs, kind treatment, a suffici-
ency of wholesome food, and monthly wages sufficient
for all the purposes of pocket money, prove often but
weak and insufficient barriers when opposed to their
innate yearning for the freedom of savage life, and their
distaste for systematic labor however light.[32]

He referred also to a 'disinclination' on the part of the Aboriginal population to leave their children in the charge of Europeans,
which he believed had some connection with the number of deaths
at the school in the previous year. A report presented at the same
time by R. H. Bland, who was the Protector of Natives for the York
region, provided further evidence that European–Aboriginal relations
were deteriorating. Bland requested that the Governor extend the
power of magistrates to deal with Aboriginal people who were
caught stealing sheep and robbing huts. The existing system, which
required that he commit them to trial at the Quarter Sessions or
dismiss the charge against them, was not a sufficient deterrent.

Symmons's last report in 1849 was submitted under his new
title, 'Guardian of Natives and Protector of Settlers', a reflection of
quite startling new perceptions of Aboriginal–European relations.[33]
In spite of the contrived and bland nature of much of the report, he
could not remain sanguine about the fate of the 'civilizing' and
'Christianizing' mission directed at Aboriginal children. The land
chosen for the new Aboriginal mission near Alder Lake had become
a swamp after heavy rains and could not be drained without
incurring great expense. Many of the Aboriginal pupils had been
married and were applying for private allotments, which were on
similarly unsuitable land.

> Thus situated it is but natural that a mutual feeling of dis-
> gust and dissatisfaction should pervade both the directors
> of the Institution and their young charges, and it is much
> to be feared that unless some radical change be shortly

effected, those feelings to which I have above alluded, and which now paralyze all exertion, may tend to revive in the breasts of the pupils a desire of recurring to their bush life and habits which under happier circumstances would, if not utterly extinguished, have remained dormant and innocuous.[34]

The issue of what was to be done about the mission was under consideration at this time by the directors and friends of the institution. Symmons appealed to the Governor to actively prevent the 'impending subversion of the labour and expense, and above all, the civilizing work of 10 long and anxious years'.[35] Eventually, the mission was moved to York, but the sickness and death of some of the Aboriginal children, and the absconding of others who wished to return to their families nearer Perth, led to the closure of the mission by 1855.[36]

There were complex reasons for the ultimate failure of the mission, but this early attempt at some degree of assimilation, and the support it received from the local settlers and the government, had depended on a perception that the Aborigines would make a valuable work force. By the end of the 1840s, Aboriginal labour was no longer so important because of the decision to import convicts into the colony, the first of whom arrived in 1850. This circumstance reduced the government's enthusiasm for providing funding for the project and helped undermine this early 'civilizing mission'.

The New Norcia experiment

The opportunity to obtain food attracted Aboriginal people to the Catholic missionary outpost at New Norcia, which was established in 1846 and admitted its first three Aboriginal boys, who were said to have 'left their families of their own free will', in December 1847.[37] The first initiative for this settlement came from Bishop Brady, who was created Bishop of Western Australia in 1845. Two Benedictine monks, the Spaniards Serra and Salvado, were chosen in Rome for the work of establishing the mission. However, before the task had truly begun, Serra was appointed first as Bishop of Port Victoria in the North West and then as coadjutor bishop to Bishop Brady. The Propaganda College in Rome then proceeded in 1849 to appoint Salvado as Bishop of Port Victoria, but, after petitioning the Pope, Salvado was allowed to continue his work at New Norcia.[38]

Before New Norcia was established, Salvado attempted to live with the Aboriginal people of the Victoria Plains. By 1846, he had settled on a grant of land and imported 710 sheep into the area. In this colonial enterprise, based on the typical settler principles of cheap land and labour, some Aboriginal children were separated from their families, but others remained with families who settled at New Norcia to live and work with the Benedictine monks. In 1849, Fathers Serra and Salvado were joined by a new group of Benedictine missionaries who were skilled workmen.[39] Two years later, Salvado, back in Europe, wrote of his experiences and condemned some of the practices he had observed in Australia. These included the employment of Aborigines without wages being paid, and the education of children who were not subsequently accepted into European society:

> It is true that schools for natives have been opened in each one of the colonies, and that the pupils have learned to read, write and do sums more quickly than was expected. But when boys or girls have finished with school, is anything done to place them in positions where they can lead a civilized life? No one has given a thought to this and so the native is forced to go back to his nomadic ways—being able to read and write does nothing to quell the pangs of hunger.[40]

Salvado's assertions may well have been largely an exercise in special pleading in order to attract financial support from overseas sources. However, at least he contemplated and condemned the worst features of the unequal relationship between the European settlers and Aboriginal workers and, by implication, the racism of this settler society. Like the Wesleyans, Salvado believed in the need to educate and 'civilize' Aboriginal children. However, even though he was critical of settler ideology and practice, part of his own civilizing process was to require that children work on the mission for several hours each day so that they would learn to be useful workers. He believed that the mission at New Norcia was a special case, in that the Spanish monks had succeeded in gaining the Aboriginal people's trust:

> These men who before would never have allowed anyone to touch their children, were happy now to entrust them to us, almost forcing us to take them into our midst…they asked us to continue the instruction and to baptize them…When the news went around that some missionary was leaving for Europe, the boys argued amongst themselves about who had first choice of going with him on the long journey, and the parents showed themselves very happy when it was their boy who was chosen.[41]

In spite of the persuasive arguments used by Salvado, the early history of this mission, which was effectively closed down while Salvado was overseas between 1849 and 1853, was fraught with difficulties. These Benedictine newcomers had attempted, first of all, to join the Aboriginal community in the Moore River area and to live a nomadic life with them. They quickly abandoned this idea and managed to secure a grant of 20 acres of land where they could settle. The first settlement failed, but a second, successful attempt was then undertaken on better land, with the help of another small grant of land and a grazing lease of 400 acres. In 1853, Salvado returned from Europe with three more priests and thirty-seven lay brothers, and it was this nucleus of permanent workers who laid the foundation for the success of New Norcia. Only then did this institution begin successfully to incorporate Aboriginal people, including children, into the settled economic and social life of the mission. They, too, now made up an important part of the work force in this self-contained community.[42]

European shepherds who cared for sheep on pastoral runs near the mission scoffed at the work of these dedicated and romantic

Spaniards, and threatened the Aborigines who visited the mission.[43] Salvado claimed, however, that the life of the Benedictine monk, which included prayer, preaching and work in the fields, was 'well adapted to the needs of these people and this part of the world'.[44] This was a notion that might have fostered good personal relationships at New Norcia but which took little account of the true nature of nineteenth-century settler capitalism. At first, Salvado and his monks did not work towards a capitalist enterprise depending on the market but envisaged a self-supporting community, which could survive and prosper in relative isolation. This was at the core of their activity, even if they also sometimes succeeded in selling and buying goods in the marketplace. Their enterprise recalls the large European estates, or *latifundia*, which provided safety and security for their communities in a very insecure world at the time of the collapse of the Roman Empire.

Bishop Salvado was also deeply embroiled in the politics of the Catholic community in Western Australia, partly because he was at first frustrated by opposition from Bishop Brady in his attempts to realize his dream of a monastic community under his personal control.[45] He sought a resolution of his conflicts with both Brady and Bishop Serra, and for his release from certain obligations to his monastic superiors. New Norcia gradually grew into a small town on the basis of the wealth created on the mission land-holdings, the size of which increased dramatically over time. His activities involved the securing of what had been Aboriginal ancestral land for his mission enterprise, the success of which depended on the labour of both the monks and the Aboriginal people. The church at New Norcia, which Salvado decorated with rich objects from Europe, celebrated a distant culture rather than the living one near at hand. The trappings of the Spanish church symbolized the limited goals and the conservative nature of this ambitious project.

Bishop Salvado had gained personal control of New Norcia by 1867, by which time he managed seventeen leases, amounting to 180,000 acres of land, quite apart from a large area that had been purchased as farmland. By this time, the labour of the monks and the Aborigines, including Aboriginal 'apprentices', had created a successful sheep run, a wheat and barley farm, a vineyard, a dairy farm and a variety of other farm activities, including horse breeding, vegetable growing and bee keeping. There were seventy-four Aboriginal men on the property in 1874, and Bishop Salvado gradually developed the policy of providing the young men with small houses and small plots of land that they could identify as their own, even though they had no title to this land. Marriages were arranged for them. By these means, he tried to keep his Aboriginal work force together and realize both his worldly and his missionary ambitions.[46]

By the 1870s, however, the Aborigines were disappearing from the Victoria Plains region around New Norcia, the prevalence of various European diseases having vastly reduced the population. The mission had also employed convict labour as part of its work force, and the convict intake had come to an end in 1868. These labour difficulties confronted Salvado and his managers at a time when the size of the monastery's land-holdings dictated an increasing labour supply. The Industrial Schools Act of 1874, which was passed largely at his instigation, allowed Salvado to take Aboriginal children from all over the colony into New Norcia and to control their movements until they were 21 years of age.

The Industrial Schools Act of 1874, which applied to both European and Aboriginal children, was designed to set rules about the treatment of children in charitable institutions, and about how they could be apprenticed out as labourers. The wording of the Act made it clear that the charitable institutions to be renamed as 'industrial schools' included those receiving Aboriginal children. In his speech introducing the Bill, the Colonial Secretary, Frederick Barlee, said that Aboriginal children placed in institutions would be subject to the controls of managers, who would be able to prevent their removal by parents. He emphasized that Bishop Salvado of New Norcia had played a major part in promoting the idea of this legislation:[47]

> Honourable members were aware of one particular institution in the Colony, where at considerable expenditure of time, money and patient labor, Aboriginal natives were admitted and trained in habits of industry and in a knowledge of their duty to God and man. He alluded, he

need hardly say, to the admirable institution under the control of Bishop Salvado at New Norcia. Now His Lordship complained, and complained with very good reason and considerable force, that *he is powerless to retain these native and half-caste children in his custody*, but that, when the parents demand it, he is obliged to surrender them.[48] [my emphasis]

This Act allowed these institutions to retain children until they were 21 years of age. It encouraged the managers to send children out to work as soon as they had proved themselves useful and to take the proceeds of their work as payment for their keep. Barlee also foreshadowed the twentieth-century practice of removing children of mixed descent from their parents when he said that he intended to compel the transfer of 'half-caste' children into one or other of these institutions, whichever would be prepared to receive them. In the debate on the third reading, Walter Padbury, a wealthy businessman and member of the Legislative Council for Swan,[49] suggested that justices of the peace might be given the power to assume guardianship 'of all Aboriginal children, whether living under the care of a father and mother or not'. He wanted the manager or director of institutions catering for Aboriginal children to have the power of guardianship over every Aboriginal child in his care until the age of 21 years, unless a younger age had been specifically agreed upon.

In this legislation, the age of 21 was set as a limit on the power of the colonial government to control a section of the population by institutionalization. This included Aboriginal children 'apparently under the age of twenty one years'. Barlee's hope of transferring all part-Aboriginal children to such institutions was partly met by clause 18 of the Act, which stated that

> [i]f it should be represented to any Justice of the Peace
> that there is in his district any person descended from the
> Aboriginal race being a child apparently under the age of
> twelve years who is not living under the care or guardian-
> ship of either father or mother, it shall be the duty of the

> said magistrate to make enquiry concerning the child referred to, and if after careful enquiry it shall be found that the child is not living under the care or guardianship of either father or mother, it shall then be lawful for the said magistrate to assume guardianship of such child in the name of the Government and to hand him or her over to the care of some person who holds a certificate of approval from His Excellency the Governor as manager of a school or institution for maintaining and teaching descendants of the Aboriginal race.[50]

When this Act was passed in 1874, there was no government administrative body directly responsible for Aboriginal affairs. This situation changed twelve years later with the passage of the Aborigines Protection Act of 1886 (see page 136).

The Benedictine Mission of New Norcia was the largest of the missions surviving from the earlier period that now operated under the Industrial Schools Act.[51] Under the Act, the managers of industrial schools were restrained from apprenticing children without parental approval, if the parents were known, and there is nothing in the Act to suggest that a different policy should be applied to Aboriginal children. However, in practice, the parents of Aboriginal children seem to have been disregarded. From September 1874, when New Norcia became an industrial school under the Act, it was granted 1s a day for each child taken in, and had the power to retain these young people until they were 21 years of age. Salvado agreed to take boys who had been convicted and would otherwise be sent to the Aboriginal prison at Rottnest. The mission now had a population of Aborigines from all over the colony, most of them children.[52]

The number of children at New Norcia rose from only thirty in 1874 to eighty-five in 1883. Thirty-four were with their families; the other fifty-one were in the mission orphanage, some without known parents and others surrendered by their parents to the care of the mission. Some were sent to the New Norcia missionary outposts at Marah and Wyening. Under the Land Regulations, institutions could apply for land grants for the use of Aborigines; in 1874, the mission had 29 acres on which Aboriginal families had been settled. The children of these families, as well as those without their parents, were trained in domestic work and in a wide variety of skills connected with this very complex farming enterprise. They were also taught to read and write, were introduced to Christian teachings and took part in sporting and musical activities.

According to David Hutchison, the holdings of the mission at New Norcia had reached more than 980,000 acres by 1900, and the number of Aboriginal workers, both adults and children, numbered 134.[53] Many of the children had been removed from their parents, who, after the passage of the Industrial Schools Act of 1874, could make no claim on them. The brothers at the monastery helped arrange the marriages of these young workers as they grew to maturity, and set them up on small-holdings, thus creating the basis for an enduring population of Aborigines who knew little of their cultural origins.[54] The relationship of master and servant, which was characteristic of labour relations elsewhere in the colony, also applied at New Norcia. The Aboriginal people had little personal independence, and they were obliged to work as dependent labourers on the land that had once been their own. However, at least the monks and Aborigines were rostered to work alongside one another, and Aborigines were paid small sums for their labour. Until Salvado died, he always claimed that the Aborigines were encouraged to look upon the mission as their home.[55]

By taking the children under the Industrial Schools Act, Bishop Salvado solved his labour problem on the huge New Norcia estate. After his death in 1900, much of the New Norcia leasehold land was resumed by the government, while some freehold land was sold by the mission, as the mission farming activities became more centralized and mechanized.

Ellensbrook

Ellensbrook, another home for Aboriginal children, was also the home of Edith Bussell, a daughter of Alfred and Ellen Bussell, early settlers in the South West, who built the original Ellensbrook house.[56] Edith Bussell extended the house and began to take in Aboriginal children in need, particularly children of mixed parentage. She continued to farm the area, using the labour of local Aboriginal people and the children in her home. They were employed as farm labourers, herding sheep and cattle, milking, making butter and cheese, as well as doing domestic work in the house. Their labour 'contributed to the survival of Ellensbrook as a farming venture'.[57] It is difficult to say when Ellensbrook began to operate under the Industrial Schools Act, but as early as 1890 the Aborigines Protection Board report stated that £750 had been spent 'for board and clothing of the half-caste children at Busselton and the Swan'.[58]

In his annual report for 1900, Henry Prinsep, Chief Inspector of Aborigines, provided a brief report on the institutions for children, and he referred to the establishment of Ellensbrook on the southwest coast, 'a small home for those who could not be taken into other institutions'. The following year, he reported that there were only four inmates at Ellensbrook, all of whom were doing well. He believed that 'they [would] all turn out, ultimately, very useful servants, as everything they learn is of a practical nature'.[59]

The Anglican Swan Native and Half-caste Home

The Swan Native and Half-caste Home was established on the outskirts of Perth in 1871 by the Anglican Church. Its origins lay in the original missionary activity of Archdeacon Wollaston, who, along with Mr and Mrs Camfield,[60] had been responsible for the opening of the Annesfield orphanage for Aboriginal children in Albany in 1852.[61] There were eleven inmates in 1856, and eighteen, including children of mixed descent, in 1858. After Wollaston died in 1856, the Camfields were unable to carry on, and in 1871 the whole mission school was transferred to Perth. The children were at first housed in a building behind Bishop Hale's home. At that time, there were eighteen children, all but two of mixed parentage. They were subsequently moved to the Native and Half-caste Mission, situated near Archdeacon Brown's rectory and the Swan Orphanage and Industrial School. Eleven of the older boys resided at this Anglican orphanage for European boys. Until 1907, the Aboriginal children were cared for by the Misses Mackintosh, who acted as matron and teacher.[62]

There is some evidence that there were objections to public funds being spent on assisting the Anglican bishop to maintain the Swan Native and Half-caste Home. In 1873, Bishop Hale was incensed by clause 8 in the Legislative Council report to the Governor on the expenditure of various departments. This report stated:

> Your Committee are of the opinion that the money voted for supporting a number of native children in an institution under the supervision of the Bishop of Perth might be more judiciously expended.

The bishop responded with a stinging attack on the un-Christian behaviour of Europeans towards Aboriginal people. His letter explains that this school was first established by the joint action of the government, Mr and Mrs Camfield, and Archdeacon Wollaston. Their intention was to train the children in the habits of civilized life, in the truths of Christianity and to be clean and industrious, and to give them a suitable and useful education.

> So strongly have I felt upon this subject that, when upon the occasion of the late Mr Camfield's illness, there seemed reason to fear that the school might fall to the ground, I signified my wish to retire from my present position in order to take charge of it. The abandonment I should have regarded in the light of a public repudiation of that duty. And I was prepared to do anything and to make any sacrifice rather than that this Colony, so long as I continue to be identified with it, should be guilty of so grievous a sin. In the same light do I regard the matter now. And I implore the members of the Legislative Council not to entertain for a moment the idea of drawing back from the attempt, feeble though it be, to discharge a great duty to God.

The letter explained that there were eighteen children at this school, which was independent of all outside help except 'in some very few particulars'. In other words, the children did most of the work to maintain the institution. He rejected criticism of the removal of some of the children to institutions in other colonies, a policy that he said was designed to provide them with suitable companions. He rejected the idea that they should necessarily remain in the colony to be despised as servants and asked that they be regarded 'as free agents, to dispose of themselves as they may desire, and as the advice and counsel of myself and other friends may guide them'.[63]

The 1899 report on the Protestant Swan River Mission, as the original home was now called, revealed that by that time the mission consisted of two branches, one for the girls and one for the boys. The girls received three hours' schooling a day and training in domestic work and sewing. The manager, David Garland, was anxious about the future of these Aboriginal girls because there seemed

> no hope of building up a strong moral character in them if they are to be discharged from this institution at the age of sixteen which is the limit now fixed by your Department for their support.
>
> With the help of your Department I should like to see a further development by which the girls could be married to natives or half castes, and provided with small cottages under the control of the institution.[64]

He was more sanguine about the boys, who were taught alongside the European boys at the Swan Orphanage and Industrial School for Protestant Boys. They received the same school instruction and practical training in handicrafts, gardening and farming. He claimed that they held their own with 'white boys' and excelled in sports. 'The boys, as a rule, do well when started in life.'

The Aborigines Protection Board

In 1886, the Aborigines Protection Act was passed and an Aborigines Protection Board was set up to deal with particular problems affecting the Aboriginal community. Solutions to problems surrounding individual cases were arrived at only after long correspondence between individuals and either the board or the subsequently established Aborigines Department. The process was slow-moving and bureaucratic. The Protectors of Aborigines, also appointed under this Act, were sometimes responsible for solving particular problems, but in many cases they were uncertain about how to proceed. In 1898, for example, it took considerable correspondence to get three Aboriginal children, who were between the ages of 3 and 6 years, from Katanning into the Protestant Swan River Mission after their 'half-caste' father died and their mother became too ill to care for them.[65] In the same year, the question arose as to whether a 15-year-old Aboriginal boy, who was said to be a hardened offender, could be sent to the reformatory at Rottnest, which normally only took children over 16 years of age, most of them European.[66] There also had to be a board ruling about what to do with a 'native boy' called Tumbler indentured to Mr T. Gerrard, who had died. He was being provided with rations, but the Protector asked whether a new master should be found for him.[67] When an Aboriginal youth charged with assaulting his mistress and her daughter was to come before the court, the Protector queried whether he should be defended in court as a European child would be defended.[68]

A long correspondence in 1900 concerned Norah, a young girl of mixed Aboriginal and Indian descent, who had been put out to service by the Protestant Swan River Mission with Mr and Mrs Crawford of Brookton. 'A young settler seduced her, she consenting, and now she is unable to perform her duties—and Mr Crawford finds that the Orphanage will not take her back or do anything for her.' The Crawfords and a friend, who had recently visited their house, wrote to the Aborigines Department for help. The Chief Inspector, Henry Prinsep, did not think that Norah should go to the general depot for women but suggested instead that she be put in the care of the Salvation Army. The latter wanted the girl to be granted 1s a day for her expenses until it could be discovered whether or not the father of the child soon to be born could be compelled to pay for its upkeep. The child was born before the case was settled, occasioning considerable detailed correspondence before the new mother could be received in Perth by the Salvation

Army. Henry Prinsep expressed his growing anxiety about the number of these problems:

> These cases are occurring more frequently than I like to see—but as yet it is hardly necessary to do more than to meet them as they occur, expense notwithstanding.
>
> But should they occur more frequently or the fact of our relieving them get abroad and the many unreported cases be in the future cast upon us—it will be necessary to establish some home, or whatever possible reproductive lines may offer [sic].[69]

These examples suggest that the operations of the board, and of the Aborigines Department that followed it, were ill adapted to solve the problems that had been created by constructing Aboriginal people as legally separate and different from Europeans.

Elementary education for Aboriginal children

Institutions, including New Norcia, which had some funding support from the colonial government, provided limited education for inmates, but otherwise no effort was made to establish educational services for Aboriginal children. The 1871 Elementary Education Act made no reference to the teaching of Aboriginal children, and there is no mention of them being present in government schools in any of the yearly reports. However, by this time, there were many children of mixed Aboriginal and European descent in Western Australia, especially in the South West, and these were the Aboriginal children most likely to be sent to school.[70] A few of these children did attend school; in fact, their presence was sometimes essential to the school maintaining the numbers it required to remain open.

However, in 1893, the amendments to the 1871 Act set up school boards that had the right, among other things, to determine which children should be excluded from a particular school. Section 22, part 4, read that children could be excluded if they were 'suffering from any infections or contagious disease, or whose presence was otherwise injurious to the health and welfare of other children'.[71] This clause, which opened the way for non-Aboriginal parents to request the removal of Aboriginal children, suggests the presence of some Aboriginal children in the government school system. The success of this strategy of removal depended on the approval of the Education Minister.

The 1886 Aborigines Protection Act specifically made Aboriginal education the responsibility of the Aborigines Protection Board, set up under that Act for this and other purposes. This move must be seen as the first deliberate legislative attempt to separate non-Aboriginal and Aboriginal children in schools. The Forrest Commission, which reported to the government not long before the passage of the 1886 Act, argued that

> the best way to teach Aborigines is through the instrumentality of men who devote their lives to the work, who are willing to endure privations and difficulties in the hope of inculcating knowledge in the natives, without hope of reward other than seeing good results in the happiness of the race on whom their labour and care is bestowed.
>
> We would like to see all philanthropic efforts of the kind liberally supported by the State, under adequate supervision, and at each mission station would recommend a small reserve, and the means of teaching useful information which would be serviceable to the native when he reaches manhood. We have no hope that the Aboriginal native will ever be more than a servant to the white man, and therefore our aim should be devoted to such instruction as will enable him to live usefully and happily among the white population...It is needless for us to deal any further with this portion of the report, as the experience of the past and the outlook of the future is far from hopeful.[72]

The Aborigines Act of 1897, under which the Aborigines Protection Board was finally abolished and a new Aborigines

Department created, further underlined the shift towards segregation in education for Aboriginal children. Clause 5 stated that the task of the newly created department included 'providing for the education of Aboriginal children (including half-castes)'. Part 3 of clause 7 referred ominously to the '*custody, maintenance, and education* of the children of Aborigines', while part 5 of clause 7 stated that the department was required 'to manage and regulate the use of all Reserves set apart for the benefit of Aborigines' (my emphasis).[73]

As a result of this emphasis on providing a separate and different kind of education for Aboriginal children, additional institutions controlled by religious bodies began to grow in the late nineteenth and early twentieth centuries. In 1890, Bishop Gibney established a mission for Aborigines near the Beagle Bay inlet. The two French priests of the Trappist order who first ran this mission were replaced by members of the German Pallottine order in 1901. A mission was also established by the Church of England on Sunday Island.[74] There was a further escalation of mission activities from 1905, after missions were given the explicit duty of educating Aborigines under the Aborigines Act of that year.[75] After the passage of this Act, many Aboriginal children were removed from government schools and sent to live on Aboriginal Reserves—for example, Carrolup, which was founded in 1915 and moved to Moore River in 1918. The complete exclusion of Aboriginal children from government schools was supposed to be in place by 1917. Before 1905, there had been five missions; by 1921 there were nine; and by 1950 there were twenty-one missions who could claim to be catering for the education and welfare of Aborigines.[76]

Hutt's special pleading about the need to integrate European and Aboriginal society reveals that many members of the settler community of the late 1830s and early 1840s hoped that Aborigines would eventually provide an important part of the work force in the Swan River Colony. The creation of a special school for Aboriginal children in the 1840s, designed to prepare these children for work on farms and in settler households, provides the clearest evidence that the Aboriginal people were regarded as an important element in the colonial work force of the future. However, as the difficulties inherent in this program became clear, the demands of the settler community for convict labour became more vociferous. The fact that the number of Aborigines in private employment had dropped considerably by 1854, after the arrival of the convicts, does not suggest a successful policy of integration into the community over the previous twenty-five years.[77]

Although historians have often represented these institutions for Aboriginal children, including New Norcia, as essentially philanthropic, their appearance and activities were irrevocably connected with the demand for cheap labour. The process of turning Aboriginal land into private property for immigrant capitalist farmers created the need for a work force. The presence of Europeans also led to the death from disease of many Aboriginal people, leaving children who were orphans. Other Aboriginal parents chose to leave their children in these institutions. The Industrial Schools Act of 1874 gave managers of institutions the right to control inmates until they were 21 years of age and to use them as they saw fit. This mixture of philanthropy and self-interest produced the nucleus of an Aboriginal working class, to some extent shut out from both their own and European culture.

CHAPTER 7

Family and child labour
in the pastoral industry

THE leasing of vast areas of Aboriginal land to European pastoralists, beginning in the 1860s, meant that whole populations of Aboriginal adults and children in any one area were available as a labour force, especially as pastoral stations were inevitably established at watering places that were already important centres for Aboriginal people. At a time when European children were obliged by law to attend school until 14 years of age, Aboriginal children were increasingly making up part of a large Aboriginal work force that would make possible these capitalist operations in the North West.[1]

The opening up of the North West

Geraldton and Dongara were settled for wheat farming in the early 1850s. The three overland expeditions of one or both of the Gregory brothers in 1846, 1848 and 1861 opened up a vast area further north, which was crossed and charted.[2] Others followed in their wake on exploring expeditions, and in some cases they settled in the area now known as the Pilbara. The first land laws concerning the North West were gazetted in 1862,[3] and in 1865 the government, fearing conflict between European settlers and Aboriginal people, sent Robert Sholl to Camden Harbour, and subsequently to Nickol Bay, to act as Government Resident in the North West.

New laws were introduced in 1872 to encourage settlement. Under clause 72 of these regulations, pastoral lands were divided into three classes, the lands in the north and the east of the colony being in the third class. Under clause 76, this third-class land was subdivided into two further classes: classes A and C. Class A, consisting of islands and areas 2 miles from the sea, could be occupied on the basis of an annual licence. Class C could only be occupied for twelve months, at which time the occupier could claim leasehold of up to 100,000 acres that he could occupy rent-free for three years; after that time, he had to lease the land for eight-year periods.[4]

The Murchison and De Grey areas were opened up in the middle of the 1870s, and by the 1880s Europeans had reached the Kimberley region, although this was not settled until the twentieth century. The newly opened up land was suitable for pastoral pursuits, and a few settlers took out millions of acres under leasehold.

Gold was also discovered first of all in the North West and was serviced from Geraldton. Its discovery in the 1890s in the Coolgardie and Kalgoorlie region led to a huge population influx and the settlement of the south-eastern region of Western Australia.[5] While the pearling and pastoral industries' reliance on unpaid Asian and Aboriginal labour suggests the weakness of their financial backing, the goldmines could attract investment more easily and generally employed a European work force.[6] However, much of the goldmining at this time was in the hands of small operators.

The opening up of the North West created a desperate need for labour, and pastoralists looked to the Aboriginal population to meet this need. However, the institutionalization of Aboriginal children that had occurred in the southern regions as a means of gaining unpaid labour was clearly not a method that could be employed for this purpose on the pastoral stations in the North West.

The Aborigines Protection Act

In 1884, Governor Broome received the report of a commission set up 'to inquire into the treatment of Aboriginal Native Prisoners of the Crown in This Colony and also certain other matters relative to Aboriginal Natives' and on 12 September sent it off to the Colonial Office.[7] The report dealt largely with the conditions on Rottnest Island. The commissioners had little to say about other matters, including inter alia 'the means to be taken to assist the young', one of the issues said to be on their agenda at the beginning of the report. However, suggestions and comments in connection with children on pages 4 and 5 of the report were to have some bearing on the legislation that followed two years later. The commissioners referred first of all to the apparent failure of past attempts to 'civilize' Aboriginal children:

> [Y]oung Aborigines have also strong tendencies to th[e] roaming life, and seem most healthy when allowed to follow it: and it has therefore happened that, with every desire to assist these people, there has been met with a great difficulty in knowing how best to set about it...Children of the native race, too, do not seem to be strong when brought up in civilized ways, and are pre-disposed to pulmonary complaints: so that, however the question is dealt with, one is met by difficulties almost, if not quite, insurmountable.[8]

They then referred to Aboriginal people as the main labour force for the Murchison River area and on the North West Cape:

> doing nearly all the shepherding, shearing, stock riding, and even fencing. They are also utilized as pearl shell divers and are in every way a most useful factor in the prosperity of the settlers.

The commissioners thought that 'their usefulness to the pioneer settlers can scarcely be over-estimated'. They recommended the appointment of a board to manage all matters connected with Aborigines.

A Bill, which became law as the Aborigines Protection Act, was introduced into parliament in 1886. It was designed, among other things, to set up an apprenticeship or indenture system, which would apply in both the pastoral and pearling industries. There were four parts to the Bill. The first dealt with the setting up of a board to handle the funds set aside to administer Aboriginal affairs through the Aboriginal Protectors, who were appointed by the Governor. The second part dealt with work contracts with Aborigines, which could only be enforced if they had been witnessed by a magistrate. The third part dealt with the use of Aboriginal prisoners as labour outside gaols, and the fourth part with Aboriginal apprentices. The fourth part of the Bill exposed the attitudes of the members of the Legislative Council to the employment of children, and, by implication, made clear what was happening in the pastoral industry.

In the original wording of the section on contracts, they were to apply to Aboriginal workers of 16 years and upwards. However, Robert Sholl, who was active in both the pastoral and pearling industries and was an elected Member of the Legislative Council for the Gascoyne, said that

> it was between the ages of 10 and 16 that they were the most useful. They were then more tractable, more easily taught, and more likely to become habituated to station life. Further than that, these Aboriginal natives matured at a much earlier age than whites did; and, at the age of 16 a native, though a boy in years, was in appearance and manners a man, and he generally considered himself a man too.

In the committee stage of the Bill, Sholl reiterated his views, and William Edward Marmion, elected Member for Fremantle, agreed that settlers should use the labour of young boys with a contract. McKenzie Grant, also a land-holder and an elected Member for Northern District, said he would be

> very sorry to see native boys, ten years of age, excluded
> from entering into contracts. Upon the stations...they
> would find all the children of the neighbourhood volun-
> teering for work long before they were ten years old...On
> some stations they were found useful at 7 or 8 years old
> minding sheep, or guarding cattle or horses, and in this
> way, they gradually became domesticated.

The elected Member for Central Province, Edward Horne Wittenoom,
supported the idea of contracts at a much earlier age and also
suggested the possibility that contracts with children could be used
to hold together whole families of workers. He said that the first
objectionable clause in the Bill was clause 18, referring to contracts at
the age of 16 years:

> The committee ventured to think that was too old; that the
> habits of these Aboriginal natives became set at an early
> age, and that the earlier their training was taken in hand
> the easier it would be to bring them into habits of
> industry. An Aboriginal at the age of ten knew probably
> as much as a white at the age of sixteen, and the com-
> mittee thought there could be nothing wrong in engaging
> them at the age of ten. Further, as a rule, the parents of
> these children would be engaged on many of the stations
> at which their offspring were employed, and it would not
> be wise to put them in a position where they could
> wander away, or be enticed away from their parents.

This part of the debate concerned the attempt to control the
movement of young Aborigines through the contract system, since,
according to Septimus Burt, the Bill did nothing to stop Aboriginal
children working, or to stop settlers looking after them, even if
there were no contract. In other words, the system of contracts was
a device to strengthen existing controls over the movement of
Aborigines. Alexander McRae, part of a family with vast pastoral
holdings and pearling interests and an elected Member for Northern
District, pointed out that, under the Pearl Fisheries Act, Aboriginal

children were employed at 15 years of age under a contract. In the end, the Bill was amended to reduce the age at which a contract could be entered into from 16 years to 14 years. The debate revealed much about the way in which children were habituated to work in the pastoral industry within a context of family labour. These patterns would continue as before, since the age clauses in the Act were effective only in connection with written contracts. However, those over 14 years could now be signed up to work under a contract. The Act recognized the difficulty of knowing the exact ages of young Aborigines when it stated that the person to be put under contract must appear 'to be of the age of fourteen years and upwards'.

This restraint on the signing up of children until they were 14 seemed to offer some safeguards against the exploitation of very young children. However, the arrangement under part 4 of the Act, whereby Aboriginal children could be indentured as apprentices at any 'suitable age', made nonsense of this caveat. Any mixed-race or Aboriginal child, having attained a 'suitable age', could be bound by indenture until 21 years of age to any master or mistress 'willing to receive such a child in any suitable trade, business or employment whatsoever'. A magistrate was to determine the child's age and see that 'reasonable provision was made for the maintaining, clothing and proper and humane treatment of any such apprentice'. Justices were to hear complaints by the employer or the apprentice, were free to visit them at any time to ascertain whether the conditions were being fulfilled, and could transfer an apprentice who was indentured from one employer to another under certain circumstances.

Under the 1886 Act, the government also established the Aborigines Protection Board, which was to consist of five persons appointed by the Governor, as well as an appointed secretary. The duties of the board, as set out in the Aborigines Protection Act of 1886, were:

1. To apportion, distribute, and supply, as it may think fit, all moneys granted by the Legislative Council for the benefit of Aborigines.

2. To distribute blankets, clothes and other relief to the Aborigines, in the discretion of the Board.

3. To submit to the Governor any proposals or suggestions relating to the care, custody, or education of the children of Aborigines.

4. To provide, as far as practicable, for the supply of medicine, medical attendance, rations, and shelter to sick, aged and infirm Aborigines.

5. To manage and regulate the use of all Reserves set apart for the benefit of the Aborigines.

6. To exercise a general supervision and care over all matters affecting the interests and welfare of the Aborigines, and to protect them against ill-treatment, imposition and fraud.[9]

'Aborigines'—those who came under the control of the board—were defined by clause 4 of the Act:

Every Aboriginal native of Australia, and every Aboriginal child or half-caste, such half-caste or child habitually associating and living with Aboriginals, shall be deemed to be an Aboriginal within the meaning of this Act, and at the hearing of any case the Justice or Justices adjudicating may, in the absence of other sufficient evidence, decide on his or their own view or judgement whether any person with reference to whom any proceedings shall have been taken under this Act is or is not an Aboriginal.

Certain administrative constraints were imposed on the Aborigines Protection Board, including the obligation to provide a report of its operations to the Governor by 15 April every year.

The Aborigines Protection Act appeared at first sight to protect both employers and employees. But in practice, employers were seldom, if ever, brought before the courts for breach of contract, while Aborigines were frequently imprisoned for not remaining with their employers. The 1886 Act was amended in 1892 to repeal the clause dealing with breach of contract between masters and servants. In the original Act, clause 44 of part 2 had limited the penalty against any Aboriginal person for breach of contract to a maximum fine of £10, or one month's imprisonment with or without hard labour. After the passage of the 1892 Act, the fine was no longer an option and the gaol term was increased to three months with or without hard labour.[10] The use of these legal devices makes it apparent that the system of indentures and apprenticeship was introduced as a means of controlling the movements of Aboriginal people.

Effects of the contract and indenture system

The system of contracts introduced under the 1886 Act could be used to control any person over the age of 14 and the apprenticeship arrangements provided for control over the rest of the young population. This was the kind of control the pastoralists wanted. Many of them agreed with Septimus Burt, who believed that Aboriginal children should be seen as the property of the settlers. He said that he had been asked for advice as to the law in a situation

> where a native or half-caste child had been brought up and trained by a settler, and afterwards, when the boy or girl began to be of some service, other people enticed them away, and those who had gone to the trouble and expense of bringing up the native had no redress. Under this Bill a master or mistress who *brought up* the native or a half-caste child would be able to exercise a sort of parental control over him [sic] until he attained a certain age. He thought that the House would see that there was nothing in the world unreasonable or objectionable about this.[11] [my emphasis]

The idea of 'ownership' of Aboriginal children by settlers explains why the system of indentures and apprenticeship was introduced. The problem of how to prevent Aboriginal children who 'belonged' to a particular homestead from absconding or going to another employer was solved by the indenture system. But, more than this, it allowed for a trade in children from one station to another. In 1898, in a letter to Prinsep, the acting Protector of Aborigines, George Brockman of Leura Station, Carnarvon, wrote that he was sending one of his 'boys' south to learn farming with a relation at Guildford:

> He is a fine specimen of my boys…he is one of five orphan children *that I bought before they were weaned about six years old*, and have been with me ever since.[12] [my emphasis]

It was also important to maintain the number of Aborigines living on any one station because of the system of rations that was set in place, ostensibly to give support to Aboriginal people. In reality, the squatters were given the equivalent of a subsidy by the Aborigines Protection Board because they were the channel for the distribution of food and blankets provided by the board. Bishop Gibney pointed out that this policy 'affords the temptation to substitute the national dole for the wages due to the native labour on their stations'.[13]

The importance attached to retaining the labour of women and children who belonged on a particular property is apparent in a letter written to the Aborigines Protection Board via its representative, C. M. Straker, by A. C. F. Canning of Pairii Downs Station in March 1893. Several Aborigines had been arrested by Mr Bresnahan for killing cattle on or near Canning's property, among them men whom he had employed for a long period.[14] These men were taken to Ashburton Downs Station, which was leased by Denis Bresnahan Jnr and George Throssell, 'together with their women and children, the women being taken down as witnesses', and handed over to the police.[15] The Aboriginal men were sentenced to imprisonment in Roebourne, and the women and children were 'signed to I. F. Hancock and detained by him'. In his letter, Canning stated that he had repeatedly asked that these women and children be returned to their own country, and was requesting help from the justice of the peace:

The following are the women and children belonging here, who have been employed. viz. Yadgemurra and child. Jacky Mingee and two children. Gniby Gniby and Tumurbah. Kyerbah and child, Minnie, and woman Mynynbah.

The girl Gniby Gniby belongs to a native resident with me for the past two years, named Tamboodie, alias Georgie, and he is naturally most desirous of getting her; I believe this girl has been given to a young native man who has no claim whatever upon her.

I have repeatedly applied to Mr. Hancock for Gniby Gniby and for Kalyugnoo[,] the child of a woman at present here, Minnerrie, but have been unable to obtain them; the woman is continually asking for her boy.

I trust you will request Mr. Hancock to return Gniby Gniby and Kayugnooher without further delay, in the meantime I shall anxiously await the decision of the Board with regard to the other women and children.[16]

This appeal to the Aborigines Protection Board reveals the complex pattern of family labour, which could not be kept intact if mothers and children, or young couples, were separated. It is clear that the pastoralists, who were dependent on Aboriginal labour for their economic survival, were at pains to retain members of their work force. However, while the ration system became a method of social control, which limited the movement of Aboriginal people, the people themselves were in any case usually anxious to remain in their own country.

The way in which the system of contracts worked in practice was revealed in 1901 by interested persons in the North West who wrote to G. S. Olivey, Travelling Inspector of Aborigines. This Aborigines Department officer received a large correspondence from pastoralists when he particularly asked for opinions on the indenture system. Most of the letters were strongly in favour of the system. They claimed that it offered protection for both parties, with Aborigines being protected from so-called 'unscrupulous' travellers who might offer them inducements to leave their employment; that it benefited the whole colony; and that, in return for labour, it provided food that Aborigines might otherwise obtain by killing stock.[17] However, John Brockman, the Resident Magistrate in Greenough, did not share the opinion of the majority. He stated that 'an indentured native was bound body and soul to his master from 10 or 11 years and got nothing in exchange except his food, shirt and trousers and perhaps a blanket'.

> It is argued that if a boy is arrested for running away, he can complain to the Court if he has been ill-treated, but this is absurd. When the boy is arrested and put in the dock, he stands there a poor, shrinking, frightened creature, he hears some talking and listens but has no idea what is being done, the only thing he knows is that his master is there and is making some complaint about him.[18]

Clear evidence about the employment of children in the pastoral industry comes from the 1894 report of the Aborigines Protection Board, gathered by Mr Charles Straker, who at that time acted as an inspector. He visited forty-eight stations on behalf of the board, and the details of his findings were included in the material sent to the Colonial Office.[19] He identified a total of 599 men, 615 women and 319 children under 10, a total of 1,533 persons, working on pastoral stations.[20] The age separation means that those estimated to be over 10 years of age were counted as adults, and were regarded as part of the work force. This report shows, therefore, that a high percentage of workers were under 14 years of age at this time, in spite of the fact that, under the Aborigines Protection Act, contracts were limited to children over 14. In fact, the total working population of Aborigines might have been much higher than this report suggested. In 1884, the Government Resident in the North West, Robert Sholl, stated that there were 1,800 Aborigines 'in the service of settlers and others between the Murchison and the Fitzroy'.[21] Twenty years later, the Roth Report estimated that there were 4,000 Aborigines working in the North West.[22]

Evidence about children employed in the pastoral industry appeared in this 1904 report. W. E. Roth, who was then Chief

Protector of Aborigines in Queensland, was appointed as a Royal Commissioner 'to enquire into the condition of the natives' in Western Australia.[23] The evidence from this commission, although it was gathered at the end of the period under study here, refers back to the practices of the previous twenty years, and leaves the reader in no doubt about the systematic exploitation of Aboriginal children during that period.[24] Roth stated in his report that he had confined his inquiries 'chiefly to the condition of the natives in the Northern and North Western areas of the State', and had interviewed forty-two witnesses, as well as receiving confidential written submissions. The detailed evidence in this report shows clearly that Aboriginal children were customarily employed in a variety of ways as unpaid labour in the North West.

The Roth Report uncovered the ways in which Aboriginal men, women and children were exploited, both sexually and as unpaid labour, and treated with contempt by many members of European society. Although there were implied criticisms of the administration of Aboriginal affairs from many of the people interviewed by Commissioner Roth, most of them gave their approval both to the system of contracts and to the apprenticeship of Aboriginal children. Axel Ostland, for example, Resident Magistrate and warden of Marble Bar, who was interviewed on 18 October 1904, answered the commissioner's questions in the following way:

> 837. With regard to indentures and apprenticeships, are there many in this district? I can trace 32 cases which should be in force in this district.
>
> 838. The Act gives power to a Justice to visit these indentured children. Do you know whether any such visits have been made? Yes. I have often done so myself but do not know whether other Justices have. I always consider myself a party to any indenture signed by myself.
>
> 839. At what age do you think Aboriginal or half-caste children should be indentured? At the age of 8 or 10 years.

840. In all such cases have you consulted the wishes of the parent of such child? Always. The mother, in most cases, has been present.

841. To what age do you think an apprenticeship should last? Until maturity: the age of 14 in the case of girls and 16 or 17 in the case of boys.

842. If there was proper supervision, do you think, on the whole, the apprenticeship system is a good one? Yes, but I think that Section No 38 of the Act, referring to the assignment of apprentices on the death of a master, should be repealed.[25]

Henry Prinsep became Chief Inspector of Aborigines after the Aborigines Protection Board was abolished and the Aborigines Department was set up in 1897. He was interviewed by Roth on 3 September 1904. Prinsep was not critical of most aspects of the system of contracts and apprenticeship, but agreed that he had no knowledge of an employer ever being fined for breaking a contract, while for this offence Aborigines were frequently imprisoned with or without hard labour. His solution to these obvious problems was to institute a system of even greater paternalistic control, particularly over Aboriginal children. He made it clear that he thought he ought to have the power to enforce the protection, care or safety of Aboriginal women and children, and the power to send children to a mission station, an orphanage or a reformatory.[26]

It is apparent that Roth agreed with Prinsep that the solution to the problems connected with the exploitation of Aboriginal children involved increased control over the victims of that exploitation, rather than taking any action against those responsible. In his summing up, he implied that much greater control would have to be exercised over Aboriginal people by the Aborigines Department, a conclusion reflected in the Aborigines Act of 1905 (see chapter 9).[27]

The system of contracts for Aboriginal persons over 14 years, and of apprenticeship for children under that age, was introduced in 1886 in order to bind the local Aboriginal people to particular pastoral holdings. If these workers absconded, they were then able to be rounded up by the police and returned to their employer. It was impossible for Aboriginal children to attempt any redress from this draconian law. It was a system of slavery that removed parents' control over their children and placed it in the hands of the pastoralists. The law did not require the payment of wages. The government could not compel the supply of adequate food or the provision of any kind of education. Children continued to live with their families on what had once been their ancestral land, but under circumstances that gradually reduced their capacity to maintain Aboriginal cultural practices. Their lives were diminished as their work laid the foundation for the wealth of the European settlers who controlled thousands of acres of pastoral land.

CHAPTER 8

Child labour in the pearling industry

PEARLING began near Roebourne in the 1860s, along with the gradual spread into the northern pastoral areas. Contemporary reports explain that much of the shell was gathered at first from very shallow water, but that skindivers in deeper water usually reached depths of about 16 feet and came to the surface after two or three minutes clutching a pearl shell in either hand.[1] By the end of the 1870s, a lucrative trade in pearl shell had been established, using the labour of Malays[2] and Aborigines. After 1885, diving apparatus was introduced and spread very gradually in the industry. By the early years of the twentieth century, it was being widely used by Japanese divers in Broome, which had become the pearling centre of Western Australia.[3]

Contemporary records about the activities of Aboriginal people seldom mention their age, both because this was not easy to determine with any accuracy, and because Europeans in the North West did not see any reason to discriminate in favour of children. Settlers who had interests in the pastoral industry often owned pearling boats and controlled the activities of young Aboriginal men, women and children as divers. The work force was difficult to find and equally difficult to keep. Correspondence provides evidence of 'blackbirding', when Aborigines were rounded up by pearlers and taken on board. Young divers were especially sought after because they were more efficient at obtaining shell and could be controlled more easily on the boats. For this reason, the industry must be recognized as one dependent on the work of young people, many of whom we would regard today as children or adolescents.

Early legislation for the pearling industry

As early as 1871, the colonial government began to legislate to control the operations of the pearl shell industry. In 1869, the impact of pearl shell fishing on the Aborigines along the coast was described by Robert Sholl, Government Resident in the North West. He referred to the coastline from Exmouth Gulf to King Sound as the area where 'the natives were made available by the traders' for the pearl shell boats.

> Were the employers of native labour all just and humane men, their presence along the coast would doubtless [be] more beneficial to the Aborigines, who receive food and clothing for their services, but it is too much to expect that a band of adventurers who are, practically, not subject to control, will always act justly or humanely, especially when their interests are at stake.
>
> So long as shells were plentiful and competition was slack, the natives had only to apprehend [sic] a sudden burst of violence on the part of individuals; but a change has taken place, and whether the number of shells be greater or less, there is no doubt that the number of adventurers is greater, and that there is every prospect of its increasing as the supply of native labour becomes unequal to the demand.
>
> This state of affairs in a settled country could be beneficial to the labouring community by increasing the rate of wages and consequently the comforts of the labouring

class; but with a savage population, unable to take advantage of the increased value of their labour, the change was productive of evil rather than good.

Native labour is at present not only the cheapest...It is to the intelligence of the native that the shell seeker owes his wealth and, as I have before said, he is maintained at little cost.

Sholl alluded to the practice of collecting Aboriginal divers by force from inland areas to make up the required numbers on the boats. He was critical of the ways in which Aboriginal people were treated, but also anxious about the evidence of conflict between the European boat owners over the control of these labourers. He did not believe that the Masters and Servants legislation could be used to control this situation and wanted to see some special legislation put in place.

I would suggest that all employers of native labour, whether on shore or at sea, be compelled to enter into some simple form of agreement with the natives, by which the one party should be bound to serve the other for a limited period; and be properly fed and clothed during that period.

The black man or white should be made personally liable for breach of contract, and provision made for the punishment of those who employ the servants of others during the currency of an agreement.[4] [my emphasis]

This can be read as a plea for protection for the Aboriginal work force, especially in connection with the provision of adequate food and clothing. But the contract system he recommended was designed to allow the owners of pearling boats to control the movements of their workers, many of whom were under the age of puberty, thus foreshadowing the 1886 Aborigines Protection Act.

Sholl's 1869 report influenced the government to introduce controls in the pearling industry. The 1871 Pearl Shell Fishery Act regulated the hiring and service of Aborigines and prohibited the employment of women.[5] Any ship's master who employed an Aboriginal person had to have a written contract signed by that Aboriginal person. The contract set out the nature and duration of the intended work, the time that 'such native' would be required to begin and the amount to be paid in wages, and stipulated that the Aboriginal person would be conveyed back to the place of first engagement before the contract expired. The debate on the Bill to introduce this Act revealed considerable scepticism about whether the introduction of a system whereby agreements had to be signed between employers and employees before a magistrate could be made to work. It revealed that Aborigines were being kidnapped and then left at any point on the coast when the season was over.[6]

The 1871 Act was repealed two years later and the Pearl Shell Fishery Regulation Act was passed. This Act obliged justices of the peace, police or other persons who were endorsing agreements between boat owners or masters and Aboriginal divers to satisfy themselves on six points before signing the contract. These included knowing that the contract was entered into voluntarily and was understood by the Aboriginal person, that the person was fit for pearl shell diving, and that the contract was for no longer than twelve months. The penalty against any ship's master for not conveying Aboriginal employees back to their place of residence was a fine of up to £50. Ship owners and masters could have their vessels searched to see that no Aboriginal persons were being held 'under duress', and to check the adequacy of the ship's provisions.

Both the 1871 and 1873 Acts stated that agreements could only be made with males, and prohibited the embarkation or employment of females on pearling boats, although anecdotal accounts of how females made the best divers suggests that they were always part of the work force.[7] These Acts seemed to offer protection for Aborigines, but the framers of the Acts knew that Aboriginal people could not, in practice, make use of them. The Acts were drawn up in such a way as to gain Colonial Office approval while also giving employers the power, through the contract system, to control the movements of their work force.

Procurement of Aboriginal labour

There are many reports of the kidnapping of young Aborigines, who were placed on board pearling luggers or kept confined until the luggers were ready to sail. In 1876, Robert Fairbairn, at that time acting Resident Magistrate in Albany, was sent by Governor Weld to inquire into the kidnapping of Aboriginal people in the North West. He concluded his report with the statement that

> just now the natives inhabiting the country between Shark's Bay and the mouth of the Gascoyne are eagerly sought for by intending pearlers. The natives are less expensive, while at the same time they are said to be more expert in procuring shell than the Malays.[8]

Other descriptions of the rounding up of Aborigines for the pearling season come from the letters of one of the McRae brothers, members of a Victorian family active in the pearling and pastoral industries. George McRae wrote to his sister in 1881 from the Ashburton River region:

> I have had a good deal of company in the way of fellows hunting up their niggers for pearling...the niggers have been a good deal of trouble this year they are getting tired of pearling and with the new regulations that have been passed pearling will hardly pay.[9]

In 1874, the Imported Labour Registry Act was passed, as owners of pearling boats were experimenting with the employment of Malays as divers for pearl shell. The Act permitted the continued employment of 'coloured labour' in the North West, even though such labour was gradually prohibited in the southern regions. After the passage of this Act, employees on the pearl shell boats were regularly counted.[10] An investigation into the treatment of workers in the pearl shell fisheries in 1875 revealed that they were not being paid, that adequate food was not being provided, and that Aboriginal divers were not being returned to their homes.[11]

A report by an anonymous 'special correspondent' from the North West, sent to the *Inquirer* in April 1875, provided an account of the ways in which the Acts of the early 1870s were being flouted by many operators in the industry:

> With respect to the pearling craft who carry native divers, I may say success has attended all; with some, quite little fortunes must have been realized, and what is more singular, *the more juvenile the native crew,* under proper management, the more successful the fishery…No employer would employ a Malay now, I should say, if he could get natives; particularly if he could work these natives some distance away from their own hunting grounds. They are apt to run away when near home.
>
> In Fremantle, Perth, Guildford, and, in fact, in all the Swan settlements, you may constantly hear it asserted 'Oh, it is no use you trying your hand at the North West, you won't get a nigger, they are all signed.'
>
> True enough they are signed, and signed, and doubly signed—from year's end to year's end—a glaring system of slavery staring the Weld policy in the teeth with a grim defiance…the horrible practice is concealed in a most accomplished manner…greatly to the advantage of the Western Australian slave holder, for he has no thousands of dollars to pay first cost for his 'nigger', and only a little flour to dispense and less clothing comforts. There are holders of niggers in the North West who don't speak twice to obtain instant obedience…Before the provisions of the agreement are fully carried out, viz, the native returned to his hunting grounds or birthplace, he gets a new pipe, some good tobacco, shirt, trousers, etc; he is then re-signed for the next season, and hunted up when the white man wants him. [This procedure] shuts out any chance of the blackfellow getting a change of masters…were he free and unfettered, and had the choice of different masters each season, he would be a different fellow altogether, and no doubt happier and longer lived.[12] [my emphasis]

The special correspondent also referred to the way in which a government official in the North West, who owned pearling luggers, rounded up his divers and kept them locked up until he was ready to sail.

At this time, Aboriginal divers, often young adolescents, were to a large extent replacing Malay divers. An 1880 report on pearl shell fishing by Robert Sholl stated that 'it was found that the cost of employing Malays was too great to allow a profit; and their employment was abandoned at once'.[13] There were 989 Malays employed in 1875, but Sholl recorded that by 1877 none were employed. By the end of the century, according to the contemporary writer Arthur Bligh, Malays, Chinese, Japanese, Filipinos, Egyptians and Indians were engaged in the pearling industry, which by that time was centred on Broome.[14] But for the 1870s, Sholl indicated that 'natives' on these boats numbered 493 in 1875, 344 in 1876, 434 in 1877, and 497 in 1878.

Point 5 of Sholl's report stated that

> native divers do not get money wages. They are allowed flour, tea and sugar. At sea they help themselves to flour, but when they are camped on shore or the vessel is anchored near the shore, they receive a ration of two pounds per diem, otherwise the flour would be wasted among their shore friends. They are also allowed tobacco, a plug of negrohead per week: for clothing, they are allowed one shirt, one pair of trousers, and one blanket at the beginning, and the same at the end of the season. I think it is fortunate that they do not receive money wages, as habits of intemperance would be encouraged, from which at present they are free.

Numerous reports about the kidnapping of young Aborigines for the pearling boats in the early 1880s suggested that some pearlers made additional sums by supplying labour for other owners of pearling boats. One report alleged that Aborigines were kept at Lacepede Islands until they were 'made available' to boat owners. A reading of the evidence leads to the conclusion that government officers were not usually prepared to bring evidence against Europeans in the North West.[15] However, a letter to the Governor from E. H. Laurence, Government Resident of Roebourne, reveals that there was a real problem about policing the age clause in the regulations that forbade children under the age of puberty to dive. Part of his letter of 31 October 1882 reads:

> My attention was called to the tender age of Ellery's natives who signed before Mr Pearse. One who was brought before that gentleman was turned back on account of youth; Mr Pearse was satisfied there were none under twelve years of age. The boy that was turned back remains at Cossack with Ellery's sister-in-law: he should be restored to his own country, and though he is probably better off where he is his remaining tends to encourage the bringing in of boys under age.[16]

Laurence raised this issue again in a letter to the Colonial Secretary on 20 April 1883, when he referred to the report of the Inspector of Pearl Shell Fisheries, Blair Mayne:

> Respecting age, however, the report is less certain and the definition of age in the Regulations leaves, necessarily, much to the discretion of the officer signing the agreements.[17]

Attempts to regulate Aboriginal labour

Letters from Governor W. C. F. Robinson to Lord Kimberley, Secretary of State for the Colonies, written in 1880, give a clear indication of the real state of affairs in the North West.[18] The Governor stated that he had devised means to protect Aborigines in the pearl shell industry through the promulgation of new regulations, because the reports he had received disclosed 'a state of things little short of slavery'. He said that his regulations had been attacked as unnecessarily severe, but had met with the general approval 'of those sections of the public which are not directly interested in the fisheries and the employment of native labour'.[19] These regulations were amended in 1881 to clarify certain issues.[20] Three years later, the Governor also sent a circular to all Government Residents and Resident Magistrates, and to all justices of the peace north of the Murchison, including the Inspector of Pearl Shell Fisheries. He referred to reports claiming that some of the methods of obtaining the services of Aboriginal divers were not in harmony with the laws of the colony, and urged that the laws be observed with the greatest vigilance.[21]

The Governor's 1880 regulations were partly the result of an inquiry into complaints against the owners and operators of the pearl shell fishing vessels, who were reported to be over-fishing the pearl shell areas and to be maltreating their employees on the fishing boats.[22] The Governor issued a circular to the owners of ships in the pearling fleet, which included a questionnaire on the costs of their establishing themselves in the industry between January 1873 and December 1879, and about the size of their hauls and the profits they had made. The circular also canvassed several options for imposing controls on the operations of the industry in order to sustain the limited resources, and asked for responses from boat owners.[23]

Predictably, the replies revealed a general dislike of controls of any kind. However, they provided evidence of the labour arrangements on the ships. Robert Sholl had about twenty-five persons on each boat, in the ratio of one European for every twelve 'natives'. He paid the Europeans between £7 and £8 a month, with a bonus of £4–6 per ton of shell collected. The Aborigines were given clothes, tobacco and rations. R. Thompson had a fleet of thirty-five boats and employed eighty to ninety Europeans, fifteen to twenty Malays and Chinese, and 600 Aborigines. He paid the Europeans between £5 and £10 a month, with bonuses of £2–5 per ton, and the Malays and Chinese between £3 and £7 a month, with bonuses of £1–2 a ton. The Aborigines were given clothes, tobacco and rations. Replies from M. Grant and F. Pearse revealed a similar pattern.[24]

The Governor's regulations listed certain practices, such as employing persons under the age of puberty, as 'unlawful', with the obvious implication that these practices were commonplace.[25] One section of the regulations was designed to prevent the practice of kidnapping, more than once alluded to in the Governor's correspondence with informants in the North West. Governor Robinson's correspondence with the Colonial Secretary, Lord Kimberley, explained how he had attempted to prevent magistrates, if they were interested parties, from taking part in witnessing agreements with Aborigines. He spoke of impressing upon the Government Resident in the North West and the Inspector of Pearl Shell Fisheries the importance of enforcing the new regulations.

Another attempt was made to clarify the situation in the North West in 1881, when Detective Constable Glover was sent to Shark Bay and the Gascoyne to collect census papers. He was also asked 'to enquire carefully' into the conduct of Aborigines and the treatment of Aborigines by Europeans, 'more especially as to the system of kidnapping natives and conveying them on board the pearling boats to work as divers'.[26] Glover reported that this was not a problem generally, and spoke highly of the good relations between Robert Sholl and his Aboriginal employees. However, he found that there were accounts of a kidnapping having been carried out by W. A. Finnerty from a place called Wooramallar. He provided a deposition from an Aborigine called Wewar, who had been a pearl shell diver. Wewar described how Finnerty came to Wooramallar on horseback looking for Aborigines:

> He galloped after me on horseback he did not tie me up he galloped after several other natives and caught them he tied them together with a rope and took them to the coast their names are Jimmy Johnny Barney Marrare Charley and another man *there were also four boys* when he got us to the coast he put us on board his own boat and told us he was going to take us to the Gascoyne he did not take us to the Gascoyne but put us on board the 'Kate' which was lying off Pelican Island.[27] [my emphasis]

That the Governor's attempts at regulation did not succeed can be seen from later reports about the continuing employment of children in the industry. In 1884, E. H. Laurence, the Government

Resident in Roebourne, wrote a report to the Colonial Secretary in which he described how a pearler called Wilson had been fined for breaking government regulations. Part of his report revealed the way in which the regulations could be evaded. He stated that Wilson

> had been allowed to carry young children as shell cleaners, and this had been specified in the agreement. It was proved that they were taken out in a dingey [sic] and dived pretty regularly: no cruelty or excessive work was alleged. The defendant pleaded that the late Inspector had told him that he might dive the boys moderately, but this agreement was made before the present Inspector who did not give any such sanction. The practice of carrying on board boys too young to dive is very liable to abuse, and I had frequent differences of opinion from the late Inspector as to the age at which he allowed them to go, but as in some ways the boys are better off on board than on shore I did not interfere with his discretions as to letting them go as shell cleaners. Should this be further abused it may be necessary to stop it altogether. I fined Wilson two pounds ten shillings in each of the four cases.[28]

There was also an unsuccessful attempt in 1882 to amend the Pearl Shell Fishery Act in order to strengthen government controls over those employers of Aboriginal labour who broke their engagement 'with these wretched people'.[29] This attempt to pass a new Bill restraining the activities of masters on pearling boats suggests that neither of the two earlier Acts, nor the Governor's regulations, had had any significant effect on the operations of the pearling industry. It is clear that the regulations were seldom enforced against the owners or masters of vessels. In spite of this, in 1883–84, the Inspector of Pearl Shell Fisheries, Blair Mayne, declared in his report that it was 'one of the best regulated and most orderly industries I have ever seen'.[30] He said that there had undoubtedly been some ill-treatment and assault of natives 'but proportionately they are not many'.[31] This report was written just two years before the arrival in the Gascoyne region of Reverend John Brown Gribble, who planned to establish an Anglican mission station in the region. His observations were to bring him into growing conflict with the Western Australian establishment over the treatment of Aborigines in the North West.[32]

Critics of Aboriginal exploitation in the pearling industry

Gribble's letters to the *West Australian* newspaper and elsewhere presented a very different picture from that of the Inspector of Pearl Shell Fisheries. Gribble described the labour arrangements in the region as 'a system of bond service bordering on slavery' and asserted that the law was openly violated. He provided accounts both of his own observations and of the descriptions given him by other people regarding the sexual violation of young girls and the capture of children taken for the pearling industry:[33]

> Frequently the natives are first brought into service by capture, and then 'assigned' afterwards. The settlers are a law unto themselves. One evening, when staying at a station, I discovered a man debauching a young black girl. I was horrified and asked him how he could do such a thing. He was astounded at the enquiry, and with the most unblushing effrontery, said, 'She has been assigned to me by the police for six months and I can do what I like with her.'[34]

The observations of other people also came to light at this time. David Carly of Perth, for example, had witnessed a kidnapping some years before the Governor's regulations were introduced, and his description was published at the time of the Gribble affair:

> In September, 1878, I was in my house at Cossack, when I heard a native woman call out to me to save her boy from a man who was kidnapping him. I went out and saw

the woman struggling with a white man for her boy. I did not interfere, as it was useless, knowing that the man's brother was a J.P., who [sic] I had seen sign away numbers of kidnapped natives. The man tore the boy from his mother, and took him to a store close by and got him assigned. The next day the boy was put on board a cutter in spite of the screams and struggles of the poor mother. I drew the attention of a constable to the case, and he said he could not interfere. I have seen hundreds of children brought into Cossack who have been torn from their mothers, and yet it is said that where the British flag flies slavery cannot exist.[35]

Concerning the system of labour contracts on the Gascoyne, Gribble wrote that

[the Aborigines] are compelled to touch the pen to an assignment paper which it is impossible for them to understand, and, as regards the witnessing of such assign-ment, the parties so acting are doubtless interested, so that in such case the poor native becomes a bond servant by force. But there is an advanced phase of this side of the question which must be disclosed. At times the wild natives are really run down and captured and taken to the stations, and then assignment as above described takes place; and then, if they run away (which they are almost certain to do), a warrant is issued for their arrest, and then the police are set in motion, and if run down or ferreted out they are taken to the Junction Police Station and there are chained up for a few weeks.[36]

The historian Neville Green comments that 'Gribble was whistling up a whirlwind that threatened the economy of the north by exposing it for what it was, a system of slavery of thousands of men, women and children'.[37] The crimes committed against Aborigines in this system included abduction, incarceration, rape and flogging, and the signing of contracts that exposed them to prison sentences.[38] Gribble failed to persuade the Perth establishment that steps should be taken to remedy the situation in the North West, and he left the colony after being subjected to almost universal vilification.[39]

But a new champion of the interests of the Aborigines in the North West now appeared in the person of Colonel Angelo, who took up an appointment as Government Resident in Roebourne in March 1886.[40] He immediately began writing confidential letters to Governor Broome about conditions in the region, over some months gradually outlining details of the ways in which Aborigines were exploited in the pearl shell industry and on pastoral stations:

> As regards the treatment of 'niggers', it is virtually slavery sanctioned by law but cannot be termed so because these 'niggers' are not to be bought or sold. [A]ll the 'niggers' in the country are claimed and monopolized by a few people who in the first instance took them with the land—but once 'signed'—a term which will need more legislation—they are to all intents and purposes their property and cannot be employed by anyone else. Thus one settler may have a crowd of natives *belonging* to him tho' not *employed* by him and another cannot get a single hand to help him.[41] [original emphasis]

Not long after his arrival, Colonel Angelo confronted Blair Mayne, the Inspector of Pearl Shell Fisheries, about the way in which Aborigines were being signed on for pearling.[42] He had obtained depositions from two Aborigines alleging their forcible removal to the pearling boats, the kidnapping of their wives, and their ill-treatment on the boats when they did not bring up enough shell. Their testimony implicated several Europeans, including Blair Mayne.[43] Angelo's actions inspired considerable hostility from some of the European pearlers, who reportedly met to plan some action against him.[44]

However, Angelo's confidential correspondence had so added to the disquiet of Governor Broome that he appointed Robert Fairbairn, then Resident Magistrate at Fremantle, to hold an inquiry into the complaints about the behaviour of Mayne, and 'various allegations bearing upon the present condition of the natives of the north west district which have been made by J. W. Cowan and David Forrest'.[45] As a result of this inquiry, Mayne was dismissed from his position as Inspector of Pearl Shell Fisheries. Angelo was commended for his activities on behalf of the Aboriginal population but rebuked for his failure to submit all his correspondence through the proper channels. However, it seems likely that he undertook the private correspondence with the Governor at the latter's request. The rebuke came from the Colonial Secretary after the correspondence was placed before the Executive Council.

Fairbairn's inquiry provided sufficient evidence to sustain the accusations that Reverend Gribble had recently made concerning violence against and rape and kidnapping of young Aborigines by various European land-holders and pearling masters in the North West. In particular, David Forrest provided an account of how some of the young Aboriginal divers were kidnapped for pearling.[46] Paragraphs 43–47 of Fairbairn's report to the Colonial Secretary read as follows:

> Mr Forrest states that it has been the practice of late years for men to leave Roebourne in parties well equipped with horses and rations.
>
> These parties travel through the Hamersley Range, thence on to the head of the Ashburton and Lyons Rivers, for the purpose of securing *all the young natives they can find.*
>
> These unfortunate natives, when caught, Mr Forrest states, are brought down by forced marches to the coast, they always camp before sunset and a strict watch is kept over the natives at night.
>
> On reaching the coast they are placed on board a vessel sent for the purpose, and then taken to Barrow Island. Men are left on the boat to look after the natives while another boat is despatched to some given point on the coast, generally to a place called Hooley's Creek, there to await the arrival of another batch—this it seems goes on

until the natives required for the season's diving are procured. From Barrow Island the natives are conveyed by sea to Cossack where they are signed in the presence of the Inspector of Pearl Shell Fisheries or some other Justice of the Peace who endorses on the agreement that, before the native signed the same, he had satisfied himself that the said native was a perfectly free and voluntary agent in the matter[,] that he was not acting under any fear or coercion[,] that before the said native signed the same he satisfied himself that he thoroughly understood and assented to the terms and the nature of the said agreement, also that the native is physically fit for the employment agreed upon.

Mr Forrest who for some years has been a settler on the Ashburton says that he is acquainted with many of the natives and he is satisfied, from what he has seen and heard from the natives themselves, that they are taken forcibly from their country.[47] [my emphasis]

Colonel Angelo believed that he had to bypass the office of the Colonial Secretary and write confidentially to the Governor about what was happening to Aborigines in the North West. But one of the settlers in the area, John W. Cowan, believed that even the Governor could not be relied upon to act.[48] He sent a voluminous correspondence to A. C. Onslow, then Chief Justice, with the request that it be sent direct to the Secretary of State for the Colonies in London. Cowan claimed that

many of the members of the Legislature are slave owners, and most of them are more or less interested in maintaining the present state of affairs. In this district, there is a powerful organization, including at least three members of the legislature and all their adherents, the only capable legal practitioner, the ruling mercantile firm here, and all working under the protection of the Government Inspector of Pearl Shell Fisheries, acting in cooperation with all the Justices of the Peace, excepting the Government Resident [Angelo] who is himself being persecuted by this wicked combination.[49]

The politics of this situation can be followed in some detail from other sources, including further correspondence sent to the Secretary of State in the following year.[50] But Cowan's letters provide details about the whipping and murder of Aborigines, their kidnapping and transport, sometimes in chains, for pearl diving, and the forging of signatures on contracts. His accusations include reference to violence against Aboriginal women and their sexual exploitation. One of his letters gives an account of the kidnapping of a young boy:

> [O]ne of this party whose name I do not know took a boy of about ten years of age away from his father and mother who were both in my employ, and put the boy on his horse in front of him, the boy shrieking with fright, and the father and mother crying, they asked me to interfere. I remonstrated with the white man, he replied laughingly, 'He'll be alright after he has been a bit away.' I told him I would report him, which I did in writing to the Government Resident. I received an answer to the effect that he had been informed that the boy had come away willingly with the party, and that he had seen the boy and that he appeared to be quite happy.[51]

It is clear from these examples that there were some outspoken contemporary critics of the treatment of Aboriginal people in the North West. But many of those involved in the worst kinds of exploitation were powerful establishment figures who were contemptuous of the culture of the Aboriginal people and believed that they had the right to make use of them as they saw fit. In 1886, for example, the acting Attorney General, Septimus Burt, who had a large leasehold property in the North West, claimed in the Legislative Council that the pearl shell industry

> had been an important factor in civilizing the native population, in making them useful, and in preventing

those outbreaks that might otherwise have occurred
between the pioneer settlers and the natives, in the
settlement of a newly discovered territory.[52]

The contract and indenture system

Burt's comments, widely endorsed by other colonists in the pastoral
and pearling industry, were expressed when he moved to introduce
the Aborigines Protection Bill in 1886. Previous Acts introduced
ostensibly to protect Aboriginal employees had in fact been used to
coerce Aboriginal labour. As discussed in chapter 7, the new
Aborigines Protection Act, passed in 1886, extended the contract
system of labour into the pastoral industry and introduced the idea of
indenturing young children into a system of apprenticeship. The
evidence shows that the idea of protecting Aboriginal people, which
was said to be the underlying purpose of the Act, was never
seriously intended.

The Roth Report of 1904 was important in uncovering
evidence about the way the indenture system worked in the pearling
industry. Graham Blick, district medical officer and acting Resident
Magistrate in Broome, was interviewed on 7 October of that year by
Commissioner Roth. Part of the transcript reads as follows:

747. What is the usual trade, business or employment to
which children are indentured? I should think quite one
half of them are indentured to the pearling industry. The
remainder are mostly girls indentured as domestic
servants.

748. Are these children thus indentured to the pearling
industry taken out on to the pearling boats? Yes.

749. Do the boys who are indentured to the pearling trade
receive any wages? There is no mention of it. I should not
think they would. It is almost certain that they do not.

750. At what age are these children signed on? I think the
ages range from 10 years upwards. The oldest I know of

was 17 years of age. He was indentured to a squatter. Little boys have been indentured on the boats at 10 or 12 years of age.

751. Are children of these early years allowed to go on the pearling boats? They have apparently been allowed to for many years. The cases I have mentioned hold good from 1897 and 1898 to the present time.

752. Are they bound down to the age of 21 years? All the boys indentured to the pearling trade were bound down to the age of 21 years, but they are generally bound down to 18 years. Lately Mr Warton did not bind them all to the age of 21 years.

753. As far as you know, are such apprenticed children signed on with the consent of their parents? I do not know.

755. Can you indenture a child without instructions from the Aborigines Department? I was under the impression that I could. I did not get permission in any case. I did not know that it was the rule to get permission from the Aborigines Department.

756. Do you personally approve of the indenture system? With reservations I do. I think the age limit should be reduced from 21 to 17 or 18 and, provided that the Justice or responsible person knows the people to whom the natives are indentured, it is generally a good thing. I do not think they should be indentured up to the age of 21 years, as at that age a boy is getting on in years and is able to shift for himself.[53]

Concerning the system of contracts, Commissioner Roth stated in 1904 that the interests of the Aboriginal people were certainly not protected against the unfitness of an employer, and that there was nothing to prevent 'the greatest scoundrel unhung', European or Asian, putting under contract 'any blacks he pleases'.[54] In any case, Roth could only find 369 Aborigines who had been employed under contract, for which no adequate records had been kept. Even without contracts, the Aborigines were not free to come and go but were often forcibly returned to their masters by the police, while none of the working Aborigines in the North West, estimated by Roth to be 4,000, were paid wages.[55]

But, as we have seen, there was a difference between the signing of a contract and the indenture system. According to the law, the contract system was intended to be used to secure the services of persons over 14 years of age. However, under the system of indentures set out in the Aborigines Protection Act of 1886, a Resident Magistrate could indenture any 'half-caste' or Aboriginal child who had reached a 'suitable age' as an apprentice, until 21 years of age.[56] Roth found that there were many more indentures than were known about by the Chief Protector of Aborigines. Children over 14 were being indentured when they should have been put under contract, none of these children received any wages, and no education was provided as part of the indenture.

> The very spirit and principles of the Pearl Shell Fishery Regulation Act of 1873, which absolutely forbids a term of aboriginal service on the boats longer than twelve months, have been stultified by recourse to the system of apprenticeship: at Broome quite one half of the children, ranging from 10 years and upwards, are indentured to the pearling industry and taken out on to the boats…One Resident Magistrate very ably expresses the present state of affairs as follows: The child is bound and can be reached by law and punished, but the person to whom the child is bound is apparently responsible to nobody.[57]

In 1887, the Pearl Shell Fishery Act was again amended, this time to tidy up an anomaly in the wording of the already revised Act, but also to put the power to endorse the agreements between employers of Aboriginal labour and their employees into different hands. Under the earlier Act, agreements could be signed by justices of the peace, a police constable or the persons appointed to implement the Pearl Shell Fishery Regulation Act of 1873.

It was proposed that, in the future, the officers who
endorse these agreements with natives employed in pearl
fishing shall be the Inspector of Pearl Fisheries, or the
Resident Magistrate, or a Protector of Aborigines.[58]

The Act proposed that the government appoint persons as Protectors
of Aborigines to ensure the carrying out of the original Act. A third
purpose of the Bill was to introduce more stringent arrangements
about the return of Aborigines, whose contracts had expired, to the
original place of residence. The Attorney General said that he was

very glad indeed that the Colony had been cleared, as it
had by the recent trial, of those gross implications cast
upon it by the most unworthy person who had recently
left the Colony

but as there were sometimes 'extreme cases', the House was anxious
to do all it could to prevent abuses.[59] The 'trial' referred to here was
the libel suit of J. B. Gribble against the editors of the *West Australian*, which Gribble had lost.[60]

It was apparent during the debate that the clause that most
upset the members was the one concerning the intention to remove
justices of the peace as persons capable of endorsing labour agreements. Three persons with interests in the pastoral and pearl shell
industries—Robert Frederick Sholl, elected Member for Gascoyne,
Daniel Keen Congdon, a nominee member of the Legislative
Council, and Alexander Joseph McRae, elected Member for the
North West—spoke forcibly against their removal. After a long
debate, the wording was changed to retain the power of justices of
the peace as endorsers of contracts, even though another nominee
member, George Randall, pointed out that 'one could easily
understand why a person directly interested in the employment of
natives might possibly be influenced, against his own judgement'.
This 1887 attempt to introduce greater controls over the activities of
those who owned pearling boats revealed more clearly than before
how men with capital resources could corrupt the process of
government.

Along the north-west coast, large numbers of young Aboriginal people were exploited by the pearling industry in ways that would have been considered unthinkable for European children, who from 1870 were required by law to attend school until 14 years of age.[61] The young work force was maintained by the owners of pearling boats by the use of contracts and the apprenticeship system, allied with a process of coercion inherent in the system of 'blackbirding'.

As a result of critical observations about what was occurring in the North West being passed on to the Governor and the Colonial Office in London, the British Government retained its power over Aboriginal people when responsible government was granted in 1890. This power was invested in a new Aborigines Protection Board under the control of the Governor, rather than being handed over to the elected parliament. The new board continued the work of the first board set up three years before under the Aborigines Protection Act of 1886. However, this reserve power lasted only until 1897, after which time the power over Aborigines lay ultimately in the hands of the Western Australian Government.

CHAPTER 9

Rehearsing the future:
'Half-castes' and reserves

The 'problem of half-castes'

The presence of whaling parties along the southern coast, well before the time of first European settlement, had produced a population of mixed descent in the South West, and this number had gradually increased from 1829. The Aboriginal people of the North West had interacted with Asian people 'for at least two centuries before the invasion of the British'.[1] A population of mixed Aboriginal and European parentage, characteristic of frontier situations where there were few European women, also began to emerge in the North West after 1860. The last years of the century saw a growing uneasiness about the fact that these children were as much European as Aboriginal. The question of what should be done with them began to exercise the minds of people who regularly dealt with Aboriginal people. The idea took shape gradually that they should be separated from both European and Aboriginal people and given special treatment. Not until the early twentieth century did this special treatment become the basis for an ambitious project in social engineering, which would see Aboriginal children forcibly removed from their parents and denied access to their culture.

But, as we have seen, the separation of children from their parents, especially their mothers, already had a long history reaching back to the earliest days of settlement. The control of Aboriginal marriages had also already been tried at New Norcia and at the Wesleyan Aboriginal Mission, as had the idea that education in industrial skills alongside Christian teaching would produce a compliant work force. However, the failure to educate Aboriginal children alongside European children reveals the limited nature of the acceptable contact between these two groups. Nor was it contemplated that mixed marriages would occur. The presence of children of mixed European and Aboriginal descent always posed a problem for administrators.

By the last decade of the century, many people concerned with the fate of Aboriginal children, especially those children being brought up in Aboriginal camps, did not favour the system of contracts and indentures as they operated under the Aborigines Protection Act of 1886. They were particularly worried about the increasing number of children of mixed descent and wanted to see more emphasis on institutions that would prepare children for a life of regular employment.[2] In 1892, for example, Bishop Gibney, the Roman Catholic Bishop of Perth, wrote:

> As regards the native and half-caste children whether in the towns or on the country stations, it seems especially important that every assistance and encouragement (to say the least) should be given to their being gathered, from the age of four years and upwards, into nursery or industrial Schools or Homes in which they should be taught to speak English, and be brought up under simple Christian training, near to their parents but apart from the influences of native camp life, with a view to their passing eventually into the regular employment of the settlers. Their training at these schools should be largely of an industrial character; in case of the boys in lighter station work, gardening, carpentering, or other handicrafts; and

in that of the girls in washing, needlework and other domestic occupations. A capitation allowance might be made by the Government for all children being so trained and taught on the stations, contingent upon results and arrangements being certified as satisfactory, either by the clergyman of the District, or some duly authorised Minister of religion or other Inspector. The establishment of Industrial Homes in the neighbourhood of the towns might in like manner be encouraged by grants-in-aid for the erection of buildings, the salaries of the necessary teachers and caretakers, and the maintenance and the clothing of the children.[3]

He believed that more might be done in the southern districts

to encourage, if not, *in the case of half-caste children at any rate, to make compulsory,* the training of all children at suitably placed industrial homes, and their regular apprenticeship as they become old enough as domestic servants and labourers. [my emphasis]

This blueprint for the future of Aboriginal children was a restatement of the old combination of institutional life and unpaid labour, with some of the detail taken from the Industrial Schools Act of 1874. However, the emphasis on 'half-caste' children showed just what racist beliefs about children of mixed parentage meant in everyday life. Clearly, it was generally believed that these children could not be accepted into European society. But neither should the government ignore their special needs. Perhaps not surprisingly, the final paragraph of Bishop Gibney's report claimed that the settlers were generally ready to cooperate in a plan such as this one, because 'their labour was to be retained at no greater cost and on terms which would make it even more permanently secure to them than under the present system'.

The question of the future of children of mixed parentage also recurred in the reports of Protectors of Aborigines, and other government officers, to the Aborigines Protection Board. In 1896,

C. A. Bailey, a Protector of Aborigines in the region of the goldfields, referred to the growing number of 'half-caste' children who were left to be brought up by Aboriginal women, the father in most cases 'disclaiming the child altogether':

> What is to be the future of such half-castes is difficult to say, but it is certain that they have all the bad points of the black, with none of the good points of the white men. It would be better if these children should be taken and brought up in one of the institutions for that purpose. *The father should be the only person to have a voice in the matter, for the mother would in most cases naturally prefer the child to remain with her, but this should be over-ruled for the child's sake.* In most cases the father would never come up and own to the child and if he did he should be compelled to, at all events contribute to the proper bringing up of his child, this would be the only feasible plan for saving the children from being like their mothers, wild in the bush. If they are placed on a station, when they grow up they are treated just like a black, and kept well at a distance, and looked down upon *although they have white blood in their veins.*[4] [my emphasis]

George Marsden, writing to the Aborigines Protection Board from the Kimberley goldfields, asked especially for direction about what to do with children of mixed descent. He wanted to know how to go about placing them in one of the schools 'set apart for the training of half-caste children'. He believed that many European fathers would contribute to their support, and that many 'half-caste' children were being destroyed by Aborigines. He knew of one 'half-caste' girl, about 10 years of age, who 'was running wild with the blacks in the bush', and predicted that she would be raped by the 'first unscrupulous white that meets her':

> I have spoken to the Warden of the Kimberley Gold Fields, also to the Doctor's House [sic] the Resident Magistrate at Derby and several of the older settlers and

they are all of opinion that it is extremely desirable that such half-castes should be taken away from their country and properly brought up[,] *not only because they are partially 'white blooded', but that growing up with the blacks and having some of the intelligence of the white, they will become extremely dangerous.* It has been suggested to me that in order to remedy to some extent the increase of the half-caste race, that a fine should be imposed on the station owner on whose run the child is born.[5] [my emphasis]

Marsden further reported that Mr Ord, the Sub-Inspector of Police for West Kimberley, believed that in nearly every case, European men would willingly contribute to the upbringing of their children. He thought that the children should not be taken from their mothers until they were 5 years old and said that they made splendid station hands when they were trained.

G. S. Olivey, who was appointed Travelling Inspector of Aborigines for the Aborigines Department in August 1899, provided detailed reports about the number, work status and health of the Aboriginal people on all the stations he visited. He, too, expressed alarm at the presence of children of mixed parentage on the stations and near the goldfields. He was especially concerned about the fate of the girls. His reports provided evidence that was used by Henry Prinsep, at that time Chief Inspector of Aborigines, in his yearly report to the government.

In his 1901 report, Prinsep identified four issues that required solutions through legislation. They were set out in his report as follows:

(a) The future dealing with half-castes;

(b) the checking of immorality with whites;

(c) the guardianship of infants; and

(d) further supervision of those employed in the pearling trade.

Prinsep wrote of the 'growing evil of miscegenation', of the 'evil influences which surrounded children during their childhood', and the intermixing of 'natives' with 'Asiatics', which was 'bad for the future of the race'. He thought that it was the government's duty 'not to allow these children, whose blood is half British, to grow up as vagrants and outcasts, as their mothers now are'.[6]

These were the sentiments that found expression in the 1905 Aborigines Act, which gave Prinsep, as Protector of Aborigines, considerable power over the lives of Aboriginal people. Before considering the 1905 Act, however, it is important to understand another contemporary debate: the need for reserves for Aboriginal people.

The idea of reserves

From the time of the passage of the Imperial Land Act of 1842, the colonial government had been empowered to reserve land for the use of Aboriginal people. Clause 3 stated that the Governor, representing Her Majesty, could exempt land from sale for a wide variety of public purposes. These were set out in detail in this clause and included reserves of land 'for the use or benefit of the Aboriginal inhabitants of the country'.[7] These words were repeated exactly in the 1872 Land Regulations, when Governor Weld proclaimed the 'Act to repeal the Acts of Parliament now in force respecting the disposal of waste lands of the Crown in the Australian Colonies, and to make other provisions in lieu thereof'.[8] However, apart from some small areas allotted to the Benedictines at New Norcia and Subiaco, no land had been reserved 'for the use or benefit' of Aboriginal people before 1878.[9]

Between 1878 and 1887, several areas were reserved for possible Aboriginal use. A large reserve of 50,000 acres was declared between the Sanford and Murchison rivers in 1878 at the request of the Anglican Bishop of Perth. On the recommendation of John Forrest, then Commissioner of Crown Lands, a further 100,000 acres was reserved in 1883 near Mount Dalgety in the Upper Gascoyne (later exchanged for a reserve on the Forrest River in the Kimberley), and in 1884 an area of 600,000 acres was reserved on the Fraser River, on the western side of King Sound.

In 1887, 2,000 acres was reserved for the Swan Native and Half-caste Mission, while small areas were set aside as reserves adjoining Roebourne and Carnarvon town sites. While at first no attempt was made to develop the areas reserved in the North West for the specific use of Aborigines, the Aborigines Protection Board, set up in 1887, was made responsible for their management.[10]

In 1882, another Imperial Land Act was passed, along with regulations, under which the Governor continued to have the power to declare Aboriginal Reserves.[11] This power was questioned by many speakers in a debate on a Bill to provide for certain matters connected with Aborigines, introduced in 1888. According to these objectors, the power to reserve land for the use of Aborigines should pass to the elected government under the system of responsible government about to be introduced.[12] The Bill under debate did not become law, and the power to proclaim Aboriginal Reserves remained with the Governor until 1898. The 1898 Land Act, under which all matters connected with land were to be controlled by the locally elected government, again contained a special section on reserves, which could be set up 'for the use or benefit of the Aboriginal inhabitants'.[13]

The idea of the government actually using its powers and setting up reserves for Aborigines was first fully canvassed in 1883 by Bishop Gibney of the Roman Catholic Church, well before the passage of the Aborigines Protection Act of 1886, under the terms of which the Aborigines Protection Board was established. He spoke of Aborigines having been deprived in the past of 'their means of natural subsistence', which had reduced their numbers. He pointed to new developments in the North West in the more recently settled areas, where the condition of Aborigines was 'little better than that of slaves', and he called on the government and the Legislative Council to give careful attention to introducing new legislation for their protection.

Bishop Gibney referred to Victoria's policy of gathering Aborigines together in 'stations' as the one most likely to satisfy the three things that the government should aim to achieve in Western Australia. He identified these goals as the protection of the 'just rights' of Aborigines, the supply of their bodily wants, and their moral and religious instruction and training.

> Stations should be formed (in the first instance on a small scale) at well selected centres, to serve at once for places of relief for the needy, the sick and the infirm, as places of religious and industrial training for the children (both native and half-caste), and as homes to which the natives not employed by the settlers might resort to find food and employment. These stations should be under managers appointed by the Government, who should, whenever practicable, be Ministers of religion or other missionary agents. It should be publicly notified that after a fixed time all relief given to the natives in the way of provisions, clothing etc., will be given at these stations: and induce-ments should be held out in other ways to them to regard these places as their homesteads. A small hospital should be provided at each station for the sick and the infirm, and arrangements should be made for the care of children of natives employed away from the station by the Settlers of the District.[14]

Gibney believed that such measures would be too late to arrest the 'apparent extinction' of the Aborigines in the older districts but that the remainder could be saved by a wise policy. He was doubtful as to how far the same system could be adopted for dealing with Aborigines in the south as well as in the north, 'where their numbers are large and their utilization as labourers is a matter of much importance to the settlers'. But he believed that their con-ditions of labour should be such as to guard against 'the deteriorating influences that have been so fatal to them elsewhere'.

Gibney recognized that these plans would involve the reser-vation of suitable blocks of land and considerable expense, which he claimed the government could meet through revenues derived from the lease and sale of Crown lands. According to him, the first step in carrying out such a policy would be the setting up of reserves in several districts; the second would be to establish a board 'for the protection and management of the Aborigines'; and the third, the appointment of local committees or guardians to act in the districts under instructions from the board.

The Forrest Commission set up in 1883, in its terms of reference, was asked to consider the question of reserves 'intended to confer benefits on the natives', which were requested by mission bodies, and to consider further

> the question of the formation of native centres or stations, whether for aged and infirm, juvenile, or able bodied Aboriginals, such as have been organized or assisted by other Australian Governments, and what part, if any, the Government of this Colony should take therein: and to state the estimated cost of carrying out any recommendation made under these heads.

The commission was clearly reluctant to address this question directly, but prevaricated with statements about the fact that the Aboriginal people were 'fast disappearing' and about the reluctance of Aborigines to leave their own country. It believed that the majority of Aborigines were in the service of settlers and not, 'as is often found in other parts of the Colony, without any fixed employment'.

> The difficulty of making large reserves for natives is, that they have a love for their own locality, and do not like to leave it under any circumstances; besides this wherever the white man goes the native will be certain to hang about the station, and will not for long go away into the bush. The native soon learns to find tobacco, tea, sugar and flour indispensable; it is therefore impossible to expect that when a country is settled the natives will for long keep away from the settlers' homes, nor is it desirable that they should do so.[15]

The reluctance of the commissioners to support the establishment of reserves for Aboriginal people is explained here in terms of the interests of the Aborigines, but the commissioners also knew that the pastoralists and pearlers of the north could not envisage doing without their Aboriginal work force.

However, the commissioners recommended that all Resident Magistrates be nominated as Native Protectors, and that they be given the authority to appoint Honorary Protectors throughout the country 'with the duty of looking after the welfare of Aborigines generally'. In the 1886 Act, this idea was followed up, but the power to appoint Protectors of Aborigines was given to the Aborigines Protection Board with each appointment being published in the *Government Gazette*.[16] Some of these Protectors were subsequently responsible for advocating the development of reserves for Aborigines. In any event, although the 1886 Aborigines Protection Act did not include any specific plan to reserve land, the board set up under the Act had responsibility for Aboriginal Reserves.

In 1892, Bishop Gibney again offered a long list of recommendations on the treatment of Aborigines of all ages and in all parts of the colony. This time, his focus was much more clearly on the north. He listed the number of Aborigines in each magisterial district, a total of nearly 14,000 persons, not including those 'said to be very numerous' in the Kimberley and in the eastern and southern districts. Of those enumerated, 9,400 were said to be in the Gascoyne and Roebourne districts, about 5,000 of whom were employed by settlers. Gibney claimed that two main principles underpinned his recommendations. The first was that

> coming here as a civilized and Christian nation, we are bound in taking away from the native races of this continent, and occupying to our own advantage the lands which are their natural heritage, to render them a full compensation in the shape of legal protection, bodily maintenance, and mental and religious instruction.[17]

His second principle, obviously tailored to appease settler interests, concerned Aboriginal labour:

> The employment of black or coloured labour in our tropical districts is almost a necessary condition to their

being settled by Europeans: and it is far better that the existing native races should be converted, if this be practicable, into the permanent labouring population of the country, than that we should be driven to import Chinese or Coolie labourers from without. It is no less to our own interests than to that of the aborigines them-selves that our mode of dealing with them should be such as to secure both these ends.

The bishop's recommendations were complex. The first was that contracts should be between the employers of Aboriginal labour and the government, rather than between the employers and the employees. While he did not advocate the payment of money wages, he thought that there ought to be strict guidelines about the pro-vision of food, clothing and other allowances, 'much as in the present Aborigines Act', but with better provisions for the care of the aged and the sick, and for the industrial training and elementary education of children. He recommended a system of reserves for 'adult natives employed as domestic servants in and about the towns', as well as for the 'wilder natives' who were not employed by settlers but who had been deprived of their means of subsistence. He, too, hoped to separate Aboriginal children from their parents and turn them into an Aboriginal working class, especially trained to be of use to the settlers.

Some of the goldfields in the north had been operating for many years, but those in the south-east of the colony near Coolgardie and Kalgoorlie were not well established before the 1890s. Here, most of the digging for gold was undertaken by European men, many of them from the eastern colonies of Australia and from overseas. At first, they had little use for the labour of the Aborigines who had inhabited the areas where gold was found. By the second half of the 1890s, the correspondence of officials working in the goldfields area began to suggest the introduction of a system of reserves for Aboriginal people who had lost their land.

In 1896, C. A. Bailey, an Inspector of Aborigines, was instructed by the Aborigines Protection Board to investigate the condition of the Aborigines in the goldfields area. He undertook a lengthy tour of the Coolgardie fields, 'embracing every mining centre from Norseman to Mount Malcolm in the North, including Kurnalpi and various other towns'. He reported that Aborigines were tending to concentrate in the settled districts near the mining centres. He had counted 290 adult Aborigines in the region of Coolgardie and another fifty at Southern Cross. He believed that Europeans had utilized the waterholes and soaks and left Aborigines with little alternative but to move nearer to settled areas where they could get water. He reported that they were sufficiently clothed, but recommended that the board establish food depots in Coolgardie and Kalgoorlie 'for the better maintenance of Aboriginal women and children'. He suggested that these Aborigines tended to quarrel with one another when congregated together. His report included the recommendation that a reserve 'within reasonable distance of the two larger centres should be set apart for the exclusive use of the natives', but he believed that 'any efforts in my opinion to establish a mission station on the fields would be futile'.[18]

In November 1895, A. G. Clifton, the warden of the East Murchison Goldfields, wrote in his report to the Under Secretary for Mines:

> I do not at all approve of the natives loitering about the camps and would like to drive them away. But in a district like this is at present where there is no game, and, as far as I can see, nothing for them to live upon, and very little water, I think it is hardly fair to drive them away from the water, unless some other arrangement can be made for their welfare…
>
> I believe from a conversation I had while in Perth with Reverend Bishop Gibney that he would take over any natives that the Government would hand over to him, but I do not remember the conditions.[19]

Another letter to the Under Secretary written the previous month from the warden of the Kimberley Goldfield, W. D. Cummins, suggested that a system of reserves for Aborigines offered a solution to this problem. He claimed he had got the idea from Sergeant Brophy, who had served in the Kimberley area for eight years.

This system has been tried in other countries, notably in America, with success. If those natives who are driven off their own hunting grounds were placed on a Reserve under the management and protection of the Aborigines Protection Board, native troubles would very soon be a thing of the past.

During the present week a white has been speared, fortunately not fatally, by natives, at Mount Dockrell: the result of natives being allowed near the workings. Both for the protection of the whites and the better management of the natives, I strongly concur in Sergt Brophy's suggestion of the system of 'native reserves'.[20]

In the following year, a report from the resident medical officer at Broome, H. W. Brownrigg, painted an appalling picture of the poor health and abject poverty of the Aboriginal people in the region around Beagle Bay. He had the task of vaccinating about one thousand Aborigines in the area, where both food and drugs were in short supply. The pearling fleet visited this region for wood and water, and Brownrigg claimed that

> the intercourse between the coloured men and the gins is the curse of this coast, [because] the majority of the former have syphilis. Most of the gins, some of them only children, are infected, and to this cause most of the loathsome diseases are attributable.

Although Brownrigg did not specifically advocate a system of reserves, he concluded that 'until the women can be protected, the future outlook of the blacks will be a gloomy one'.[21]

Support for reserves also came from Bishop Riley of the Anglican Church[22] after a tour of the north in 1896. He wrote to the Governor upon his return, setting out some of his impressions of Aboriginal–European relations, and revealing that he had changed his mind about some issues as a result of his tour. He referred first of all to his belief that the Aborigines Protection Board should be replaced by a government department and minister for Aboriginal affairs who would be responsible to parliament. 'Public opinion, or rather the Opposition would keep him up to the mark.' He referred to the cruelty of the system whereby 'natives' were indentured to the settlers. 'This is only a form of slavery, as the natives for the most part do not know what it means or for the rest do not dare to refuse to sign the document.' He believed that the policy of 'dispersing the natives' should be defined so that it could be understood, and that a policeman should not be permitted to shoot a 'native' unless he was really attacked. He added in a footnote to his letter that 'dispersing the natives' was a euphemism for murder. On some stations, he reported, Aborigines were only fed while they were actively employed by Europeans. 'Afterwards they are turned out into the bush to feed themselves. It is when this happens that they spear the cattle and then are hunted down.' Bishop Riley believed that

> there should be hospitals on Native Reserves for the old, the sick and the infirm. The Reserve question is most pressing—at present if natives have to leave a station when it has been fenced in—or a goldfield when it has been taken up, they have no where to go to, as hostile tribes or families would kill them. Under these circumstances they ought to have Cities [sic] or Reserves of refuge.
>
> I believe these reserves might be made almost self supporting, as from what I have seen from the work of the natives at Roebourne, I feel certain that if properly managed they would work very well—they can in the north do better work than white men.
>
> From what I gather from men who have been on the distant goldfields, the worst places for the natives are near these fields.[23]

Some of the most disturbing reports on other matters came to the board from George Marsden in the North West. In May 1896, the Governor was so disturbed by Marsden's reports of the flogging of Aborigines that he sent a request to the Premier that the matter be investigated.[24] Marsden also reported on the practice of Aboriginal men offering their women to Malay pearlers in return for food, and wrote of the prevalence of syphilis among Aborigines and the presence of many old people in desperate need of food and medical care.[25] Marsden was anxious that 'half-caste' children, whom he encountered on his tour of the North West stations, be removed by the board. In one instance, he referred to a boy who was developing 'a cruel and cunning nature. He will not look at a white man, but remains with blacks the whole time or with the cook'.[26]

These debates about 'half-castes' and reserves for Aboriginal people, which were increasingly common in the 1890s, reflected a growing sense of unease by many Western Australian citizens about the fate of Aboriginal men, women and children whose cultures and livelihoods had been destroyed by many decades of settler capitalism. However, there was almost universal underlying contempt for Aboriginal culture, a taken-for-granted assumption that the land belonged to Europeans, and a belief in the continuing importance of Aboriginal labour. These ideas combined to persuade apparently reasonable people that the only solution to the Aboriginal 'problem' was to be found in some system of reserves, selectively applied.

As a solution to the problems of poverty, homelessness and sickness that the Aborigines Protection Board was beginning to confront, the government began allotting large areas as reserves to be managed by mission bodies. Although they would continue to need financial assistance, as they had in the past, these missions were essentially offering to take over the huge problems that the colony had to confront as a result of six decades of alienation of Aboriginal land and exploitation of Aboriginal labour.

The 1905 Aborigines Act

The 1901 report of the Aborigines Department contained references to a draft Bill that would deal with Aboriginal affairs. This Bill was a precursor to the final passage of the 1905 Aborigines Act, which would be a decisive step in determining the future treatment of Aboriginal people. The remarks on the draft Bill, written by Henry Prinsep, the Chief Inspector of Aborigines, reiterated the views

REHEARSING THE FUTURE: 'HALF-CASTES' AND RESERVES

expressed in the 1901 Aborigines Department report. He not only underlined his racist beliefs, shared by most Western Australians at that time, but also foreshadowed a policy that would eventually lead to the systematic removal of Aboriginal children from their parents and the attempt to control marriage relations.[27] Prinsep was alarmed at the growing pattern of prostitution of Aboriginal women, which he believed was often encouraged by the men; he deplored the mixing of Aboriginal and Asian 'blood', even though he recognized that Asian men often treated their wives well, because these marriages would 'probably fill some of the Northern districts with a mongrel race, very inimical to their future quietude'. The fate of children of mixed descent was a major concern.

In December 1904, Walter Roth submitted his report as commissioner investigating the 'condition of the natives' in Western Australia. His ideas about children of mixed descent were closely aligned with those of Henry Prinsep, who was by then the Chief Protector of Aborigines. Roth wrote in his report of the future of 'vagabondism and harlotry' that would be the fate of 'the many hundred half-caste children' in the State, and of the treatment of these children as described to him by the many people he had interviewed. He referred to several clauses in the draft Bill, which would eventually become the 1905 Aborigines Act, as essential for solving the problems connected with children of mixed descent, including the sections that ultimately gave the Chief Inspector great power over them as their guardian. Roth also argued for a wide-ranging policy on reserves for Aboriginal people, as hunting grounds, as sanctuaries and asylums for the indigent, and as places set aside for the removal of 'undesirable' people from particular districts.[28]

In order to respond to these widely held fears about miscegenation, and about the number and fate of children of mixed descent, the 1905 Aborigines Act prohibited the movements of Aboriginal women and young Aboriginal persons.[29] No woman or no male or female Aborigine or 'half-caste' under 16 years was permitted to be on board a ship, and Aboriginal women and girls under 16 were not to be near creeks used by pearlers. It would be an offence for non-Aboriginal persons to cohabit with Aborigines, and an old Act was given new life under clause 44, which made it an offence to entice girls away from schools or institutions. Under clause 42, 'no marriage of a female Aboriginal with any person other than an Aboriginal shall be celebrated without the permission, in writing, of the Chief Protector'.

Clause 60 set out twelve subclauses about which the Governor might make regulations, including 'enabling any aboriginal or half-caste child to be sent to and detained in an aboriginal institution, industrial school, or orphanage'. The Chief Protector was to be 'the legal guardian of every Aboriginal or half-caste child until such child attains the age of 16 years'. In this way, the Chief Protector would set out to remove children of mixed descent from their parents, and to control Aboriginal marriage relations in order to favour the dominance of European physical characteristics.

The Act gave the Governor wide powers to declare Aboriginal Reserves, to alter their boundaries, or to abolish them. He could also appoint superintendents of reserves. Through the Chief Protector, he could compel any Aboriginal person to live on a reserve, except for those persons who were employed or who held a permit allowing their absence from a reserve, or any female married to a non-Aboriginal person. Non-Aboriginal people were not entitled to enter an Aboriginal reserve. These powers left open the possibility that some Aborigines would be left alone, but also allowed that any or all Aborigines, except for those who were specifically exempted, could be forced to live quite apart from European society. These clauses added to the possibility of controlling both the labour force and the inter-marriage of European and Aboriginal people.[30]

The first experiment in economic assimilation, in the first half of the nineteenth century, involved some of the same features as the second attempt beginning early in the twentieth century. Aboriginal children were removed from contact with their parents, they were obliged to work in a variety of ways without wages, and they were taught basic skills in literacy and numeracy so that they would be useful workers for a European elite. The children were to be prevented, if possible, from returning to their own people, but were married to one another wherever possible. It was hoped that they would become the nucleus of an Aboriginal working class, assimilated only to the extent necessary for them to become rural workers and domestic servants. These arrangements were put in place by missionaries who, while professing to believe in their roles as agents of civilization and education, also recognized and promoted the obvious value of Aboriginal child labour to the local settlers. The twentieth-century planning for partial future assimilation, as expressed in the 1905 Act, envisaged the gradual breeding out of the 'black blood', by forcibly separating so-called 'half-caste' children from their Aboriginal families and controlling their future marriages, so that their offspring would be of lighter skin colour.

Other legislative controls on Aboriginal people

During the 1890s, a number of other attempts had been made to control Aboriginal people by the introduction of new laws. In 1892, the Aboriginal Offenders Act of 1883 was amended to make whipping the preferred method of dealing with offenders, although they could still be imprisoned for two years as well as being whipped.[31] In his second reading speech on the Bill in the House of Assembly, the Attorney General, Septimus Burt, said that depredations by 'natives' were becoming more frequent:

> Year after year we are told that Rottnest is no prison whatever for these natives; that they simply come back from there worse than when they went there; they get sleek and fat there; and that in fact they rather like it. That being so, we have to consider what punishment is more likely to have any deterrent effect upon these natives. I have come to the conclusion myself, and have done so for years, that the only way of effectually dealing with all these coloured races, whether blackfellows, or Indians, or Chinamen, is to treat them like children. I have proved it, in my own small experience. You can only deal with them effectually, like you deal with naughty children—whip them. It is the only argument they recognize, brute force.

> ...Moreover, it will save a great deal of trouble and expense if we whip these natives and let them go, instead of sending them hundreds of miles all the way to Rottnest.[32]

In the same year, the Aborigines Protection Act was amended to give magistrates the power to imprison Aborigines for three months, with or without hard labour, for breach of contract.[33]

The passage of the 1892 Police Act, which consolidated earlier Acts and strengthened police powers, added to the controlling mechanisms that were now closing in on Aboriginal people, thus foreshadowing further restraints in the early twentieth century.[34] In the following year, the Constitution Act Amendment Act, which enfranchised all male Europeans for the election of members of the Legislative Assembly, specifically denied Aboriginal men the right to vote. The Act declared that 'no Aboriginal native of Australia...shall be entitled to be registered, except in respect to a freehold qualification, for the Legislative Council and the Legislative Assembly respectively'. Section 26 stated that 'in this Act the words "Aboriginal native" shall include persons of half blood'.[35] In these ways, the government of Western Australia used its legislative powers to prevent any possibility of future assimilation of the Aboriginal population.

The history of the treatment of Aboriginal children reveals that, from the time of settlement until the passage of the Aborigines Act of 1905, there were no policies that were designed to protect Aboriginal culture and none that aimed at genuine assimilation. The Aboriginal people were removed from their land, which was essential for their economic and cultural survival. Their children were not incorporated into the education system, while those designated as 'half-castes' were removed into institutions. Finally, all Aboriginal people near centres of European settlement who were not active workers in the European economy were removed to reserves. These policies reflected the self-interest and the racism of settler society.

CONCLUSION:

Holding a work force in bondage

ECONOMIC imperatives explain why the first European settlers in Western Australia used their own children, and children of the poor, as a work force in the early days of settlement, until the arrival of convicts in 1850. For the same reason, European settlers involved in opening up the North West in the last four decades of the nineteenth century had to rely almost entirely on Aboriginal family and child labour in order to establish themselves. The wealth of the elite families of Western Australian society was thus created by a European work force of family and child labour paid a minimum wage, and by Aboriginal men, women and children who were not paid a wage but provided with rations.

The colonial elite inherited an ideology that justified the passage of legislation holding this work force in bondage. Ideas about class differences, and the payment of minimum wages to labourers, had their origins in English society, where much of the wealth, held in a few hands, had been made in earlier centuries, first of all from the expropriation of peasant land through the system of enclosures, and then out of the slave trade and various early imperial and colonial enterprises. Ideas about the barbarism of the black races were also embedded in English society and had been used for several centuries as justification for the treatment of Africans as slaves. In this new frontier situation of Western Australia, laws were passed to control the movement of workers, to allow the exploitation of child labour and to bind Aboriginal children into a system of apprenticeships. In this way, the settler elite sought to realize the dream of owning or controlling vast land-holdings, made productive by a compliant work force.

A system of education in the colony developed slowly. Compulsory education was not introduced until 1870, and even then there were few schools outside the closely settled areas. Secondary schooling in the nineteenth century was available only to children of the wealthiest families who could afford private schools. Therefore, there was little chance of upward mobility for the children of the working poor. The education of Aboriginal children was not even addressed until 1886, when it was officially declared that this burden belonged to the Aborigines Protection Board—a responsibility that was then passed on to the Aborigines Department in 1897. European authority figures believed that mission bodies were best able to educate Aboriginal children, and this solution kept European and Aboriginal children separated.

The pattern of child labour was complex. The first unaccompanied child workers arrived in the 1830s, followed in the 1840s by the Parkhurst boys, who were hired out to the settlers. Aboriginal children were first taken from their parents and institutionalized at the Wesleyan Mission School from 1840, and later at other institutions, including New Norcia, in order to provide a cheap labour force for settlers. Many European children worked with their parents on sheep runs and farms in a pattern of family labour, while in the North West, Aboriginal children worked on cattle stations and as divers on pearling boats, some of them taken by force from their parents by 'blackbirders'.

Until the 1860s, there was no safety net for European children whose family circumstances left them penniless or abandoned. When Catholic and Anglican churches established orphanages providing a place for these children, it was in return for various kinds of labour. By the end of the century, both European and Aboriginal children were inmates in a complex pattern of institutions designed to assist abandoned or delinquent children to become a useful part of a future work force. So-called delinquent children often found themselves incarcerated for extended periods, even though the courts may have given them only a light sentence of a few weeks.

These working children of European descent, unaccompanied or with parents, were the servants of the settler elite. Aboriginal children, on the other hand, were essentially slaves who received no wages and had no accessible legal rights. And by the last decade of the century, as male authority figures considered what they called 'the problem' of children of mixed descent, new discourses began to develop that would provide the rationale for the large-scale removal of children from their parents in the twentieth century.

ABBREVIATIONS USED IN NOTES

AJCP	Australian Joint Copying Project
ANZHESJ	*Australia New Zealand History of Education Society Journal*
ASW	*Australian Social Work*
BL	Battye Library
CO	Colonial Office, London
COR	Colonial Office Records, London
CSO	Colonial Secretary's Office, Western Australia
CSR	Colonial Secretary's Records, Western Australia
Ed.	King Edward VII
H. of C.	House of Commons
JAS	*Journal of Australian Studies*
JRAHS	*Journal of the Royal Australian Historical Society*
SROWA	State Records Office of Western Australia
UWA	The University of Western Australia
Vict.	Queen Victoria
WAGG	*Western Australian Government Gazette*
WAHSJP	*Western Australian Historical Society Journal and Proceedings*
WA Leg. Co. V&P	Western Australian Legislative Council Votes and Proceedings
WA Parl. V&P	Western Australian Parliament Votes and Proceedings
WAPD	Western Australian Parliamentary Debates

NOTES

Introduction: Understanding childhood in nineteenth-century Western Australia

1   For historiographical articles on the history of childhood, with detailed footnotes, see Penelope Hetherington, 'Childhood and youth in Australia', *JAS*, no. 18, 1986, pp. 3–18, and 'Writing the history of childhood in Western Australia', in Hetherington, ed., *Childhood and Society in Western Australia*, Perth, 1988. For histories of Australian children that deal at least partly with the nineteenth century, see S. Fabian & M. Loh, *Children in Australia: An Outline History*, Melbourne, 1980; G. Featherstone, ed., *The Colonial Child*, Melbourne, 1981; Ken McNab & Russell Ward, 'The nature and nurture of the first generation of native-born Australians', *Historical Studies*, vol. 10, 1962, pp. 289–308; Beverley Earnshaw, 'The colonial children', *Push from the Bush*, vol. 9, 1981, pp. 28–43; Portia Robinson, *The Hatch and Brood of Time: A Study of the First Generation of Native Born White Australians, 1888–1928*, Melbourne, 1985; and Jan Kociumbas, *Australian Childhood: A History*, Sydney, 1997.

2   For a discussion of historical constructions of 'childhood', see Ian Jackson, 'Children of the fourth estate: Public representations of "children" and "childhood"', *JAS*, no. 36, 1993, pp. 65–79.

3   Halsbury's *Statutes of England*, 2nd edn, London, 1949, vol. 12, p. 928.

4   For a discussion of the concept of 'slavery' in connection with Aboriginal labour, see Raymond Evans, ' "Kings in brass crescents": Defining Aboriginal labour patterns in colonial Queensland', in Kay Saunders, ed., *Indentured Labour in the British Empire, 1834–1920*, London, 1984, pp. 183–204. See also Alison Holland, 'Feminism, colonialism and Aboriginal workers: An anti-slavery crusade', *Labour History*, no. 69, 1995, pp. 52–64.

5   See I. H. van den Driesen, 'Convicts and migrants in Western Australia, 1850–1868: Their number, nature and ethnic origins', *JRAHS*, vol. 73, part 1, 1986, pp. 40–58.

6   For the early political history of the Swan River Colony, see B. K. de Garis, 'Political tutelage 1829–1830', in C. T. Stannage, ed., *A New History of Western Australia*, Perth, 1981, pp. 304–25. For a detailed social history, see C. T. Stannage, *The People of Perth: A Social History of Western Australia's Capital City*, Perth, 1979.

7   I especially value two articles on child and family labour. They are W. Minge-Kalman, 'The Industrial Revolution and the European family: The institutionalization of "childhood" as a market for family labour', *Comparative Studies in Society and History*, vol. 20, 1978, pp. 454–68; and V. Goddard & B. White, 'Child workers and capitalist development:

An introductory note and bibliography', *Development and Change*, vol. 13, 1982, pp. 465–77.

8   SROWA, AN 24, CSR, vol. 137, Incoming Correspondence. See, for example, the indenture agreement of Frederick Friend made in May 1829, which states that he agrees for himself, his wife Frances, and his daughter, Mary Anne, to serve Henry Campbell for seven years in return for a passage to the colony for himself and family and such food and fuel as the regulations provide for. His daughter was 1 year old at this time.

9   There was no Hansard recording of the debates of the Legislative Council for the first six years, but in 1990, as a way of celebrating 100 years of responsible government, an edition entitled *WA Parliamentary Debates, 1870–1876* was published, reconstructed in 1970 out of the contemporary reporting of the proceedings in the *Inquirer and Commercial News*, the *Perth Gazette and Western Australian Times*, the *Herald* and the *Official Votes and Proceedings of the Legislative Council*, which had recorded the 'Business of the Chamber' but not the debates. See the foreword to this volume by N. J. Burrell, chief Hansard reporter.

10   See Paul Buddee, *Fate of the Artful Dodger: Parkhurst Boys Transported to Australia and New Zealand, 1842–1852*, Perth, 1984; and Andrew Gill, *Forced Labour for the West: Parkhurst Convicts 'Apprenticed' in Western Australia, 1842–1851*, Perth, 1997.

11   The classic text on education is that of David Mossenson, *State Education in Western Australia, 1829–1960*, Perth, 1972. There is some literature on education provided by church schools and on many other aspects of education in the nineteenth century. Aboriginal children are simply not mentioned in most of these texts.

Chapter 1: Counting the European population

1   There is a substantial literature about demographic transition in Australian society, discussing the gradual reduction in the size of European families in the nineteenth century. See Helen Ware, ed., *Family and Fertility Formation: Australian Bibliography and Essays*, Canberra, 1972; J. C. Caldwell et al., *Towards an Understanding of Demographic Change*, Canberra, 1976; L. T. Ruzicka & J. C. Caldwell, *The End of Demographic Transition in Australia*, Canberra, 1977; P. F. McDonald, *Marriage in Australia: Age at First Marriage and Proportions Marrying 1860–1971*, Canberra, 1978; J. C. Caldwell, 'Towards a restatement of demographic transition theory', ch. 2, in Caldwell, ed., *The Persistence of High Fertility*, Canberra, 1978; and Gordon A. Carmichael, *With This Ring: First Marriage Patterns, Trends and Prospects in Australia*, Canberra, 1988. For Western Australia, see Margaret Grellier, 'The family: Some aspects of its demography and ideology in nineteenth century Western Australia', in C. T. Stannage, ed., *A New History of Western Australia*, Perth, 1981; and

Margaret Anderson, 'Marriage and children in Western Australia, 1842–1849', in P. Grimshaw, C. McConville & E. McEwan, eds, *Families in Colonial Australia*, Sydney, 1985, pp. 49–56. For Australia generally, see Alison MacKinnon, 'The state as agent of demographic change? The higher education of women and fertility decline, 1880–1930', *JAS*, no. 37, 1993, pp. 58–71.

2   The *Colonial Blue Books* for the period 1837–69 (except for 1849) provided a compilation of official figures about the people of the Swan River Colony and their activities and, after 1848, included the information gained from the most recent census. After the introduction of self-government, this information was published in the *Western Australian Blue Books* from 1870 to 1905, except for the consolidation of the issues from 1896 to 1898 in the *Statistical Register*, an alternative source of information that began publication in 1896. See *Checklist of Censuses, Blue Books and Statistical Registers of Western Australia*, BL, 1981.

3   I. H. van den Driesen, essay 3 in *Essays on Immigration Policy and Population in Western Australia, 1850–1901*, Perth, 1986.

4   These economic developments and demographic variables are examined in R. T. Appleyard, 'Western Australia: Economic and demographic growth, 1850–1914', in C. T. Stannage, ed., *A New History of Western Australia*, Perth, 1981, ch. 6.

5   *Checklist of Censuses*. For the population figures on 1 January 1836, BL, AJCP Reel 301, CO 18, Governor's Despatches nos 99 and 118. The first census in the Swan River Colony, the only one for which schedules are extant, was in 1832.

6   *Historical Records of Australia*, Stirling to Murray, 30 January 1830, pp. 622 ff., 'Abstract of the General Muster Book, showing the Amount and Description of Population at the End of the Year'.

7   SROWA, AN 24, CSR, Acc. 36, vol. 4, folio 79. Inward Correspondence, 1 January to 10 February 1830.

8   SROWA, AN 24, CSR, Acc. 36, vol. 5, folio 141. Inward Correspondence, 11 February to 30 March. See the details about the family of John Burdett Wittenoom.

9   SROWA, AN 24, CSR, Acc. 36, vol. 6, folio 2. Inward Correspondence, 2 April to 20 May 1830.

10   SROWA, AN 24, CSR, Acc. 36, vol. 110, folios 166–169, 1842.

11   Two children died on the voyage and two children were born.

12   SROWA, AN 24, CSR, Acc. 36, vol. 110, folios 178–183, 1842.

13   ibid. William and Frederick.

14   See Pamela Statham, 'Swan River Colony, 1829–1850', in Stannage, ed., *A New History*, pp. 181–210. Footnote 46 provides details about the seven ships that brought these boys.

15   *Checklist of Censuses*; and Ian Berryman, 'The early censuses of the Swan River Colony', *Push from the Bush*, no. 5, 1979, pp. 55–62.

16   BL, AJCP Reel 298, 1832, CO 18/10, pp. 112–56. See also Ian Berryman,
      A Colony Detailed: The First Census of Western Australia, 1832, Perth, 1979.

17   BL, AJCP Reel 31, 1836, CO 18/16, pp. 78–97.

18   H. of C. *Sessional Paper* 687 of 1837–38.

19   Ann Bryan, W. Kelly and M. Stenson are listed as servants; T. Burges,
      G. Wall, G. Watt and M. Watt as labourers.

20   *Blue Book*, 1834–37.

21   Military establishment: fifty-five children in 1844, seventy-three in 1846
      and forty-four in 1850. There were 126 children of Enrolled Pensioners in
      1850.

22   *WAGG*, 19 December 1848. Census, 10 October 1848, General Summary.

23   N. G. Butlin, J. Ginswick & P. Statham, 'Colonial statistics before 1850',
      ANU Source Papers in Economic History, no. 12, 1986, p. 85. I have taken
      the total of females from the *Blue Book* figures as approximate.

24   Reached by subtracting the emigrant total from the immigrant total.

25   See M. Anderson, 'Marriage and children in Western Australia'.

26   See ch. 2 for more details about this group of children.

27   Statham, 'Swan River Colony', footnote 46, p. 712; and Paul Buddee, *Fate
      of the Artful Dodger: Parkhurst Boys Transported to Australia and New
      Zealand, 1842–1852*, Perth, 1984, p. 165.

28   6 Vict., No. 8, 1842. *An Act to Regulate the Apprenticeship and otherwise
      Provide for the Guardianship and Control of a Certain Class of Juvenile
      Immigrants*.

29   Buddee, *Fate of the Artful Dodger*, p. 51.

30   *Census of the Population, and Return of Stock and Crops*, Western
      Australia, 1848; *Statistics of Western Australia, Registrar General's Office*,
      Perth, 1854; *Western Australia, Census of 1859*, Perth, 1859.

31   van den Dreisen, *Essays*, for details of the claim that an 1861 census was
      also conducted.

32   *Census of the Colony of Western Australia, taken on 31st March, 1870,
      also the General Statistics of the Colony for the Year Ending 31st December
      1869*, Perth, 1870.

33   *Census of the Colony of Western Australia taken on 3rd of April 1881.
      Statistical Tables Relating to the Colony from 1872–1881 Inclusive*, Perth,
      1882.

34   *Census of Western Australia, April 1891*, General Report with Appendices
      by Walter Gale, Superintendent of Census, Perth, 1892.

35   *Seventh Census of Western Australia, taken for the Night of 31st March,
      1901*, compiled under the direction of Malcolm A. C. Fraser, Registrar
      General, Government Statistician and Superintendent of Census, Perth,
      1904.

Chapter 2: Family and child labour

1   Pamela Statham, comp., *Dictionary of Western Australia, 1829–1914*,
         vol. 1, Perth, 1981. The Governor, Sir James Stirling, was granted 100,000
         acres; the Surveyor General, J. S. Roe, 5,600 acres; the Colonial Secretary,
         N. Broun, 9,626 acres; and the Attorney General, G. F. Moore, 12,000
         acres. Peter Latour, whose grant was managed by Richard Wells for his
         absent master, claimed 103,000 acres and Thomas Peel was finally granted
         250,000 acres.

2   G. C. Bolton, 'The idea of a colonial gentry', *Historical Studies*, vol. 13,
         1968, pp. 307–28; J. V. Beckett, *The Aristocracy of England, 1660–1914*,
         Oxford, 1986, pp. 87–8. For an analysis of the size of the first capital
         investment in the Swan River Colony, see J. M. R. Cameron, *Ambition's
         Fire: The Agricultural Colonization of Pre-Convict Western Australia*,
         Perth, 1981.

3   George Fletcher Moore, *Diary of Ten Years Eventful Life of an Early Settler
         in Western Australia and also A Descriptive Vocabulary of the Language of
         the Aborigines*, Perth, 1978 [1884], pp. v–vi.

4   For a discussion of the celebratory historiography of so many Western
         Australian historians, see C. T. Stannage, *Western Australia's Heritage: The
         Pioneer Myth*, UWA Extension Services, monograph, no. 1, 1985.

5   J. S. Battye, *Western Australia: A History from its Discovery to the Inaugu-
         ration of the Commonwealth*, Oxford, 1924; F. K. Crowley, 'Master and
         servant in Western Australia, 1829–1851', *WAHSJP*, vol. 4, part 5, 1953,
         pp. 94–115; Alexandra Hasluck, *Thomas Peel of Swan River*, Melbourne,
         1965; Pamela Statham, 'Swan River Colony, 1829–1850', in C. T. Stannage,
         ed., *A New History of Western Australia*, Perth, 1981, pp. 181–210; and
         Jenny Gregory, 'The Gallops of Dalkeith: A re-examination of a pioneer
         family', *Push from the Bush*, no. 22, 1986, pp. 48–72. Gregory's work
         takes account of the economic value of women's work.

6   There is some literature in this field concerning children and family
         labour in other colonies, including G. P. Walsh, 'Factories and factory
         workers in New South Wales, 1788–1900', *Labour History*, no. 21, 1971,
         pp. 1–16; D. McDonald, 'Child and female labour in Sydney 1876–1898',
         ANU Historical Journal, vol. 10/11, 1973–74, pp. 40–9; Beverley
         Earnshaw, 'The convict apprentices, 1820–1838', *Push from the Bush*,
         vol. 5, 1979, pp. 82–97; Michael Horsbrough, 'The apprenticing of
         dependent children in New South Wales between 1850 and 1885', *JAS*,
         no. 7, 1980, pp. 33–54; Shirley Fisher, 'The family and the Sydney
         economy', *Australia 1888*, vol. 9, 1982, pp. 83–7; Michael Gelding,
         'Economic relations in the bourgeois family: Sydney 1870–1940', *Australia
         1888*, vol. 9, 1982, pp. 66–71; Anne O'Brien, 'Poor families in 19th
         century New South Wales', *Australia 1888*, vol. 9, 1982, pp. 29–33. See
         also an analysis of the findings of the 1875 select committee into the
         employment of young people, *Labour History*, no. 21, 1971, pp. 73–5.

7   Enid Russell, *A History of the Law in Western Australia: And its Development from 1829–1979*, Perth, 1980, p. 50.

8   9 Vict., No. 2, 1845. *An Ordinance to Provide for the Maintenance and Relief of Deserted Wives and Children and other Destitute Persons and to Make the Property of Husbands and near Relatives, to whose Assistance they have a Natural Claim, in Certain Circumstances, Available for Support.*

9   ibid., clause 4.

10   ibid., clause 11.

11   *Historical Records of Australia*, vol. 6, pp. 606–8, 'Regulations for the guidance of those who may propose to embark, as settlers, for the new Settlement on the Western Coast of New Holland', 13 January 1829.

12   ibid.

13   Statham, *Dictionary*, for details of the later history of this family.

14   COR, vol. 4, 1829, pp. 170, 172; vol. 2, pp. 43, 44.

15   K. D. M. Snell, *Annals of the Labouring Poor: Social Change and Agrarian England, 1660–1900*, Cambridge, 1985, ch. 3; K. E. Knorr, *British Colonial Theories, 1570–1850*, Toronto, 1968. Ch. 9 provides a detailed analysis of the debates about 'overpopulation', 'surplus labour' and emigration.

16   See Alexandra Hasluck, *Thomas Peel*, pp. 21 ff., for the original proposals with which Thomas Peel was associated, including the idea of shipping 10,000 people to the Swan River in return for a land grant of 4 million acres.

17   *Historical Records of Australia*, p. 613, Under-Secretary Twiss to Mr T. Peel, 29 January 1829.

18   ibid., p. 608, Under-Secretary Twiss to Sir F. Vincent and Messrs. Peel and Schenley, 21 January 1829.

19   *British Parliamentary Papers: Colonies: Australia*, vol. 5, sessions 1837–40, no. 3, pp. 27–37. Copy of a dispatch from Governor Sir James Stirling to Lord Glenelg, Western Australia, Perth, 3 December 1837.

20   Statham, *Dictionary*, vol. 1. William Tanner, 1801–45, arrived in the *Drummore* in 1831. He left the colony in 1844 due to ill-health.

21   Pamela Statham, comp., *The Tanner Letters: A Pioneer Saga of Swan River and Tasmania, 1831–1845*, Perth, 1987, p. 30. William Tanner to his mother and sisters, 3 January 1832.

22   ibid., p. 23. William Tanner to his mother, October 1831.

23   ibid.

24   Nathaniel Ogle, *The Colony of Western Australia: A Manual for Emigrants*, London, 1837. See appendix showing sizes of early land grants.

25   Peter Cowan, ed., *A Faithful Picture: The Letters of Eliza and Thomas Brown at York in the Swan River Colony 1841–1852*, Fremantle, 1977.

26   John Ramsden Wollaston, *Journals and Diaries 1841–1846*, collected by Canon A. Burton, vol. 1, Perth, 1954.

27   ibid., p. 125.

NOTES TO CHAPTER 2

28   *WAGG*, 8 September 1838.

29   ibid., 13 June 1840.

30   ibid., 2 October 1840. Copy of Instructions addressed by Lord John Russell to the Land and Emigration Commissioner, 14 January 1840.

31   6 Vict., No. 5, 1842. *An Act to Provide Summary Remedy in Certain Cases of Breach of Contract*. For analysis of these early Acts, see Crowley, 'Master and servant', pp. 100, 113.

32   The idea that the overseas colonies represented a suitable destination for children who were orphans, or permanently separated from their parents, already had a long history. The first children who emigrated to Australia without their parents were those identified as criminals and transported to New South Wales after 1788 and later to Van Diemen's Land. In the eighteenth century, children over 7 years of age were not distinguished from adults before the law and a great many crimes were punished with sentences of transportation. After 1853, this sentence could not be imposed on children under 14 years, which meant the gradual ending of this kind of juvenile emigration.

33   *Perth Gazette*, 13 July 1833.

34   ibid., 24 August 1833.

35   ibid., 20 July 1833.

36   ibid., 13 September 1834.

37   ibid.

38   I. Pinchbeck & M. Hewitt, *Children in English Society: From the 18th Century to the Children's Act, 1948*, London, 1973, pp. 549 ff. The South African colony at Cape Town began importing these children before the process began in the Swan River Colony. Information about this use of child labour in South Africa was published in the *Perth Gazette* in the 1840s.

39   Alex G. Scholes, *Education for Empire Settlement: A Study of Juvenile Migration*, London, 1932, pp. 1–3.

40   Jillian Wagner, *Children of the Empire*, London, c. 1982, p. 7.

41   Pinchbeck & Hewitt, *Children in English Society*, p. 555.

42   See Andrew Gill, *Forced Labour for the West: Parkhurst Convicts 'Apprenticed' in Western Australia, 1842–1851*, Perth, 1997.

43   Paul Buddee, *Fate of the Artful Dodger: Parkhurst Boys Transported to Australia and New Zealand, 1842–1852*, Perth, 1984. Only eighteen boys arrived in 1842 but 334 boys came between 1842 and 1852. See p. 51.

44   Andrew Gill is responsible for making this point very strongly in his study.

45   7 Vict., No. 11, 1844; and 12 Vict., No. 16, 1849.

46   Buddee, *Artful Dodger*, p. 5. Buddee provides a graphic picture of the ill-treatment and inhumanity towards children in nineteenth-century England.

47   For details about the history of Parkhurst, see Buddee, *Artful Dodger*.

48   See Buddee, *Artful Dodger*, and Gill, *Forced Labour for the West*, for details about these 'children'.

49   This is essentially the view of Scholes, *Education for Empire*, and Buddee, *Artful Dodger*, who both have a Whig view of history.

50   6 Vict., No. 8, 1842. *An Act to Regulate the Apprenticeship and otherwise to Provide for the Guardianship and Control of a Certain Class of Juvenile Immigrants.*

51   *WAGG*, 23 September 1842.

52   ibid., 20 January 1843. See Buddee, *Artful Dodger*, p. 37, for an account of Governor Arthur's confinement of small boys at Point Puer, partly because of their small stature and unsuitability as labourers.

53   The first eighteen boys were apprenticed as follows: butchers 3, carpenters 3, bakers 2, tailor 1, harness maker 1, gardener 1, gent's service 2, farm hands 5.

54   *WAGG*, 20 January 1843.

55   *British Parliamentary Papers: Colonies: Australia*, pp. 99–100. 'Tabular Report of the Guardian of Government Juvenile Emigration, for the half year ending 31 December 1845'.

56   The names of the Parkhurst boys, as far as they have been identified, appear in Buddee, *Artful Dodger*, p. 166. Their ages and alleged crimes appear on p. 51.

57   See ibid., pp. 33, 53, 56 and 143, for references to the scheme by which boys were divided into four classes for emigration.

58   *British Parliamentary Papers: Colonies: Australia*, p. 92. Enclosure No. 4, Governor Hutt to Lord Stanley, 3 December 1845. See also Buddee, *Artful Dodger*, p. 143.

59   *British Parliamentary Papers: Colonies: Australia*, p. 94. Enclosure No. 6 in the Despatch from Governor Hutt to Lord Stanley, 14 January 1846.

60   ibid., p. 97.

61   WA Leg. Co. V&P, no. A3, 1885. Letters advocating the Establishment of a Training Home for Girls in Western Australia, with the object of Supplying the Demand for Female Servants.

62   WAPD, 1885, vol. 10.

63   Andrew Gill, *Orphans of the Empire*, Sydney, 1997; Barry M. Coldrey, *The Scheme: The Christian Brothers and Childcare in Western Australia*, Perth, 1993; Ivor A. Knight, *Out of Darkness: Growing up with the Christian Brothers*, Fremantle, 1998.

Chapter 3: Parsimony and discrimination in education

1   There is a considerable literature on the history of education in Western Australia, including monographs and journal articles. There are also dissertations held in university departments, especially in the departments of Education.

2   D. P. Leinster-Mackay, 'On the un-English character of Western Australian public schools, 1846–1976', *Early Days*, vol. 7, part 8, 1976, pp. 43–54; Noreen Riorden, 'Private Venture Schools in Western Australia between 1829 and 1914: An Analysis of their Constitution and Education', MEd, UWA, 1990.

3   Martin Newbold, 'The Sisters of Mercy, first teaching order in Australia', *Early Days*, vol. 7, part 6, 1974, pp. 26–34; Anne McLay, *Women out of their Sphere: Sisters of Mercy in Western Australia from 1846*, Perth, 1992, pp. 69–73.

4   *WA Blue Book*, 1847.

5   See David Mossenson, *State Education in Western Australia, 1829–1960*, Perth, 1972, ch. 2.

6   SROWA, WAS 582, cons. 526, item 1. General Education Committee Outward Letters, 9 September 1847 to 24 September 1856. Letter to R. R. Maddern, Perth, 19 May 1848.

7   *WA Blue Book*, 1848.

8   Two-thirds of 2,487 gives a figure of 1,658 who were potentially school pupils—a rough estimate.

9   BL, AJCP Reel 752, 1854, CO 18/87, p. 168. His Excellency the Governor to the Colonial Office, 3 May 1855.

10   BL, AJCP Reel 298, 1854, CO 18/87-89, pp. 171–4.

11   ibid.

12   SROWA, WAS 582, cons. 526, item 1, 1850. Education Committee Outward Letters, 9 September 1847 to 24 September 1856. Letter to Mr Carter, York, 6 June 1850.

13   SROWA, WAS 582, cons. 526, item 1, 1854. Education Committee Outward Letters. Third Report of the General Board of Education to His Excellency the Governor, 7 August 1854.

14   SROWA, WAS 582, cons. 526, item 1, 1855. Education Committee Outward Letters. Letter from the board to the Colonial Secretary, 6 December 1855.

15   SROWA, WAS 582, cons. 526, 1856. Education Committee: Outward Correspondence, 1868–71. 16 June 1868.

16   SROWA, WAS 582, cons. 526, 1870. Education Committee: Outward Correspondence, 1868–71. 29 March 1870, 13 July 1870.

17   For more detail about early abortive attempts to set up schools, see Mossenson, *State Education*, ch. 1.

18   WAPD, 1871, vol. 1.

19   See Maree Seeto, 'The Significance of the Catholicism of Frederick Aloysius Weld for the Development of Education in Western Australia, 1869–1875', MEd, UWA, 1989, for an analysis of the politics surrounding the passage of this Bill and the role played by the Governor.

20   49 Vict., No. 27, 1895. *An Act to Amend the Education Acts, 1871–1894, and to Provide for the Payment of Compensation to the Managers of Assisted Schools on the Cessation of the Grant-in-aid from Public Funds.*

21   35 Vict., No. 14, 1871. *An Act to Provide for Public Elementary Education, and to Encourage Voluntary Efforts in Support of Schools.*

22   WAPD, 1871. The Colonial Secretary, F. P. Barlee, introducing the second reading of the 1871 Bill.

23   38 Vict., No. 5, 1874. *An Act to Amend the Elementary Education Act, 1871.*

24   41 Vict., No. 11, 1877. *An Act to Further Amend the Elementary Education Act.*

25   *Census of the Colony of Western Australia taken on 3rd of April, 1881. Statistical Tables Relating to the Colony from 1872–1881 Inclusive*, Perth, 1882.

26   *Census of Western Australia, April 1891.* General Report with Appendices by Walter Gale, Superintendent of Census, Perth, 1892.

27   Education Department, *Rural and Isolated Schools Series*, Schools of the Cuballing Shire Region, p. 6.

28   SROWA, WAS 582, cons. 526, item 205, 1874. Minutes of the Central Board of Education, 1873–76. 14 January 1874.

29   WA Leg. Co. V&P, no. 11, 1883. Report of the Central Board of Education to His Excellency the Governor, for the Year ending December 1882.

30   WA Leg. Co. V&P, no. 8, 1881. Report of the Central Board of Education for the Year ending 31 December 1880.

31   WA Leg. Co. V&P, no. 11, 1883. Report of the Central Board of Education for the Year ending 31 December 1882.

32   WA Leg. Co. V&P, no. 11, 1885. Report of the Central Board of Education for the Year ending 1884.

33   WA Leg. Co. V&P, no. 15, 1887. Report of the Central Board of Education for the Year ending 1886.

34   WA Leg. Co. V&P, paper 13, 1888. Report of the Commissioners Appointed to Inquire into the System of Education pursued in Government Primary Schools, 1887–1888 (known as the Shearer Report after the chairman, Reverend David Shearer).

35   WA Leg. Co. V&P, no. 7, 1889. Report of the Central Board of Education for the Year ending 31 December 1888.

36   WAPD, 1893, vols 4, 5, new series. Elementary Education Amendment Bill.

37   57 Vict., No. 16, 1893. *An Act to Amend the Law relating to Public Elementary Education.*

38   WA Parl. V&P, no. 17, 1895. Report of the Secretary for Education for the Year 1894, Outlining Wide-ranging Changes.

39   ibid., Education Report, p. 44.

40   58 Vict., No. 30, 1894. *An Act to Further Amend the Law relating to Public Elementary Education.*

41   WA Parl. V&P, paper 31, 1898.

42   63 Vict., No. 3, 1899, clauses 12, 13.

43   For the debate on the Bill, see WAPD, 1899, vol. 14, new series.

44   See John D. Woods, 'The State Aid Issue in Western Australia, 1885–1895', MEd, UWA, 1978.

45   59 Vict., No. 27, 1895. *An Act to Amend the Education Acts, 1871–1894, and to Provide for the Payment of Compensation to the Managers of Assisted Schools on the Cessation of the Grant-in-Aid from Public Funds.*

46   Geraldine Byrne, 'Ursula Frayne, Sister of Mercy', in Laaden Fletcher, ed., *Pioneers of Education in Western Australia*, Perth, 1982; McLay, *Women out of their Sphere*, pp. 69–73.

47   This building still stands in St Georges Terrace.

48   See Mossenson, *State Education*, pp. 32–4; and A. deQ Robin, 'Mathew Blagden Hale, father of secondary education', in Fletcher, ed., *Pioneers of Education.*

49   49 Vict., No. 19, 1885. *An Act to Dissolve the Corporation of the Governors of the Perth Church of England Collegiate School, and for other Purposes.*

50   60 Vict., Private Act, 1896. *An Act to Empower the Diocesan Trustees of the Church of England in Western Australia to Sell, Mortgage, or Lease Perth Allotments H7 and H1, and to Apply the Proceeds or Rents and Profits thereof Subject to and in Accordance with Certain Trusts.*

51   40 Vict., No. 8, 1876. *An Act to Make Provision for the Higher Education of Boys.*

52   W. Robinson, Governor from 1875 to 1877, from 1880 to 1883 and from 1890 to 1895.

53   WA Leg. Co. V&P, no. 9, 1875–76. Schedule of Despatches from the Governor of Western Australia to the Secretary of State for the Colonies, p. 9. His Excellency the Governor to the Right Hon. Secretary of State, 25 January 1876.

54   47 Vict., No. 11, 1883. *An Act to Enable 'The Governors of the High School, Perth' to Raise Money on Mortgage.*

55   55 Vict., No. 29, 1892. *An Act to Make Better Provision for the Appointment of Governors of the High School, Perth, and for other Purposes.*

56   WA Leg. Co. V&P up to 1889, or WA Parl. V&P from 1890. Reports of the Governors of the High School from 1879 to 1900.

57   WAPD, 1897, vol. 2, new series, p. 610.

58   See Mossenson, *State Education*, pp. 62–3; and Donald Leinster-McKay & David Adams, 'The education of colonial gentleman and lady', in W. D. Neal, ed., *Education in Western Australia*, Perth, 1979, ch. 3.

59   See Kelly Islay, 'The Secondary Education of Girls in Government Schools, 1829–1950', MEd, UWA, 1981.

60   David Adams, 'Frederick Charles Faulkner, a classicist in the Antipodes', in Fletcher, ed., *Pioneers of Education.*

61   For a history of the development of secondary schools in Western Australia, see Gregory G. Hancock, 'The Origins and Early Years of Independent Secondary Schools in Western Australia 1891–1911', BEd,

UWA, 1976; and David Adams, 'The Schools of the Public Schools' Association, and their Antecedents, 1829–1929', PhD, UWA, 1979.

62 Barry M. Coldrey, *The Scheme: The Christian Brothers and Childcare in Western Australia*, Perth, 1993. See the introduction and ch. 1 for the origins of this order in Ireland and its arrival in Western Australia.

63 These bare facts are set out in F. K. Crowley, *Australia's Western Third: A History of Western Australia from the First Settlements to Modern Times*, Melbourne, 1960, pp. 144–5.

64 Michael White, *TAFE in WA: A Selection of Significant Historical Documents, 1832–1929*, Perth, vol. 1, 1982.

65 R. L. Weiland, 'The Development of Special Education in Western Australia, 1896–1945', MEd, UWA, 1975.

Chapter 4: Paupers, bastards, delinquents and larrikins

1 There is a considerable literature about such institutions from other States of Australia. See Brian Dickey, 'The establishment of industrial schools and reformatories in New South Wales, 1800–1875', *JRAHS*, vol. 54, part 2, 1968, pp. 135–51; Dickey, 'The evolution of care for destitute children in New South Wales, 1875–1901', *JAS*, no. 4, 1979, pp. 38–57; Dickey, 'Care for dependent children in South Australia in 1988', *Journal of the Historical Society of South Australia*, vol. 10, 1982, pp. 84–91; Michael Horsbrough, 'Child care in NSW in 1890', *ASW*, vol. 30, no. 3, 1977, pp. 15–24; Horsbrough, 'Subsidy and control: Social welfare activities of the NSW Government, 1858–1910', *JAS*, no. 2, 1977, pp. 64–92; Horsbrough, 'The Randwick Asylum: Organizational resistance to social change', *ASW*, vol. 30, no. 1, 1877, pp. 15–24; Horsbrough, 'Government policy and the Benevolent Society', *JRAHS*, vol. 63, part 2, 1977, pp. 77–92; John Ramsland, 'The development of boarding-out systems in Australia: A series of welfare experiments in child care, 1860–1910', *JRAHS*, vol. 60, part 3, 1974, pp. 186–98; Ramsland, 'The Sydney ragged schools: A 19th century voluntary approach to child welfare and education', *JRAHS*, vol. 68, no. 3, 1982, pp. 222–37; Ramsland, 'Henry Parkes and the development of industrial and reformatory schools in colonial New South Wales', *ASW*, vol. 35, no. 1, 1982, pp. 3–10; Ramsland, 'An anatomy of a 19th century child-saving institution: The Randwick asylum for destitute children', *JRAHS*, vol. 70, part 3, 1984, pp. 194–209; Ramsland, '"A place of refuge from dangerous influences": Hobart Town Industrial School for Girls, 1862–1945', *JRAHS*, vol. 71, part 3, 1985, pp. 207–17; Ramsland, *Children of the Back Lanes: Destitute and Neglected Children in Colonial New South Wales*, Sydney, 1986; Ramsland, 'The development of the ragged school movement in 19th century Hobart', *JRAHS*, vol. 73, part 2, 1987, pp. 126–34; Noeline Williamson, 'Factory to reformatory: The founding and failure of industrial reform

schools for girls in 19th century NSW', *ANZHESJ*, vol. 9, no. 1, 1980, pp. 32–41; Williamson, 'Hymns, songs and blackguard verses: Life in the Industrial and Reformatory School for Girls in NSW, part 1, 1867–1887', *JRAHS*, vol. 67, part 4, 1982, pp. 375–87; Williamson, 'Laundry maids or ladies: Life in the Industrial and Reformatory School for Girls in NSW, part 2, 1887–1910', *JRAHS*, vol. 68, part 4, 1983, pp. 312–24. See also Sheila Bignell, 'Orphans and destitute children in Victoria up to 1864', *Victorian Historical Magazine*, vol. 44, 1972, pp. 5–18; L. Ritter, 'Boarding out in New South Wales and South Australia: Adoption, adaption or innovation', *JRAHS*, vol. 64, part 2, 1978, pp. 120–6; Elizabeth Windschuttle, 'Discipline, domestic training and social control: The Female School of Industry, 1826–1847', *Labour History*, no. 39, 1980, pp. 1–14; Sabina Willis, 'Purified at Parramatta: The Industrial School for Girls', in Judy Mackinolty & H. Radi, eds, *In Pursuit of Justice: Australian Women and the Law, 1788–1979*, Sydney, 1979; M. Barbalet, *Far from a Low Gutter Girl: The Forgotten World of State Wards: South Australia 1887–1940*, Melbourne, 1983; Robert van Krieken, 'Children and the state: Child welfare in New South Wales 1890–1915', *Labour History*, no. 51, 1986, pp. 33–53; Stephen Garton, 'Frederick William Neitenstein: Juvenile reformatory and prison reform in New South Wales, 1878–1909', *JRAHS*, no. 75, part 1, 1989, pp. 51–64; Christina Twomey, 'Gender, welfare and the colonial state: Victoria's 1864 Neglected and Criminal Children's Act', *Labour History*, no. 73, 1997, pp. 169–86; Maree Murray, ' "The child is not a servant": Children, work and the boarding-out scheme in New South Wales, 1880–1920', *Labour History*, no. 76, 1999, pp. 190–206; Gladys Scrivener, 'Parental imposition or police coercion? The role of parents and police in committals to the Industrial Schools in New South Wales, 1867–1905', *JRAHS*, vol. 86, part 1, 2000, pp. 23–38. Very little has been published on the institutionalization of European children in the nineteenth century in Western Australia, but see the first part of A. Roy Peterkin, *The Noisy Mansions: The Story of Swanleigh 1868–1971*, Perth, 1986.

2   9 Vict., No. 2, 1845. *An Ordinance to Provide for the Maintenance and Relief of Deserted Wives and Children, and other Destitute Persons, and to Make the Property of Husbands and near Relatives, to whose Assistance they have a Natural Claim, in Certain Circumstances Available for Support.*

3   35 Vict., No. 4, 1871. *An Act to Make Further Provision for the Maintenance of Bastard Children by their Putative Fathers.*

4   39 Vict., No. 8, 1875. *An Act to Amend the Bastardy Laws.*

5   ibid., clause 15.

6   60 Vict, No. 35, 1896. *An Act to Amend the Bastardy Laws Act 1875.* See WAPD, 1896, vol. 9, new series.

7   Anne McLay, *Women out of their Sphere: Sisters of Mercy in Western Australia from 1846*, Perth, 1992, p. 101.

8   *Link*, Sisters of Mercy, vol. 2, no. 1, Manuscript Stack, Q B/GIB. See also Philomena Lowe, *Friend of the Orphan: Matthew Gibney, Missioner, Priest, Bishop*, Perth, 1994.
9   Peterkin, *The Noisy Mansions*.
10   ibid., pp. 7, 8, for the rules.
11   ibid., p. 12.
12   38 Vict., No. 11, 1874. *An Act to Promote the Efficiency of Certain Charitable Institutions*.
13   WAPD, 1877 session. Industrial Schools Bill, 1874, Amendment Bill, 1877.
14   41 Vict., No. 7, 1877. *An Act to Amend the Industrial Schools Act, 1874.*
15   44 Vict., No. 3, 1880. *An Act to Amend the Police Ordinance, 1861.*
16   *West Australian*, 9 March 1883.
17   WA Leg. Co. V&P, no. 3, 1887. Report on Gaols and Prisons for the Year 1886.
18   Prue Joske, Chris Jeffery & Louise Hoffman, *Rottnest Island: A Documentary History*, Perth, 1995.
19   WA Leg. Co. V&P, no. 6, 1881. Report on Gaols and Prisons for the Year 1880.
20   WAPD, 1882, vol. 7. The Industrial Schools Act 1874, Amendment Bill, 1882.
21   WA Parl. V&P, no. 14, 1900. Report on the Prison at Rottnest, p. 27.
22   WA Leg. Co. V&P, no. 5, 1883. Report on Gaols and Prisons for the Year 1882.
23   48 Vict., No. 5, 1884. *An Act to Regulate the Punishment of Whipping.*
24   WA Leg. Co. V&P, no. 30, 1882. Report on Gaols and Prisons for the Year 1881.
25   WA Leg. Co. V&P, no. 13, 1882. Report on the Reformatory at Rottnest Island.
26   WA Leg. Co. V&P, 1882. Colonial Secretary to the Governor concerning the Report on Rottnest Prison, 1882.
27   Legislative Council Debates, 1882, p. 157.
28   56 Vict., No. 5, 1893. *An Act to Provide for the Establishment of Industrial and Reformatory Schools.*
29   See F. K. Crowley, *Australia's Western Third: A History of Western Australia from the First Settlements to Modern Times*, Melbourne, 1960.
30   WA Parl. V&P, no. 7, 1900. See the report of the Superintendent of Public Charities and Inspector of Industrial and Reformatory Schools for the year ending 1899. This report lists eight institutions operating under the two Acts of 1874 and 1893.
31   63 Vict., No. 3, 1899. *An Act to Amend the Law relating to Public Elementary Education.*
32   56 Vict., No. 5, 1893, clause 9.

33   Aboriginal children were not mentioned in the Industrial and Reformatory Schools Act of 1893, because they were now dealt with separately under the 1886 Aborigines Protection Act.

34   WA Parl. V&P, part 1, no. 12, 1895. Report on Rottnest Prison for the Year 1894.

35   The Fremantle Gaol was controlled by the Imperial Convict Establishment until 1886, when it was handed over to the colonial establishment.

36   Report of the Commission Appointed to Inquire into the Penal System of the Colony, Perth, 1899 (Jameson Report).

37   Joske, Jeffery & Hoffman, *Rottnest Island*.

38   For reproductions of the plans for the reformatory and its extensions, and for photographs of the buildings, see R. J. Ferguson, *Rottnest Island: History and Architecture*, Perth, 1986, pp. 56–8.

39   WA Parl. V&P, 1889. Report on Gaols and Prisons for the Year 1888. Table: Nominal Return of Juvenile Prisoners at the Rottnest Reformatory during 1888.

40   SROWA, AN 24, CSO, Acc. 527, item 858, 1897. The Reformatory and Industrial School at Rottnest.

41   WA Parl. V&P, no. 7, 1901–02. Report of the Superintendent of Public Charities and Inspection of Industrial and Reformatory Schools for the Year ending 31st December 1900, p. 18.

42   ibid., p. 19.

43   SROWA, AN 24, CSO, Acc. 527, item 858, 1897. The Reformatory and Industrial School at Rottnest.

44   SROWA, AN 24, CSO, Acc. 527, item 638, 1897. William Dale to Under-Secretary Burt, 4 March 1897.

45   SROWA, AN 24, CSO, Acc. 527, item 130/6, 1880. Resident Magistrate of Fremantle to the Colonial Secretary, 11 December 1880.

46   SROWA, AN 24, CSO, Acc. 527, item 130/7, 1880. W. Dale, Superintendent of Poor Houses, to the Colonial Secretary, 14 December 1880.

47   SROWA, AN 24, CSO, Acc. 527, item 1083, 1883. Orphanages: William Dale to the Colonial Secretary.

48   WA Parl. V&P, no. 7, 1901–02, p. 20. Report of the Superintendent of Public Charities and the Inspector of Industrial and Reformatory Schools for 1900.

49   ibid., p. 10. Return showing the number of children maintained at the expense of the state in reformatory, industrial schools and industrial orphanage schools; the number admitted and discharged during the year 1900; the number remaining on 31 December 1900.

50   See Darren J. Foster, 'Neglected Children in WA: A Case Study 1897–1908: John George Foster', held in Battye Library (BL, Stack, Q362.76 FOS), for a vivid history of Fremantle in the 1890s, with the huge influx of population attracted by the gold rush. Foster describes the life of one child and the process whereby he was committed to a reformatory.

51   WA Parl. V&P, no. 7, 1900. The Report of the Superintendent of Public
      Charities and the Inspector of Industrial Schools and Reformatories,
      p. 26.
52   P. Irvine, 'The History of the Roman Catholic Establishment at
      Glendalough', Honours thesis, Graylands Teachers' College, 1962.
53   Matthew Gibney was the Roman Catholic Bishop of Western Australia
      from 1886 to 1910. The Oblate brothers, with headquarters in Paris,
      worked in Ireland, England, Canada and South Africa.
54   WA Parl. V&P, no. 7, 1900. The Report of the Superintendent of Public
      Charities and the Inspector of Industrial Schools and Reformatories,
      pp. 24–5.
55   Editorial, *West Australian*, 31 January 1894, p. 4.
56   J. E. Thomas & Alex Stewart, *Imprisonment in Western Australia:
      Evolution, Theory and Practice*, Perth, 1978.
57   Jameson Report, 1899, First Progress Report.
58   ibid., p. 7.
59   ibid., paras 992–3.
60   ibid., paras 983–5.
61   ibid., paras 994–9.
62   ibid., paras 954–5.
63   SROWA, AN 24, CSO, Acc. 527, item 858, 1897. The Reformatory and
      Industrial School at Rottnest, His Excellency the Governor.
64   Jameson Report, pp. 8, 9.
65   Brad Halse, *The Salvation Army in Western Australia: Its Early Years*,
      Nedlands, 1990. See also WA Parl. V&P, 1902, 1903. Report of the Super-
      intendent of Public Charities and Inspector of Industrial and Reformatory
      Schools for the Years ending 1901 and 1902.
66   Criminal Code Act (2 Ed., No. 14). For the debate on the Bill, see WAPD,
      1901, vol. 19, new series.
67   *Western Australian Criminal Code*, 1902.

Chapter 5: Estimating the Aboriginal population
1   *Census of the Colony of Western Australia taken on 3rd of April 1881.
      Statistical Tables Relating to the Colony from 1872–1881 Inclusive*, Perth,
      1882. See the introductory comments by the Superintendent of Census,
      Laurence Elliot.
2   For a detailed and critical analysis of Western Australian census material
      and its shortcomings, see I. H. van den Driesen, *Essays on Immigration
      Policy and Population in Western Australia, 1850–1901*, Perth, 1986.
      See also R. T. Appleyard, 'Western Australia: Economic and demographic
      growth, 1850–1914', in C. T. Stannage, ed., *A New History of Western
      Australia*, Perth, 1981. There is also useful demographic material in
      Rica Erickson, *The Bride Ships: Experiences of Immigrants Arriving in*

Western Australia 1849–1889, Perth, 1992. The publication by S. J. Hallam, *Aboriginal Demography in South West Australia: 1858 Census Lists*, Centre for Pre-History, UWA, 1988, is one of the few attempts to discuss the Aboriginal demography of the second half of the nineteenth century.

3   *Census of Western Australia, April 1891*. See the report of the Superintendent of Census, Walter A. Gale.

4   For a brief history of the relationship between Aborigines and European settlers in the Swan River Colony, see Neville Green, 'Aborigines and white settlers in the 19th century', in Stannage, ed., *A New History*, pp. 72–123.

5   The most detailed work on Aboriginal demography in Western Australia before 1850 is that by Sylvia J. Hallam, who combines archaeological and ethnohistorical data. I am greatly indebted to her for correspondence on this issue. See S. J. Hallam, 'Population and resource usage on the Western Littoral', *Memoirs of the Victorian Archaeological Survey, Collection of Papers presented to ANZAAS, 1977*, section 25A, vol. 2, Melbourne, 1978, pp. 16–36; *Fire and Hearth: A Study of Aboriginal Usage and European Usurpation in South Western Australia*, Canberra, 1979, especially pp. 104–10; and 'The first Western Australians', in Stannage, ed., *A New History*.

6   *British Parliamentary Papers: Colonies: Australia*, vol. 5, pp. 237–8. Sir James Stirling to Lord Glenelg, 15 October 1837.

7   Hallam describes these early attempts at recording the size of the Aboriginal population in her article 'Population and resource usage'.

8   F. Armstrong, 'Manners and habits of the Aborigines of Western Australia', *Perth Gazette and Western Australian Journal IV*, 29 October 1836, pp. 789–90; 5 November 1836, pp. 793–4; 12 November 1836, p. 797; George Fletcher Moore, *Diary of Ten Years Eventful Life of an Early Settler in Western Australia*, Perth, 1978 [1884]; Sir George Grey, *Journals of Two Expeditions of Discovery in North West and Western Australia, during the years 1837, 38 and 39*, London, 1841.

9   See E. J. Stormon, trans., ed., *The Salvado Memoirs: Historical Memoirs of Australia and Particularly of the Benedictine Mission of New Norcia and the Habits and Customs of the Australian Natives*, Perth, 1977 [Rosendo Salvado, *Memorie Storiche dell'Australia*, Rome, Society for Propagation of the Gospel, 1851], p. 114.

10   Nathaniel Ogle, *The Colony of Western Australia: A Manual for Emigrants*, Sydney, 1977 [1839], pp. 62–3.

11   *WAGG*, 30 May 1841.

12   ibid., 12 April 1844.

13   ibid., 28 February 1845.

14   For an analysis of all the census material concerning Aborigines in Australia, see L. R. Smith, *The Aboriginal Population of Australia*, Canberra, 1980.

15   *WAGG*, 19 December 1848, for the report of the Registrar General, G. F. Stone.

16   Smith, *The Aboriginal Population*, pp. 156–69, including ten pages of tables for the period up to modern times.

17   Hallam, 'The first Western Australians', p. 66.

18   ibid., p. 67.

19   Paul Hasluck, *Black Australians: A Survey of Native Policy in Western Australia, 1829–1897*, Perth, 1970 [1942].

20   Lois Tilbrook, 'Shadows in the Archives: An Interpretation of European Colonization and Aboriginal Responses in the Swan River Area', PhD, UWA, 1987, pp. 68–72.

21   Hasluck, *Black Australians*, p. 29, n. 24 p. 216.

22   Gillian Cowlishaw, 'The determinants of fertility among Australian Aborigines', *Mankind*, vol. 13, no. 1, 1981, p. 37.

23   Hallam, 'The first Western Australians', p. 67.

24   Stormon, *Salvado Memoirs*, pp. 137–8, 169.

25   Hallam, 'Population and resource usage'.

26   Stormon, *Salvado Memoirs*, p. 137.

27   ibid., p. 138.

28   ibid., p. 31.

29   Neville Green & Lois Tilbrook, comps, eds, *Aborigines of New Norcia 1845–1914*, vol. 7, *The Bicentennial Dictionary of Western Australia*, Perth, 1989.

30   S. J. Hallam, 'Aboriginal demography in Southwestern Australia', in ibid., pp. 179–99.

31   *Census 1891*, ch. 13.

32   ibid., ch. 14, appendix.

33   ibid., ch. 14, appendix, table 4.

34   ibid., p. 91, para. 324.

35   The words of Christopher W. Coppin, who supplied information to H. W. Baker, author of 'A North-West tragedy: The big blow of 1887', *Early Days: Journal and Proceedings, Royal Western Australian Historical Society*, December 1947. This excerpt is quoted in Kathy De La Rue, *Pearl Shell and Pastures*, Cossack, 1979, p. 97.

36   See also De La Rue, *Pearl Shell and Pastures*, especially ch. 8.

37   WA Parl. V&P, vol. 1, no. 14, 1897. The Report of the Aborigines Protection Board for the Year ending December 31st, 1896. Appendix no. 1, General Report of the Kimberley District.

38   ibid. Appendix no. 2, General Report on the Aborigines of the Southern and Eastern Goldfields.

39   WAPD, 1888, vol. 14. *A Bill to Provide for Certain Matters Connected with the Aborigines*.

40   WAPD, 1889, vol. 15. Debate on the Constitution Bill clause 70.

41   *British Parliamentary Papers: Colonies: Australia,* 1895–99, vol. 34. John Forrest, Premier, Memorandum for His Excellency, Acting Governor Onslow, 20 April 1892.
42   WA Parl. V&P, vol. 1, no. 18, 1896. Further Correspondence on the Subject of the Position of the Aborigines' Protection Board in Western Australia.
43   ibid., vol. 1, no. 8, 1896. Report of the Aborigines' Protection Board in Western Australia for 1895.
44   ibid., vol. 2, no. 40, 1899. Report of the Aborigines' Department for the Year ending June 30, 1899.
45   *Seventh Census of Western Australia, taken for the Night of 31st March, 1901,* Perth, 1904, p. 60.

Chapter 6: Institutions for Aboriginal children in the south

1   See Christine Bolt, *Victorian Attitudes to Race,* London, 1971.
2   BL, Private Archives, Acc. 332. A. Alexander Collie to his brother, 4 August 1831.
3   An earlier version of this chapter appeared in an article entitled 'Aboriginal children as a potential labour force in Swan River Colony, 1829 to 1850', *JAS,* vol. 23, 1992, pp. 41–58. See also Neville Green, *Broken Spears: Aborigines and Europeans in the South West of Western Australia,* Cottesloe, 1995.
4   *British Parliamentary Papers: Colonies: Australia,* 1841, pp. 381–3. Governor Hutt to Lord John Russell, 15 May 1841.
5   *British Parliamentary Papers, Aborigines: Australian Colonies,* 1844, p. 372. Instructions issued to the Protector of Aborigines, Western Australia, enclosed in a dispatch by Hutt to Normandy, 11 February 1840.
6   *WAGG,* January 1841, no. 235. Report by Charles Symmons, Protector of Aborigines, to the Colonial Secretary.
7   *British Parliamentary Papers, Colonies: Australia.* Governor Hutt to Secretary of State for the Colonies, Lord Stanley, 8 April 1842.
8   *WA Blue Book,* 1844. Population Return, p. 102.
9   *WAGG,* 9 July 1841.
10   For details about these events, see Green, *Broken Spears,* pp. 124–8; and Henry Reynolds, *This Whispering in Our Hearts,* Sydney, 1998, ch. 4.
11   Green, 'Aborigines and white settlers in the 19th century', in C. T. Stannage, ed., *A New History of Western Australia,* Perth, 1981, p. 90.
12   Francis Armstrong was a young man with some knowledge of Nyungar culture. He held the position of Constable of Police for Perth and Interpreter to the Natives.
13   *WAGG,* 9 July 1841.
14   See W. McNair & H. Rumley, *Pioneer Aboriginal Mission: The Work of Wesleyan Missionary, John Smithies, in the Swan River Colony 1840–1855,*

Perth, 1981, for the early history of the founding of the mission and for biographical details about the Wesleyans. See also John J. Brown, 'Policies in Aboriginal Education in Western Australia, 1829–1897', MEd, UWA, 1979, especially ch. 3.

15   *WAGG*, 8 January 1841.

16   ibid.

17   *British Parliamentary Papers: Colonies: Australia*, 1844, pp. 387–8; and also *WAGG*, 13 August 1841, 'Regulations and Arrangements relative to Native Children who may be provided with Situations in the Houses of Settlers, and who attend the Wesleyan Missionary School at Perth', enclosure 3, attached to Governor Hutt's dispatch to Lord John Russell, 15 May 1841.

18   *WAGG*, 13 August 1841, 'Regulations', clause 15.

19   *British Parliamentary Papers: Colonies: Australia*, 1844, p. 385. Report to the Colonial Secretary by Charles Symmons, Protector of Natives, Perth, 7 January 1841.

20   ibid.

21   *British Parliamentary Papers: Colonies: Australia*, 1844. Enclosure 3 in the dispatch from Governor Hutt to Lord John Russell, 15 May 1841.

22   *WAGG*, 13 January 1843.

23   ibid., 10 February 1843.

24   ibid.

25   ibid., 12 January 1844.

26   ibid., 12 April 1844.

27   8 Vict., No. 6, 1844. *An Act to Prevent the Enticing away of Girls of the Aboriginal Race from School, or from any Service in which they are Employed.*

28   *WAGG*, 12 April 1844.

29   ibid., 17 January 1844.

30   ibid., 16 January 1844.

31   Green, *Broken Spears*, p. 185.

32   *WAGG*, 22 January 1847.

33   This change of title was reported in the *Gazette* on 3 April 1849. It was made by Governor Fitzgerald.

34   *WAGG*, 8 June 1850.

35   ibid.

36   McNair & Rumley, *Pioneer Aboriginal Mission*, ch. 5.

37   E. J. Stormon, trans., ed., *The Salvado Memoirs: Historical Memoirs of Australia and Particularly of the Benedictine Mission of New Norcia and the Habits and Customs of the Australian Natives*, Perth, 1977 [Rosendo Salvado, *Memorie Storiche dell'Australia*, Rome, Society for Propagation of the Gospel, 1851], p. 69.

38   George Russo, *Lord Abbot of the Wilderness: The Life and Times of Bishop Salvado*, Melbourne, 1980. The complex relationship between these men can be followed in this biography. See also George Russo, 'Dom Rosendo

Salvado: The abbot', in Lyall Hunt, ed., *Westralian Portraits*, Perth, 1979, pp. 29–36.

39   Stormon, *Salvado Memoirs*, p. 104, for the list of missionaries who arrived in December 1849.

40   ibid., p. 119.

41   ibid., p. 85.

42   D. E. Hutchison, ed., *A Town Like No Other: The Living Tradition of New Norcia*, Fremantle, 1995, pp. 38–72.

43   Stormon, *Salvado Memoirs*, p. 77.

44   ibid., p. 71.

45   Russo, *Lord Abbot*.

46   ibid., pp. 87 ff. While I have relied on George Russo's biography for certain information, this is not his interpretation of the activities of Bishop Salvado.

47   See George Russo, 'Bishop Salvado's Plan to Civilize and Christianize Aborigines', MA, UWA, 1972, pp. 160–4. See also Russo, 'Religion, politics and Western Australian Aborigines in the 1870s: Bishop Salvado and Governor Weld', *Twentieth Century*, October 1974, pp. 5–19.

48   For the debate, see WAPD, 1874. Before this Act was passed, the Bill was referred to as the Charitable Institutions Bill.

49   John Nairn, *Walter Padbury: His Life and Times*, Perth, 1985.

50   38 Vict., No. 11, 1874. *An Act to Promote the Efficiency of Certain Charitable Institutions*.

51   See Anna Haebich, *For Their Own Good: Aborigines and Government in the South West of Western Australia, 1900–1940*, Perth, 1988, chs 2, 3; and Peter Biskup, *Not Slaves, Not Citizens: The Aboriginal Problem in Western Australia, 1898–1954*, St Lucia, 1973, ch. 1.

52   See Neville Green & Lois Tilbrook, comps, eds, *Aborigines of New Norcia, 1845–1914*, vol. 7, *The Bicentennial Dictionary of Western Australia*, Perth, 1989, pp. xii–xix.

53   Hutchison, *A Town Like No Other*, p. 63.

54   Neville Green, 'Aboriginal lifestyles at New Norcia, 1845–1909', in Green & Tilbrook, *Aborigines of New Norcia*, pp. xii–xix; Haebich, *For Their Own Good*, p. 9.

55   See Green & Tilbrook, *Aborigines of New Norcia*, pp. xviii–xix, for the changes that were occurring at New Norcia by the end of the century.

56   Andrew Broughton, 'Ellensbrook, Margaret River', Architecture thesis, no detail, held in BL. In 1878, Edith Bussell took over the property, which she bought from her brother, who had inherited it.

57   Len Collard, *A Nyungar Interpretation of Ellensbrook and Wonnerup Homesteads*, compiled in 1994 for the National Trust, p. 68.

58   WA Parl. V&P, no. 20, 1890–91. Aborigines Protection Board Report, 1890.

59   Aborigines Department Annual Reports, 1900, 1901.

60   Henry Camfield had taken up the post of Government Resident in Albany
      in 1848.
61   Donald Garden, *Albany: A Panorama of the Sound from 1827*, West
      Melbourne, 1977, pp. 148–50.
62   A. Roy Peterkin, *The Noisy Mansions: The Story of Swanleigh 1868–1971*,
      Perth, 1986, pp. 32–3.
63   WA Leg. Co. V&P, no. 2, 1873–75. Letter from the Lord Bishop of Perth
      concerning the support of Aboriginal Native Children in the Establishment
      under his care.
64   WA Parl. V&P, no. 40, 1899, p. 10. Aborigines Department Report for 1899.
65   SROWA, AN 24, Acc. 255, item 15, 1898. Correspondence of the
      Aborigines Department.
66   SROWA, AN 24, Acc. 255, item 330, 1898. Correspondence of the
      Aborigines Department.
67   SROWA, AN 24, Acc. 255, item 452, 1898. Correspondence of the
      Aborigines Department.
68   SROWA, AN 24, Acc. 255, item 544, 1898. Correspondence of the
      Aborigines Department.
69   SROWA, AN 24, Acc. 255, item 57, 1900. Correspondence of the
      Aborigines Department.
70   See Haebich, *For Their Own Good*, pp. 47–51.
71   54 Vict., No. 16, 1893. *An Act to Amend the Law relating to Public
      Elementary Education.*
72   Report of a Commission Appointed by His Excellency the Governor to
      Inquire into the Treatment of Aboriginal Native Prisoners of the Crown in
      the Colony, 1884 (Forrest Commission), pp. 5–6.
73   61 Vict., No. 5, 1897. *An Act to further Amend the Constitution Act of 1889,
      and for the Better Protection of the Aboriginal Race of Western Australia.*
74   P. Biskup, 'Native Administration and Welfare in Western Australia,
      1897–1954', MLaw, UWA, 1966.
75   5 Ed., No. 14, 1905. *An Act to Make Provision for the Better Protection and
      Care of the Aboriginal Inhabitants of Western Australia.*
76   See Michael Howard, 'Aboriginal society in South Western Australia', in
      R. M. Berndt & C. H. Berndt, eds, *Aborigines of the West: Their Past and
      Their Present*, Perth, 1979, ch. 7.
77   *Statistics of Western Australia, Registrar General's Office*, Perth, 1854 (also
      known as the 1854 Census).

Chapter 7: Family and child labour in the pastoral industry

1   For an Aboriginal perspective on these events, see Frank Rijavek, *Know
      the Song, Know the Country: The Ngarda-Ngali Story of Culture and
      History in the Roebourne District*, Roebourne, c. 1995 (booklet that
      accompanies the film of the same name, BL, Stack, 781.629 RIJ).

2   For a detailed account of the early explorers and the gradual opening up of the North West, see G. C. Bolton, 'A Survey of the Kimberley Pastoral Industry from 1885 to the Present', MA, UWA, 1953; and Martyn & Audrey Webb, *Edge of Empire*, Perth, 1983. The most detailed published history of the North West is by K. Forrest, *The Challenge and the Change: The Colonization and Settlement of the North West, 1861–1914*, Perth, 1996.

3   *WAGG*, 21 December 1862.

4   ibid., 20 March 1872. Governor Weld proclaimed the new land regulations based on an imperial Act: *An Act to Repeal the Acts of Parliament now in Force respecting the Disposal of Waste Lands of the Crown in the Australian Colonies, and to Make Other Provisions in lieu thereof.*

5   F. K. Crowley, *Australia's Western Third: A History of Western Australia from the First Settlements to Modern Times*, Melbourne, 1960. For a contemporary account, see David W. Carnegie, *Spinifex and Sand: A Narrative of Five Years' Pioneering and Exploration in Western Australia*, London, 1898.

6   I am indebted to Eddie Lutze for his insights on this point.

7   The commissioners were John Forrest, E. A. Stone, George Shenton, Maitland Brown, W. E. Marmion, John F. Stone, A. R. Waylen and Charles Harper. This was known as the Forrest Commission.

8   Report of a Commission Appointed by His Excellency the Governor to Inquire into the Treatment of Aboriginal Native Prisoners of the Crown in the Colony, 1884 (Forrest Commission), p. 4.

9   50 Vict., No. 25, 1886. *An Act to Provide for the Better Protection and Management of the Aboriginal Natives of Western Australia, and to Amend the Laws relating to certain Contracts with such Aboriginal Natives.*

10   55 Vict., No. 25, 1892. *An Act to Amend the Aborigines Protection Act, 1886, and to Provide a Summary Remedy for Breach of Contract.*

11   WAPD, vol. 2, 1886, p. 459. Septimus Burt speaking on the Aborigines Protection Act.

12   BL, Manuscript Note, 773, 3594A/65/5. G. Brockman to H. Prinsep.

13   SROWA, AN 1/1, Acc. 495, item 55, 2120/1896. Report by M. Gibney.

14   For more detail about Bresnahan and Canning, see Forrest, *The Challenge and the Change*, pp. 203–12.

15   SROWA, Lands and Surveys Registers, cons. 5000, item 779.

16   SROWA, AN 1/1, Acc. 495, vol. 886, 1893. A. C. Canning to C. M. Straker, Records of the Aborigines Protection Board.

17   SROWA, AN 1/2, Acc. 255, item 51, 1901. Correspondence with G. S. Olivey, Travelling Inspector of Aborigines.

18   SROWA, AN 1/2, Acc. 255, item 51, 1901. John Brockman, Resident Magistrate, Roebourne, to the Chief Protector of Aborigines.

19   *British Parliamentary Papers: Colonies: Australia*, vol. 34, 1895. Report of the Aborigines Protection Board for the Year ending 1894. See table p. 114.

20   WA Parl. V&P, no. 5, 1895. Report of the Aborigines Protection Board for 1894.

21   WA Leg. Co. V&P, no. 32, 1884. Report of a Commission to Enquire into the Treatment of Aboriginal Native Prisoners of the Crown in this Colony. Evidence from R. J. Sholl, p. 18.

22   W. E. Roth, Report of the Royal Commission on the Condition of the Natives, 1904 (Roth Report).

23   See Peter Biskup, *Not Slaves, Not Citizens*, pp. 55–64, for details of the background to the setting up of the Roth Royal Commission.

24   Roth Report.

25   ibid., p. 105.

26   ibid., p. 40.

27   5 Ed., No. 14, 1905. *An Act to Make Provision for the Better Protection of the Aboriginal Inhabitants of Western Australia.*

Chapter 8: Child labour in the pearling industry

1   Edwin W. Streeter, *Pearls and the Pearling Life*, London, 1886, provides a clear contemporary account of the process of skindiving in north-west Australia. See pp. 144–60.

2   For a discussion of the complex pattern of culture contact between Aboriginal and Asian people, see Christine Choo, 'The impact of Asian–Aboriginal Australian contact in northern Australia, particularly in the Kimberley, Western Australia', *Asian and Pacific Migration Journal*, vol. 3, no. 2–3, 1994, pp. 295–310; and Choo, *Mission Girls: Aboriginal Women on Catholic Missions in the Kimberley, Western Australia, 1900–1950*, Perth, 2001.

3   See W. B. Kimberly, comp., *History of West Australia: A Narrative of her Past together with Biographies of her Leading Men,* Melbourne, 1897, for an early history of the pearling industry. See also J. P. S. Bach, 'The pearling industry in Western Australia and the White Australia Policy', *Historical Studies*, vol. 10, no. 38, 1962, pp. 203–13; and Arthur C. V. Bligh, *The Golden Quest: The Roaring Days of West Australian Gold Rushes and Life in the Pearling Industry*, Sydney, 1938.

4   SROWA, AN 24, CSO, Acc. 36, vol. 646, item 17, 1869. Sholl to the Colonial Secretary.

5   34 Vict., No. 14, 1871. *An Act to Regulate the Hiring and Service of Aboriginal Natives Engaged in Pearl Shell Fishery; and to Prohibit the Employment of Women therein.*

6   WAPD, 1870–71. Debate on the Pearl Shell Fishery Bill.

7   See Ron Bunney, *The Hidden*, Perth, 2000, for a novel about the fate of a young Aboriginal girl in the pearling industry.

8   *Inquirer*, 1 March 1876. This is a report of Fairbairn's visit to the North West to investigate a claim that three pearlers were holding Aborigines

against their will on Faure Island off Shark Bay. He visited the island and found evidence of the presence of Aborigines, although they had been hurriedly removed before his arrival. Fairbairn was Resident Magistrate at Greenough from 1873 to 1875, in the Kimberley in 1883, and in Fremantle from 1886 to 1908.

9   SROWA, 286A. Eight letters from George McRae to his sister 1881–82. See the letter of 16 November 1881.

10   I. H. van den Driesen, *Essays on Immigration Policy and Population in Western Australia 1850–1901*, Perth, 1986. In 1886, anti-Chinese legislation prevented Chinese persons having a licence on the goldfields until two years after a field had been opened. A poll tax of £10 was levied on every Chinese who entered the colony. Chinese persons were not granted a licence to operate pearl shell boats.

11   WA Leg. Co. V&P, no. 12, 1875. Correspondence relative to the State of Affairs on the North West Coast and the Treatment of Malay and other Laborers employed in the Pearl Shell Fisheries.

12   *Inquirer*, 18 April 1875, p. 3, col. 2.

13   WA Leg. Co. V&P, paper A16, 1880. Report by R. J. Sholl, Government Resident at Roebourne, on the Pearl Shell Fisheries of the North West.

14   Bligh, *The Golden Quest*, book 2, ch. 1 and pp. 159 ff.

15   SROWA, AN 1/1, Acc. 388, item 575/1883: Government Resident, Kimberley, Kidnapping; item 575/1884: Native Blue Book; item 575/1885: Newspaper Cuttings, Aborigines.

16   SROWA, AN 1/1, Acc. 388. Native Blue Book, item 3, 575, 1882.

17   ibid.

18   WA Leg. Co. V&P, paper A13, 1881. Correspondence relating to the question of Police Protection to Settlers in Outlying Districts, Promulgation of Pearl-Shell Fisheries Restrictions, and Protection of Aboriginal Natives.

19   39 Vict., No. 13, 1875. This Pearl Shell Fishery Regulation Act was passed in 1875 and the regulations made under the Act were printed in *WAGG* on 8 December 1880.

20   *WAGG*, 16 August 1881.

21   ibid., 24 April 1884.

22   Some of the boat owners sent the Aborigines 'up the rigging' until they were told they could come down, if they did not bring up enough shell.

23   SROWA, AN 24, CSO, Acc. 488, vol. 527, item 1282. Questionnaire sent to the owners of ships in the Pearling Fleet, n.d.

24   SROWA, AN 24, CSO, Acc. 488, vol. 527, item 1282. Replies to the Questionnaire, n.d.

25   WA Leg. Co. V&P, paper A15, 1881. Pearl Shell Fishery Regulations.

26   SROWA, AN 24, CSO, Acc. 488, vol. 527, item 1314/1881. Letter from the Colonial Secretary to Detective Constable Glover.

27   SROWA, AN 24, CSO, Acc. 488, vol. 527, item 1314/1881. Letter and depositions from Detective Constable Glover to the Colonial Secretary.

28   SROWA, AN 1/1, Acc. 388, item 1, 4528, 16 May 1884. The Government
        Resident, Roebourne, to the Colonial Secretary.
29   47 Vict., No. 10, 1883. *An Act to Amend the Pearl Shell Fishery Regulation
        Act, 1875.* The Act of 1883 aimed to close certain loopholes in the 1875
        Act, and that of 1886 set out certain new laws concerning the licensing of
        vessels and the payment of duty.
30   Blair Mayne was Inspector of Pearl Shell Fisheries from 1883 to 1887,
        when he was dismissed by the Governor.
31   WA Leg. Co. V&P, no. 28, 1884. Report of the Inspector of Pearl Shell
        Fisheries for the season 1883–84.
32   Rev. J. B. Gribble, *Dark Deeds in a Sunny Land: Blacks and Whites in
        North-West Australia,* Introduction by Bob Tonkinson, Perth, 1987. This
        text is a reprint of the 1905 edition, which was itself a compendium of
        reports, letters and articles from the 1880s surrounding this case. This
        edition also contains an account of these events by Su-Jane Hunt, 'The
        Gribble affair: A study in colonial politics'. Neville Green also writes of
        the Gribble affair and provides a context for understanding the response
        of the settlers to Gribble's criticisms in his article called 'Aborigines and
        white settlers in Western Australia in the 19th century', in C. T. Stannage,
        ed., *A New History of Western Australia,* Perth, 1981, pp. 101–6. The most
        recent reconstruction of Gribble's conflict with the Western Australian
        elite is that of Cavan Brown, *The Blackfellow's Friend,* Perth, 1999.
33   Gribble, *Dark Deeds,* pp. 35, 45, 49, 50, 51.
34   *Daily Telegraph,* Melbourne, 9 July 1886. Interview with Rev. J. B. Gribble.
35   Gribble, *Dark Deeds,* pp. 48–9.
36   ibid., p. 33.
37   Green, 'Aborigines and white settlers', p. 105.
38   Gribble, *Dark Deeds.*
39   See Henry Reynolds, *This Whispering in Our Hearts,* Sydney, 1998, ch. 7.
40   Colonel Edward Fox Angelo was Resident Magistrate in Roebourne from
        1886 to 1889. For more detail about his experiences in the North West,
        see Reynolds, *This Whispering,* ch. 8.
41   SROWA, AN 24, CSO, Acc. 1172, C34. Confidential letter from Colonel
        Angelo, Government Resident in the North West, to Governor Napier
        Broome, 31 March 1886.
42   SROWA, AN 24, CSO, Acc. 1172, C43. Confidential letter from Colonel
        Angelo, Government Resident at Roebourne, to Governor Napier
        Broome, 9, 10 September 1886.
43   SROWA, AN 24, CSO, Acc. 1172, C42. Confidential letter from Colonel
        Angelo, Government Resident in Roebourne, to Governor Napier
        Broome, 21 September 1886.
44   SROWA, AN 24, CSO, Acc. 1172, C63. A report of a meeting of magistrates
        with the object of taking measures hostile to the Government Resident,
        5 November 1886.

45   SROWA, AN 24, CSO, Acc. 1172, C63. Report of an Investigation of Differences between Colonel Angelo, Government Resident at Roebourne, and the Inspector of Pearl Shell Fisheries, and an inquiry into the general condition of the Aborigines, 24 January 1887. This file contains copies of the letters setting up the inquiry, depositions and letters sent to Fairbairn, and Fairbairn's report to the Colonial Secretary. It also contains copies of letters from the Colonial Secretary to Angelo and to Mayne as a result of the findings by Fairbairn.

46   David Forrest had a large holding in the North West. See K. Forrest, *The Challenge and the Change: The Colonization and Settlement of the North West, 1861–1914*, Perth, 1996, for the personal history of John W. Cowan.

47   SROWA, AN 24, CSO, Acc. 1172, C63. R. Fairbairn to the Colonial Secretary, 24 January 1887.

48   See Forrest, *The Challenge and the Change*, for the personal history of John W. Cowan.

49   BL, AJCP, Reels 1702–1703, CO 18, piece no. 207, July–December 1886. Letter of John W. Cowan to the Secretary of State for the Colonies, 21 October 1886.

50   BL, AJCP, Reels 1704–1705, CO 18, piece no. 208, January–August 1887.

51   BL, AJCP, Reels 1702–1703, CO 18, piece no. 208, July–December 1886. Letter from John W. Cowan to the Secretary of State for the Colonies, 15 October 1886.

52   WAPD, 1886, vol. 11. Septimus Burt introducing the Aborigines Protection Bill.

53   W. E. Roth, Report of the Royal Commission on the Condition of the Natives, 1904 (Roth Report), p. 64.

54   ibid., p. 6.

55   See C. D. Rowley, *The Destruction of Aboriginal Society*, Canberra, 1970, especially chs 4, 9 and 11, for details about the pearling and pastoral industries generally.

56   50 Vict., No. 25, 1886. The Aborigines Protection Act.

57   Roth Report, p. 9.

58   WAPD, 1887, vol. 12. See the second reading speech of the Attorney General, Hon. C. N. Warton, in introducing the Bill.

59   51 Vict., No. 18, 1887. *An Act to further Amend 'the Pearl Shell Fishery Regulation Acts 1873 and 1875'.*

60   See Gribble, *Dark Deeds*, p. 68.

61   SROWA, AN 24, CSO, Acc. 488, vol. 527, folio 2812, 1887. The use of diving apparatus began in a small way in the 1880s, but Mayne wrote at that time that the swimming system allowed for much larger profits for the owners. See E. Mayne to Colonial Secretary.

Chapter 9: Rehearsing the future: 'Half-castes' and reserves

1   Christine Choo, *Mission Girls: Aboriginal Women on Catholic Missions in the Kimberley, Western Australia, 1900–1950*, Perth, 2001, p. 97.

2   See Anna Haebich, *For Their Own Good: Aborigines and Government in the South West of Western Australia, 1900–1940*, Perth, 1988, ch. 2, for a detailed discussion of the attitudes and beliefs of the European population about Aborigines of mixed descent.

3   SROWA, AN 24, Acc. 495, item 61, 1892. The Bishop of Perth, Suggestions with Reference to the Treatment and Employment of the Aboriginal Natives in the Northern Districts of Western Australia, clause 4.

4   SROWA, AN 24, Acc. 495, item 49, 1896. A. C. Bailey to the Secretary, Aborigines Protection Board.

5   SROWA, AN 24, Acc. 495, item 35, 1896. George Marsden, Protector of Aborigines, Kimberley Region, to the Aborigines Protection Board, 24 October 1896.

6   WA Parl V&P, vol. 2, 1901–02. Aborigines Department Report for the Financial Year Ending 30th June 1901.

7   *WAGG*, 31 March 1843.

8   ibid., 20 March 1872.

9   Paul Hasluck, *Black Australians: A Survey of Native Policy in Western Australia, 1829–97*, Melbourne, 1970 [1942], p. 116.

10   ibid., pp. 114–16. Hasluck discusses this issue in more detail.

11   *WAGG*, 11 October 1882. *An Act to Repeal the Acts of Parliament now in Force respecting the Disposal of the Waste Lands of the Crown in the Australian Colonies, and to Make other Provisions in lieu thereof.*

12   WAPD, 1888, vol. 14.

13   62 Vict., No. 37, 1898. *An Act to Consolidate and Amend the Laws relating to the Sale, Occupation, and Management of Crown Lands, and for other Purposes.*

14   SROWA, AN 24, Acc. 495, item 53, 1883. Bishop Gibney, Suggestions as to Measures to be Adopted with a View to the Improvement of the Condition of the Aboriginal Natives.

15   WA Leg. Co. V&P, 1884. The Forrest Commission Report.

16   50 Vict., No. 25, 1886. *An Act to Provide for the Better Protection and Management of the Aboriginal Natives of Western Australia, and to Amend the Laws Relating to Certain Contracts with such Aboriginal Natives*, part 1, clause 4.

17   SROWA, AN 24, Acc. 495, item 61, 1892. The Bishop of Perth, Suggestions with Reference to the Treatment and Employment of the Aboriginal Natives in the Northern Districts of Western Australia, clause 4.

18   SROWA, AN 24, Acc. 495, item 2, 1896. C. A. Bailey, Protector of Aborigines, to the Secretary, Aborigines Protection Board, 1 December 1896.

19   SROWA, AN 24, Acc. 495, item 4, 1895. A. G. Clifton, Warden of the East Murchison Goldfields, to Under Secretary of Mines, 1 November 1895.

20   SROWA, AN 24, Acc. 495, item 4, 1895. W. D. Cummins, Warden of the Kimberley Goldfield, to the Under Secretary for Mines, 23 October 1895.

21   SROWA, AN 24, Acc. 495, item 42, 1896. H. W. Brownrigg, Resident Medical Officer at Broome, to the Secretary, Aborigines Protection Board, 6 November 1896.

22   Charles Owen Leaver Riley was Anglican Bishop of Perth from 1894 to 1929.

23   SROWA, AN 24, Acc. 495, item 58, 1896. Bishop Riley to the Governor, Sir Gerard Smith, 21 July 1896.

24   SROWA, AN 24, Acc. 495, item 5, 1896. Governor Gerard Smith to Premier John Forrest, 11 May 1896.

25   SROWA, AN 24, Acc. 495, item 37, 1897. George Marsden to the Aborigines Protection Board from La Grange Bay, 9 March 1897.

26   SROWA, AN 24, Acc. 495, item 44, 1897. George Marsden to the Aborigines Protection Board reporting on Oobagooma Station, n.d.

27   For more details about Prinsep and the 1905 Act, see Pat Jacobs, *Mister Neville*, Fremantle, 1990, pp. 56–7.

28   Report of a Royal Commission on the Condition of the Natives, 1904, pp. 25–30.

29   5 Ed., No. 14, 1905. *An Act to Make Provision for the Better Care and Protection of the Aboriginal Inhabitants of Western Australia.*

30   ibid., clauses 10–15.

31   55 Vict., No. 18, 1892. *An Act to Amend 'the Aboriginal Offenders Act 1883' and to Authorize the Whipping of Aboriginal Native Offenders.*

32   WAPD, 1891–92, vol. 15, new series, pp. 398–400.

33   55 Vict., No. 25, 1892. *An Act to Amend 'the Aborigines Protection Act, 1886' and to Provide a Summary Remedy for Breach of Contract by Aborigines.*

34   56 Vict., No. 16, 1892. *An Act to Consolidate and Amend the Law relating to the Police in Western Australia.* For relations between Aboriginal people and the police, see Andrew Gill, 'Aborigines, settlers and police in the Kimberleys, 1887–1905', *Studies in Western Australian History*, vol. 1, 1977, pp. 1–27; Tom Austen, *A Cry in the Wind: Conflict in Western Australia 1829–1929*, Darlington, 1998.

35   57 Vict., No. 14, 1893. The Constitution Act Amendment Act.

SELECT BIBLIOGRAPHY

OFFICIAL SOURCES

Census material

Census of the Colony of Western Australia, taken on 31st March, 1870, also the General Statistics of the Colony for the Year Ending 31st December 1869, Perth, 1870.

Census of the Colony of Western Australia taken on 3rd of April 1881. Statistical Tables Relating to the Colony from 1872–1881 Inclusive, Perth, 1882.

Census of the Population and Return of Stock and Crops, Western Australia, 1848.

Census of Western Australia, April 1891, General Report with Appendices by Walter Gale, Superintendent of Census, Perth, 1892.

Checklist of Censuses, Blue Books and Statistical Registers of Western Australia, Battye Library, 1981.

Colonial Blue Books, 1837–69.

Seventh Census of Western Australia, taken for the Night of 31st March, 1901, compiled under the direction of Malcolm A. C. Fraser, Registrar General, Government Statistician and Superintendent of Census, Perth, 1904.

Statistics of Western Australia, Registrar General's Office, Perth, 1854 (also known as the 1854 Census).

WA Blue Books, 1870–1905.

WA Statistical Register, 1896–1900.

Western Australia, Census of 1859.

Official records

Aborigines Protection Board.

Aborigines Department.

British Parliamentary Papers: Colonies: Australia.

British Parliamentary Papers: Aborigines: Australian Colonies.

Central Board of Education.

Colonial Office Records: Inward Correspondence.

Colonial Office Records: Outward Correspondence.

Education Department.

General Board of Education.

Historical Records of Australia.

Statutes of Western Australia.

Western Australian Colonial Secretary's Office.

Western Australian Government Gazettes.

Western Australian Legislative Council Debates.
Western Australian Parliamentary Debates.
Western Australian Votes and Proceedings.

Special reports and commissions of inquiry

Report by R. J. Sholl, Government Resident at Roebourne, on the Pearl Shell Fisheries of the North-West, 1880.

Report of the Select Committee of the Legislative Council Appointed to Consider and Report upon the Question of Immigration, 1882.

Report of the Central Board of Education to His Excellency the Governor, for the Year ending December 1882.

Report of a Commission Appointed by His Excellency the Governor to Inquire into the Treatment of Aboriginal Native Prisoners of the Crown in the Colony, 1884 (Forrest Commission).

The Report of the Bishop of Perth to the Colonial Secretary, Malcolm Fraser, of the Native and Half-caste Homes under his Charge, June 9th 1885.

Report of an Investigation of Differences between Colonel Angelo, Government Resident at Roebourne, and the Inspector of Pearl Shell Fisheries, and an Enquiry into the General Condition of the Aborigines, 24 January, 1887.

Report of the Commissioners Appointed to Inquire into the System of Education pursued in Government Primary Schools, 1887–1888 (Shearer Report).

Report as to a Regular System of Profitable Employment for the Prisoners Confined in Fremantle Gaol, 1888.

Report on the Employment of Native Prisoners from Rottnest Island at Fremantle Bar and on the Mainland, 1890.

Report of the Commission Appointed to Inquire into the Penal System of the Colony, Perth, 1899 (Jameson Report).

Report of a Royal Commission on the Condition of the Natives, 1904, undertaken by Walter Edmund Roth (Roth Report).

Government reports published yearly in the WA Legislative Council Votes and Proceedings and in the WA Parliament Votes and Proceedings

Reports of the Aborigines Protection Board.

Reports of the Aborigines Department.

Reports of the General Board of Education, the Central Board of Education and the Education Department.

Reports by the Board of Immigration.

Reports on Gaols and Prisons.

Reports of the Governors of the High School.

Reports of the Inspector of Pearl Shell Fisheries.

Reports on the Prison at Rottnest.

Reports of the Superintendent of Public Charities and Inspector of Industrial and
Reformatory Schools.

Reports of the Superintendent of Poor Houses.

NEWSPAPERS

Daily Telegraph, Melbourne.

Perth Gazette and Western Australian Journal.

Inquirer, Perth.

West Australian.

BOOKS AND ARTICLES ON NINETEENTH-CENTURY WESTERN AUSTRALIAN HISTORY

Adams, David, 'The education of a colonial gentleman and lady', in Neal, W. D.,
ed., *Education in Western Australia*, Perth, 1979, ch. 3.

—— 'Frederick Charles Faulkner, a classicist in the Antipodes', in Fletcher, Laaden,
ed., *Pioneers of Education in Western Australia*, Perth, 1982, pp. 129–54.

Anderson, M., 'Marriage and children in Western Australia, 1842–49', in Grimshaw,
P., McConville, C. & McEwan, E., eds, *Families in Colonial Australia*,
Sydney, 1985, pp. 49–56.

Anderson, M. & Gill, A., 'The history of the Swan River Guardian, or, the death of
the free press in Western Australia in 1838', *Push from the Bush*, no. 10,
1981, pp. 4–30.

Appleyard R. T., 'Western Australia: Economic and demographic growth,
1850–1914', in Stannage, C. T., ed., *A New History of Western Australia*,
Perth, 1981, ch. 6.

Austen, Tom, *A Cry in the Wind: Conflict in Western Australia 1829–1929*,
Darlington, 1998.

Bach, J. P. S., 'The political economy of pearl shelling', *Economic History Review*,
Second Series, vol. 14, 1961–62, pp. 105–14.

—— 'The pearling industry in Western Australia and the White Australia Policy',
Historical Studies, vol. 10, no. 38, 1962, pp. 203–13.

Baines, Patricia & Hume, Lorna, 'Children of the Chief Protector: Some Nyungar
childhood experiences during the time of the Aborigines Act, 1905–1929',
in Hetherington, Penelope, ed., *Childhood and Society in Western
Australia*, Perth, 1988, ch. 4.

Baker, H. W., 'A North-West tragedy: The big blow of 1887', *Early Days: Journal
and Proceedings, Royal Western Australian Historical Society*, December
1947, pp. 37–40.

Barley, Sheila, 'Out of step: The failure of the early Protestant missions', in Reece, Bob & Stannage, Tom, eds, *Studies in Western Australia History*, vol. 7, *European–Aboriginal Relations in Western Australian History*, 1984, pp. 26–32.

Battye, J. S., *Western Australia: A History from its Discovery to the Inauguration of the Commonwealth*, Oxford, 1924.

Berman, Muriel, 'Bishop Salvado: A re-appraisal', in Reece, Bob & Stannage, Tom, eds, *Studies in Western Australian History*, vol. 7, *European–Aboriginal Relations in Western Australian History*, 1984, pp. 36–41.

Berryman, Ian, 'The early censuses of the Swan River Colony', *Push from the Bush*, no. 5, 1979, pp. 55–62.

—— *A Colony Detailed: The First Census of Western Australia, 1832*, Perth, 1979.

Biskup, Peter, *Not Slaves, Not Citizens: The Aboriginal Problem in Western Australia, 1898–1954*, St Lucia, 1973.

Bligh, Arthur C. V., *The Golden Quest: The Roaring Days of West Australian Gold Rushes and Life in the Pearling Industry*, Sydney, 1938.

Bolton, G. C., 'The idea of a colonial gentry', *Historical Studies*, vol. 13, 1968, pp. 307–28.

Bourke, D. F., *The History of the Catholic Church in Western Australia*, Perth, 1979.

Bridges, B., 'Aboriginal education in Australia', *Australian Journal of Education*, vol. 12, no. 3, 1968, pp. 225–43.

Brown, Cavan, *The Blackfellow's Friend*, Perth, 1999.

Buddee, Paul, *Fate of the Artful Dodger: Parkhurst Boys Transported to Australia and New Zealand, 1842–1852*, Perth, 1984.

Bunney, Ron, *The Hidden*, Perth, 2000.

Burges, Lockier Clere, *The Pioneers of the Nor'-West, Australia, Pastoral and Pearling: Being the Reminiscences of Lockier Clere Burges*, Geraldton, 1913.

Butlin, N. G., Ginswick, J. & Statham, P., 'Colonial statistics before 1850', *ANU Source Papers in Economic History*, no. 12, 1986.

Byrne, Geraldine, 'Ursula Frayne, Sister of Mercy', in Fletcher, Laaden, ed., *Pioneers of Education in Western Australia*, Perth, 1982, ch. 1.

Cameron, J. M. R., *Ambition's Fire: The Agricultural Colonization of Pre-Convict Western Australia*, Perth, 1981.

Carnegie, David W., *Spinifex and Sand: A Narrative of Five Years' Pioneering and Exploration in Western Australia*, London, 1898.

Carter, Jennie, 'Two historians and convictism', in Stannage, C. T., ed., *Studies in Western Australian History*, vol. 4, *Convictism in Western Australia*, 1981, pp. 68–73.

—— *History of the Removal of Aboriginal Children from their Families in Western Australia, 1829–1972*, Aboriginal Affairs Department contribution to the State's submission to the Human Rights and Equal Opportunity Commission National Inquiry into Separation of Aboriginal and Torres Strait Islander Children from their Families, Aboriginal Affairs Department, 1996.

Choo, Christine, 'The impact of Asian–Aboriginal Australian contact in northern Australia, particularly in the Kimberley, Western Australia', *Asian and Pacific Migration Journal*, vol. 3, no. 2–3, 1994, pp. 295–310.

—— 'The role of the Catholic missionaries at Beagle Bay in the removal of Aboriginal children from their families in the Kimberley region from the 1890s', *Aboriginal History*, vol. 21, 1997, pp. 14–29.

—— *Mission Girls: Aboriginal Women on Catholic Missions in the Kimberley, Western Australia, 1900–1950*, Perth, 2001.

Clement, Cathie, comp., *A Guide to the Printed Sources for the History of the Kimberley Region of Western Australia*, Perth, 1996.

Coldrey, Barry M., *The Scheme: The Christian Brothers and Childcare in Western Australia*, Perth, 1993.

Collard, Len, *A Nyungar Interpretation of Ellensbrook and Wonnerup Homesteads*, compiled in 1994 for the National Trust.

Cowan, Peter, ed., *A Faithful Picture: The Letters of Eliza and Thomas Brown at York in the Swan River Colony 1841–1852*, Fremantle, 1977.

Crowley, F. K., 'Master and servant in Western Australia, 1829–1851', *Western Australian Historical Society Journal and Proceedings*, vol. 4, part 5, 1953, pp. 94–115.

—— *Australia's Western Third: A History of Western Australia from the First Settlements to Modern Times*, Melbourne, 1960.

—— *Big John Forrest, 1847–1918: A Founding Father of the Commonwealth of Australia*, Perth, 2000.

Davidson, W. S., *Havens of Refuge: A History of Leprosy in Western Australia*, Perth, 1978.

de Garis, B. K., 'Political tutelage 1829–1830', in Stannage, C. T., ed., *A New History of Western Australia*, Perth, 1981, ch. 9.

De La Rue, Kathy, *Pearl Shell and Pastures*, Cossack, 1979.

deQ Robin, A., 'Mathew Blagden Hale, father of secondary education', in Fletcher, Laaden, ed., *Pioneers of Education in Western Australia*, Perth, 1982, pp. 39–64.

Durack, Mary, *Kings in Grass Castles*, London, 1959.

—— *To Be Heirs Forever*, London, 1976.

Elkin, A. P., 'Aboriginal–European relations in Western Australia: An historical and personal record', in Berndt, R. M. & Berndt, C. H., eds, *Aborigines of the West: Their Past and Their Present*, Perth, 1979, ch. 24.

Erickson, R., *The Victoria Plains*, Perth, 1971.

—— *The Dempsters*, Perth, 1978.

—— *The Bride Ships: Experiences of Immigrants Arriving in Western Australia 1849–1889*, Perth, 1992.

Ewers, J. K., *Perth Boys' School, 1848–1947*, Perth, 1947.

Ferguson, R. J., *Rottnest Island: History and Architecture*, Perth, 1986.

Forrest, K., *The Challenge and the Change: The Colonization and Settlement of the North West, 1861–1914*, Perth, 1996.

Garden, Donald, *Albany: A Panorama of the Sound from 1827*, West Melbourne, 1977.

Garrick, Phyllis, 'Two historians and the Aborigines: Kimberly and Battye', in Reece, Bob & Stannage, Tom, eds, *Studies in Western Australian History*, vol. 7, *European–Aboriginal Relations in Western Australian History*, 1984, pp. 111–30.

—— 'Children of the poor and industrious classes in Western Australia, 1829–1880', in Hetherington, P., ed. *Childhood and Society in Western Australia*, Perth, 1988, pp. 13–27.

Gill, Andrew, 'Aborigines, settlers and police in the Kimberleys, 1887–1905', *Studies in Western Australian History*, vol. 1, 1977, pp. 1–27.

—— *Forced Labour for the West: Parkhurst Convicts 'Apprenticed' in Western Australia, 1842–1851*, Perth, 1997.

Goddard, E. & Stannage, T., 'John Forrest and the Aborigines', in Reece, Bob & Stannage, Tom, eds, *Studies in Western Australian History*, vol. 7, *European–Aboriginal Relations in Western Australian History*, 1984, pp. 52–8.

Green, Neville, 'Aboriginal and settler conflict in Western Australia, 1826–1852', *Push from the Bush*, no. 3, 1979, pp. 70–94.

—— 'Aborigines and white settlers in the 19th century', in Stannage, C. T., ed., *A New History of Western Australia*, Perth, 1981, ch. 3.

—— *Broken Spears: Aborigines and Europeans in the South West of Western Australia*, Cottesloe, 1995.

Green, Neville & Moon, Susan, *Far From Home: Aboriginal Prisoners on Rottnest Island, 1838–1931*, vol. 10, *Dictionary of Western Australians*, Perth, 1997.

Green, Neville & Tilbrook, Lois, comps, eds, *Aborigines of New Norcia, 1845–1914*, vol. 7, *The Bicentennial Dictionary of Western Australia*, Perth, 1989.

Gregory, Jenny, 'The Gallops of Dalkeith: A re-examination of a pioneer family', *Push from the Bush*, no. 22, 1986, pp. 48–72.

Grey, Sir George, *Journals of Two Expeditions of Discovery in North West and Western Australia, during the years 1837, 38 and 39, under the authority of Her Majesty's Government*, London, 1841.

Gribble, J. B., *Dark Deeds in a Sunny Land: Blacks and Whites in North-West Australia*, Perth, 1987 [1905].

Haebich, Anna, 'European farmers and Aboriginal farmers in South Western Australia, mid-1890s–1914', in Reece, Bob & Stannage, Tom, eds, *Studies in Western Australian History*, vol. 7, *European–Aboriginal Relations in Western Australian History*, 1984, pp. 59–67.

—— *For Their Own Good: Aborigines and Government in the South West of Western Australia, 1900–1940*, Perth, 1988.

—— *Broken Circles: Fragmenting Indigenous Families 1800–2000*, Fremantle, 2000.

Hallam, S. J., 'Population and resource usage on the Western Littoral', *Memoirs of the Victorian Archaeological Survey, Collection of Papers presented to ANZAAS, 1977*, section 25A, vol. 2, Melbourne, 1978, pp. 16–36.

—— *Fire and Hearth: A Study of Aboriginal Usage and European Usurpation in South Western Australia*, Canberra, 1979.

—— 'The first Western Australians', in Stannage, C. T., ed., *A New History of Western Australia*, Perth, 1981, ch. 2.

—— *Aboriginal Demography in South West Australia: 1858 Census Lists*, Centre for Pre-History, University of Western Australia, 1988.

—— 'Aboriginal demography in Southwestern Australia', in Neville Green & Lois Tilbrook, comps, eds, *Aborigines of New Norcia, 1845–1914*, vol. 7, *The Bicentennial Dictionary of Western Australia*, Perth, 1989.

Halse, Brad, *The Salvation Army in Western Australia: Its Early Years*, Nedlands, 1990.

Hasluck, Alexandra, *Thomas Peel of Swan River*, Melbourne, 1965.

Hasluck, Paul, *Black Australians: A Survey of Native Policy in Western Australia, 1829–1897*, Melbourne, 1970 [1942].

Hetherington, Penelope, 'Childhood and youth in Australia', *Journal of Australian Studies*, no. 18, 1986, pp. 3–18.

—— 'Writing the history of childhood in Western Australia', in Hetherington, P., ed., *Childhood and Society in Western Australia*, Perth, 1988.

—— 'Aboriginal children as a potential labour force in Swan River Colony, 1829 to 1850', *Journal of Australian Studies*, no. 23, 1992, pp. 41–58.

Hodson, Sally, 'Nyungar and work: Aboriginal experiences in the rural economy of the Great Southern Region of Western Australia', *Aboriginal History*, vol. 17, no. 1, 1993, pp. 73–92.

Howard, Michael C., 'Aboriginal society in South Western Australia', in Berndt, R. M. & Berndt, C. H., eds, *Aborigines of the West: Their Past and Their Present*, Perth, 1979, ch. 7.

Hunt, Su-Jane, 'The Gribble affair: A study in colonial politics', in Reece, Bob & Stannage, Tom, eds, *Studies in Western Australian History*, vol. 7, *European–Aboriginal Relations in Western Australian History*, 1984, pp. 42–51.

Hutchison, David, *A Town Like No Other: The Living Tradition of New Norcia*, Fremantle, 1995.

Jacobs, Pat, *Mister Neville*, Fremantle, 1990.

Jebb, Mary Anne, 'The Lock hospitals experiment: Europeans, Aborigines and venereal disease', in Reece, Bob & Stannage, Tom, eds, *Studies in Western Australian History*, vol. 7, *European–Aboriginal Relations in Western Australian History*, 1984, pp. 68–87.

Joske, Prue, Jeffery, Chris & Hoffman, Louise, *Rottnest Island: A Documentary History*, Perth, 1995.

Kerr, Alex, *North Western Australia*, Perth, 1962.

Kimberly, W. B., comp., *History of West Australia: A Narrative of her Past together with Biographies of her Leading Men*, Melbourne, 1897.

Knight, Ivor A., *Out of Darkness: Growing up with the Christian Brothers*, Fremantle, 1998.

Leinster-Mackay, D. P., 'On the un-English character of Western Australian public schools, 1846–1976', *Early Days*, vol. 7, part 8, 1976, pp. 43–54.

Leinster-Mackay, Donald & Adams, David, 'The education of colonial gentleman and lady', in W. D. Neal, ed., *Education in Western Australia*, Perth, 1979.

Lowe, Philomena, *Friend of the Orphan: Matthew Gibney, Missioner, Priest, Bishop*, Perth, 1994.

McLay, Anne, *Women out of their Sphere: Sisters of Mercy in Western Australia from 1846*, Perth, 1992.

McLeod, Don, *How the West Was Lost: The Native Question in the Development of Western Australia*, Port Hedland, 1984.

McNair, W. & Rumley, H., *Pioneer Aboriginal Mission: The Work of Wesleyan Missionary, John Smithies, in Swan River Colony, 1840–1855*, Perth, 1981.

Marchant, Leslie, *Aboriginal Administration in Western Australia, 1886–1905*, Canberra, 1981.

Millett, Mrs Edward, *An Australian Parsonage, or the Settler and the Savage in Western Australia*, London, 1872; facsimile edition Perth, 1980.

Moore, George Fletcher, *Diary of Ten Years Eventful Life of an Early Settler in Western Australia and also A Descriptive Vocabulary of the Language of the Aborigines*, Perth, 1978 [1884].

Mossenson, David, *State Education in Western Australia, 1829–1960*, Perth, 1972.

Mounsey, C. F., 'Aboriginal education—a new dawning', in Berndt, R. M. & Berndt, C. H., eds, *Aborigines of the West: Their Past and Their Present*, Perth, 1979, ch. 30.

Nairn, John, *Walter Padbury: His Life and Times*, Perth, 1985.

Newbold, Martin, 'The Sisters of Mercy, first teaching order in Australia', *Early Days*, vol. 7, part 6, 1974, pp. 26–34.

Ogle, Nathaniel, *The Colony of Western Australia: A Manual for Emigrants*, Sydney, 1977 [1839].

Peterkin, A. Roy, *The Noisy Mansions: The Story of Swanleigh 1868–1971*, Perth, 1986.

Reece, Bob, 'Laws of the white people: The frontier of authority in Perth in 1838', *Push from the Bush*, no. 17, 1984, pp. 2–28.

—— 'Prisoners in their own country: Aborigines in Western Australian historical writing', in Reece, Bob & Stannage, Tom, eds, *Studies in Western Australian History*, vol. 7, *European–Aboriginal Relations in Western Australian History*, 1984, pp. 131–40.

Reynolds, Henry, *This Whispering in Our Hearts*, Sydney, 1998.

—— comp., *Dispossession: Black Australians and White Invaders*, Sydney, 1989.

Reynolds, Tom, 'Records relating to Aborigines in the Western Australian Government Archives', in Reece, Bob & Stannage, Tom, eds, *Studies in Western Australian History*, vol. 7, *European–Aboriginal Relations in Western Australian History*, 1984, pp. 88–101.

Richardson, A. R., *Early Memories of the Great Nor-West, and a Chapter in the History of WA*, Perth, 1909.

Rijavec, Frank, *Know the Song, Know the Country: The Ngarda-Ngali Story of Culture and History in the Roebourne District*, Roebourne, Ieramugadu Group, c. 1995 (booklet that accompanies the film of the same name).

Rowley, C. D., *The Destruction of Aboriginal Society*, Canberra, 1970.

Rowse, Tim, 'Were you ever savages? Aboriginal insiders and pastoralists patronage', *Oceania*, vol. 58, no. 1, 1987, pp. 81–99.

Russell, Enid, *A History of the Law in Western Australia: And its Development from 1829–1979*, Perth, 1980.

Russo, George, 'Religion, politics and Western Australian Aborigines in the 1870s: Bishop Salvado and Governor Weld', *Twentieth Century*, October 1974, pp. 5–19.

—— 'Dom Rosendo Salvado: The abbot', in Hunt, Lyall, ed., *Westralian Portraits*, Perth, 1979, pp. 29–36.

—— *Lord Abbot of the Wilderness: The Life and Times of Bishop Salvado*, Melbourne, 1980.

Shann, E. O. G., *Cattle Chosen: The Story of the First Group Settlement in Western Australia, 1829–1841*, Perth, 1926.

Smith, L. R., *The Aboriginal Population of Australia*, Canberra, 1980.

South, Robin, 'Photographic sources of Aboriginal history in Western Australia: A guide to major collections in the J. S. Battye Library of Western Australian History', in Reece, Bob & Stannage, Tom, eds, *Studies in Western Australian History*, vol. 7, *European–Aboriginal Relations in Western Australian History*, 1984, pp. 102–10.

Stannage, C. T., *The People of Perth: A Social History of Western Australia's Capital City*, Perth, 1979.

—— *A New History of Western Australia*, Perth, 1981.

—— ed., *Convictism in Western Australia*, vol. 4, *Studies in Western Australian History*, 1981, pp. 57–61.

—— 'Bishop Salvado: A review of the memoirs', in Reece, Bob & Stannage, Tom, eds, *Studies in Western Australian History*, vol. 7, *European–Aboriginal Relations in Western Australian History*, 1984, pp. 33–5.

—— *Western Australia's Heritage: The Pioneer Myth*, University of Western Australia Extension Services, monograph, no. 1, 1985.

Statham, Pamela, comp., *Dictionary of Western Australia, 1829–1914*, vol. 1, Perth, 1981.

—— comp., *The Tanner Letters: A Pioneer Saga of Swan River and Tasmania, 1831–1845*, Perth, 1987.

—— 'Swan River Colony, 1829–1850', in Stannage, C. T., ed., *A New History of Western Australia*, Perth, 1981, ch. 5.

Storman, E. J., trans., ed., *The Salvado Memoirs: Historical Memoirs of Australia and Particularly of the Benedictine Mission of New Norcia and the Habits and Customs of the Australian Natives*, Perth, 1977 [Rosendo Salvado, *Memorie Storiche dell'Australia*, Rome, Society for Propagation of the Gospel, 1851].

Streeter, Edwin W., *Pearls and the Pearling Life*, London, 1886.

Thomas, J. E. & Stewart, Alex, *Imprisonment in Western Australia: Evolution, Theory and Practice*, Perth, 1978.

van den Driesen, I. H., 'The Census of 1861: An intriguing incident in Western Australian history', in Stannage, C. T., ed., *Convictism in Western Australia*, vol. 4, *Studies in Western Australian History*, 1981, pp. 57–61.

—— 'Demographic grumbles: Some problems with population data in Western Australia 1850–1900', *Australian Historical Statistics*, vol. 6, 1983, pp. 4–36.

—— *Essays on Immigration Policy and Population in Western Australia, 1850–1901*, Perth, 1986.

—— 'Convicts and migrants in Western Australia, 1850–1868: Their number, nature and ethnic origin', *Journal of the Royal Australian Historical Society*, 73, part 1, 1986, pp. 40–68.

Watson, Edward Jack, *Rottnest: Its Tragedy and its Glory*, Perth, 1998.

Webb, Martyn & Webb, Audrey, *Edge of Empire*, Perth, 1983.

White, Michael, *TAFE in WA: A Selection of Significant Historical Documents, 1832–1929*, Perth, vol. 1, 1982.

Whittington, Vera, *Sister Kate: A Life Dedicated to Children in Need of Care*, Perth, 1999.

William, Dom, 'Bishop Salvado's work', *Early Days: Journal and Proceedings, WA Historical Society*, December 1947, pp. 27–36.

Wilson, John, 'The Pilbara Aboriginal social movement: An outline of the background and significance', in Reece, Bob & Stannage, Tom, eds, *Studies in Western Australian History*, vol. 7, *European–Aboriginal Relations in Western Australian History*, 1984, ch. 13.

Wollaston, John Ramsden, *Journals and Diaries 1841–1846*, collected by Canon A. Burton, vol. 1, Perth, 1954.

Zucker, Margaret, *From Patrons to Partners: A History of the Catholic Church in the Kimberley, 1884–1984*, Fremantle, 1994.

UNPUBLISHED MANUSCRIPTS AND DISSERTATIONS

Adams, David, 'The Schools of the Public Schools' Association, and their Antecedents, 1829–1929', PhD, University of Western Australia, 1979.

Biskup, Peter, 'Native Administration and Welfare in Western Australia, 1897–1954', MLaw, University of Western Australia, 1966.

Bolton, G. C., 'A Survey of the Kimberley Pastoral Industry from 1885 to the Present', MA, University of Western Australia, 1953.

Broughton, Andrew, 'Ellensbrook, Margaret River', Architecture thesis, no detail. Held in Battye Library.

Brown, John J., 'Policies in Aboriginal Education in Western Australia, 1829–1897', MEd, University of Western Australia, 1979.

Carter, Jennie, 'History of the Removal of Aboriginal Children from their Families in Western Australia, 1829–1972', Aboriginal Affairs Department, 1996.

Foster, Darren J., 'Neglected Children in WA: A Case Study 1897–1908: John George Foster'. No details. Held in Battye Library.

Hancock, Gregory G., 'The Origins and Early Years of Independent Secondary Schools in Western Australia 1891–1911', BEd, University of Western Australia, 1976.

Irvine, P., 'The History of the Roman Catholic Establishment at Glendalough', Honours thesis, Graylands Teachers' College, 1962.

Islay, Kelly, 'The Secondary Education of Girls in Government Schools, 1829–1950', MEd, UWA, 1981.

McCarthy, Michael, 'Charles Edward Broadhurst (1826–1905): A Remarkable Nineteenth Century Failure', MPhil, Murdoch University, 1990.

Riordan, Noreen, 'Private Venture Schools in Western Australia between 1829 and 1914: An Analysis of their Constitution and Education', MEd, University of Western Australia, 1990.

Russo, George, 'Bishop Salvado's Plan to Civilize and Christianize Aborigines', MA, University of Western Australia, 1972.

Seeto, Maree, 'The Significance of the Catholicism of Frederick Aloysius Weld for the Development of Education in Western Australia, 1869–1875', MEd, University of Western Australia, 1989.

Shepherd, Brian, 'A History of the Pearling Industry off the North West Coast of Australia from its Origins until 1916', MA, University of Western Australia, 1973.

Tilbrook, Lois, 'Shadows in the Archives: An Interpretation of European Colonization and Aboriginal Responses in the Swan River Area', PhD, University of Western Australia, 1987.

Weiland, R. L., 'The Development of Special Education in Western Australia, 1896–1945', MEd, University of Western Australia, 1975.

Woods, John D., 'The State Aid Issue in Western Australia, 1885–1895', MEd, University of Western Australia, 1978.

INDEX

A

Aboriginal children
    contracts for, 144–55, 173–5
    education of, 7, 115–26, 138, 198
    indenture system for, 145–55, 173–5
    in institutions, 115–36
    as a labour force, 101, 104, 107, 109, 113–14, 141–55, 156–77
    of mixed descent, 178–83, 192
Aboriginal Offenders Act 1883, 195
Aboriginal Offenders Act Amendment Act 1892, 195
Aborigines
    citizenship, 6, 196
    counted in censuses, 100–1
    definition of, 148
    see also Nyungar people
Aborigines Act 1897, 139
Aborigines Act 1905, 140, 154, 183, 192–6
Aborigines Department, 192–3
Aborigines Protection Act 1886, 2, 136, 139, 144–9, 173, 179, 184, 187
Aborigines Protection Act Amendment Act 1892, 149, 196
Aborigines Protection Board, 110, 112, 136–9, 147–51, 180–1, 184, 192
Agricultural Society of Swan River Colony, 36
Angelo, Colonel E. F., 83, 96, 169–72
Anglican Church, 64, 66–7
Anglican Swan Native and Half-caste Home (later Protestant Swan River Mission), 8, 134–7, 184
apprenticeship of Aboriginal children, *see* Aboriginal children, indenture system for

Armstrong, Francis, 102, 118–21
Assisted Schools Abolition Act 1895, 63–4
Atkinson, William, 55

B

Bailey, C. A., 110, 181, 188–9
Barlee, Ellen, 14, 44
Barlee, Frederick, 17, 54–5, 130–1
Barrow, Peter, 103
Bastardy Act 1871, 70
Bastardy Act Amendment Act 1875, 70
Bastardy Laws Act 1875 Amendment Act 1896, 70
Beagle Bay, Roman Catholic Mission, 9, 140
Benedictine missionaries, 126–33, 183
Bishop's Girls' School, 66
Bishop's School, 64
'blackbirding', 157, 160–2, 170–1, 198
Bland, R. H., 125
Blick, Graham, 173
'boarding out', 94
Booth, Commandant of the Salvation Army, 93
Brady, Bishop of the Catholic Church, 47, 126, 129
Bresnahan, Denis, 150
Briggs, Henry, 66
Brockman, Fanny, 26
Brockman, George, 150
Brockman, John, 152
Brockman, William Locke, 26–7
Broome, Governor, 144, 169
Brown, Archdeacon, 72
Brown, Eliza, 32
Brown, Maitland, 45
Brown, Thomas, 32
Brownrigg, H. W., 190